The Harvard Guide to Influential Books

THE HARVARD GUIDE TO INFLUENTIAL BOOKS

*113 Distinguished Harvard Professors
Discuss the Books That Have Helped
to Shape Their Thinking*

Edited by

C. Maury	Claudia M.	Kim D.
Devine	Dissel	Parrish

1817

HARPER & ROW, PUBLISHERS, New York
*Cambridge, Philadelphia, San Francisco, Washington
London, Mexico City, São Paulo, Singapore, Sydney*

FIRST EDITION

Designer: Sidney Feinberg

Library of Congress Cataloging-in-Publication Data

The Harvard guide to influential books.

Includes index.
 1. Bibliography—Best books. 2. College teachers—Books and reading.
3. Harvard University—Faculty—Books and reading. 4. Books and reading.
I. Devine, C. Maury. II. Dissel, Claudia M. III. Parrish, Kim D.
Z1035.H38   1986   011'.7   86-45090
ISBN 0-06-055013-9   86 87 88 89 90 MPC 10 9 8 7 6 5 4 3 2 1
ISBN 0-06-096084-1 (pbk.)   86 87 88 89 90 MPC 10 9 8 7 6 5 4 3 2 1

In Appreciation

To our parents—the most
eminent and influential
teachers of all

Jim and Rita in Maryland
J. K. and 'Rene in California
Cactus and Dot in Oklahoma

Dedicated
To the Memory of
John F. Kennedy, A.B. '40
A Passionate Reader
A Student of Life
and
35th President of the United States
Whose Leadership Still Challenges Us
"To Strive, to Seek, to Find and Not to Yield"

CONTENTS

ACKNOWLEDGMENTS

No literary work or creative effort is without its silent partners —those who give of their time, ideas and enthusiasm without formal recognition. This publication is no exception.

We are particularly grateful to the members of the Harvard faculty without whose encouragement and participation this book would never have come to be.

The Harvard Guide to Influential Books began in the spring of 1985 as a privately printed book entitled *The Harvard Guide to Reading for the Future.* We would like to thank specifically those who helped with that first book: Win Knowlton, whose enthusiasm for our idea during our first visit to his home inspired us to go on; Dick Fahey, whose artistic and practical sense helped us through design; Karen Davison, whose proficiency with a word processor brought us to print; and Harvard's Kennedy School of Government Mid-Career Class of 1985, who worked with us and whose spirit enabled us to meet extraordinary publication deadlines. They should know that we would never have made it without them.

We would especially like to thank those who made this revised and expanded book possible: Laura McGarry, whose skill and judgment with the word processor enhanced every rewrite; Nancy Hardy and Judy Albright, whose research at the Library of Congress was invaluable and time-saving for us; and Hugh Van Dusen, our editor at Harper & Row, whose patience and understanding of first-time editors sustained us.

We would like to extend special thanks to the secretaries and administrative assistants of Harvard who managed successfully to walk the fine line between protecting their employers and representing them in this project. We are grateful for those special friends in Boston and Cambridge who went out of their way to conduct interviews, pick up and deliver forms and do some research when we could not be there. When we were commuting to Cambridge we were the guests of many kind friends and classmates who fed and sheltered us after long days on the Harvard campus. Their hospitality was fortifying then and truly appreciated now.

Finally, our most heartfelt thanks are reserved for our families and dear friends who tolerated our single-mindedness and who kept giving when we were too preoccupied to respond in kind.

To the Reader:

The editors gratefully acknowledge the cooperation of all the individual faculty members who participated in our book. Each faculty member's participation was a matter of personal choice. Harvard University, the President and Fellows of Harvard College and the Board of Overseers have not sponsored, endorsed or profited financially from this book's production.

Hoc est verum et nihi nisi verum.

PARTICIPANTS

Daniel Aaron
James Ackerman
S. James Adelstein
William Alfred
Graham T. Allison
Kenneth Andrews
Clarissa Atkinson
Bernard Bailyn
Walter Jackson Bate
Daniel Bell
Nicolaas Bloembergen
William Bossert
Alan Brinkley
Robert Brustein
Constance H. Buchanan
Jeanne S. Chall
Hale Champion
Alfred D. Chandler
Mary V. Chatfield
C. Roland Christensen
Robert Coles
John Williams Collins III
Richard N. Cooper
Clare Dalton
Dante Della-Terza
Paul M. Doty
John T. Dunlop
Diana Eck
Christopher Edley
Archie C. Epps
Myron B. Fiering
Franklin Ford
Howard Frazier
Emanuel A. Friedman

Gerald E. Frug
John Kenneth Galbraith
Carney Gavin
Sheldon Glashow
Nathan Glazer
Stephen J. Gould
Oleg Grabar
Patricia Albjerg Graham
Howard Green
Kenneth W. Haskins
Hugh Heclo
Richard J. Herrenstein
Howard Hiatt
James Hodgson
Stanley Hoffman
Gerald Holton
Matina Horner
Harold Howe II
Jerome Kagan
John Kao
Gordon D. Kaufman
John V. Kelleher
Duncan Kennedy
Francis Keppel
Winthrop Knowlton
Martin A. Linsky
David M. Livingston
George C. Lodge
Albert Lord
Roderick MacFarquhar
John E. Mack
Harvey C. Mansfield, Jr.
Ernest R. May
Colin McArdle

Thomas K. McCraw
Elizabeth McKinsey
Margaret R. Miles
D. Quinn Mills
Martha Minow
John D. Montgomery
Mark Moore
Richard E. Neustadt
Richard R. Niebuhr
Robert Nozick
Joseph S. Nye, Jr.
Laurie D. Olin
Richard D. Parker
Orlando Patterson
Reginald Phelps
Richard Pipes
Willard V. Quine
Howard Raiffa
Robert B. Reich
David Riesman
Marc Roberts
Jeffrey Sachs
Moshe Safdie

Michael J. Sandel
Thomas C. Schelling
Bruce Scott
Ihor Ševčenko
Judith Shklar
B. F. Skinner
Anne Whiston Spirn
Zeph Stewart
John R. Stilgoe
Samuel Thorne
C. Peter Timmer
Helen Vendler
Sidney Verba
Avis C. Vidal
Ezra F. Vogel
Luise Vosgerchian
Lloyd Weinreb
Fred R. Whipple
Gordon R. Willey
Edward O. Wilson
James Q. Wilson
Abraham Zaleznik

PARTICIPANTS BY COLLEGE AND SCHOOL

Harvard College and Graduate School of Arts and Sciences

Daniel Aaron
James Ackerman
William Alfred
Bernard Bailyn
Walter Jackson Bate
Daniel Bell
Nicolaas Bloembergen
William Bossert
Alan Brinkley
Robert Brustein
Robert Coles*
Richard N. Cooper
Dante Della-Terza
John T. Dunlop*
Diana Eck*
Archie C. Epps
Myron B. Fiering
Franklin Ford
John Kenneth Galbraith
Carney Gavin
Sheldon Glashow
Stephen J. Gould
Oleg Grabar
Hugh Heclo
Richard J. Herrenstein
Stanley Hoffman

Gerald Holton
Jerome Kagan
John V. Kelleher
Albert Lord
Roderick MacFarquhar
Harvey C. Mansfield, Jr.
Robert Nozick
Orlando Patterson
Reginald Phelps
Richard Pipes
Willard V. Quine
David Riesman
Jeffrey Sachs
Michael J. Sandel
Ihor Ševčenko
Judith Shklar
B. F. Skinner
Zeph Stewart
Helen Vendler
Sidney Verba
Ezra F. Vogel
Luise Vosgerchian
Fred R. Whipple
Gordon R. Willey
Edward O. Wilson
James Q. Wilson

*Joint appointment

Harvard Business School

Kenneth Andrews
Alfred D. Chandler
Mary V. Chatfield
C. Roland Christensen
John Kao
George C. Lodge

Thomas K. McCraw
D. Quinn Mills
Howard Raiffa*
Bruce Scott
C. Peter Timmer
Abraham Zaleznik

Graduate School of Design

James Hodgson
Laurie D. Olin
Moshe Safdie

Anne Whiston Spirn
John R. Stilgoe

Divinity School

Clarissa Atkinson
Constance H. Buchanan
Gordon D. Kaufman

Margaret R. Miles
Richard R. Niebuhr

Graduate School of Education

Jeanne S. Chall
John Williams Collins III
Nathan Glazer
Patricia Albjerg Graham

Kenneth W. Haskins
Harold Howe II
Francis Keppel

Kennedy School of Government

Graham T. Allison
Hale Champion
Paul M. Doty*
Winthrop Knowlton
Martin A. Linsky
Ernest R. May*
John D. Montgomery

Mark Moore
Richard E. Neustadt
Joseph S. Nye, Jr.
Robert B. Reich
Thomas C. Schelling
Avis C. Vidal

Harvard Law School

Clare Dalton   Martha Minow
Christopher Edley   Richard D. Parker
Gerald E. Frug   Samuel Thorne
Duncan Kennedy   Lloyd Weinreb

Harvard Medical School

S. James Adelstein   David M. Livingston
Emanuel A. Friedman   John E. Mack
Howard Green   Colin McArdle
Howard Hiatt

School of Public Health

Howard Frazier   Marc Roberts*

Radcliffe College

Matina Horner   Elizabeth McKinsey

PREFACE

All too often life's demands leave us little time to look back on what has influenced our thinking. Life's major events have an obvious effect on us, but these life-shaping experiences can sometimes be triggered by the most apparently insignificant and inconsequential things—a word, a thought, an idea, a book. Here we have an annotated listing of books that have mattered, books that have had a major influence on the thinking of over a hundred Harvard University faculty members.

The *Guide* is the offspring of a modest book we published privately in the spring of 1985. In that book, we tried to develop a reading list for the future—a list that would continually focus our thinking. *The Harvard Guide to Reading for the Future*, as it was called, grew out of our own frustration, when we left Harvard upon graduation, at having only touched the surface of a wealth of exciting and challenging issues and problems.

We were not unlike most graduate students who, upon seeing an end to their formal education, collect course syllabi with the firm intention of pursuing the course readings on their own later in life. We were, however, unlike most graduate students in that we had begun our studies at Harvard midway in our careers. We were students in the Mid-Career Masters in Public Administration program at Harvard's Kennedy School of Government, and recognized the tremendous self-discipline we would need to stick with a reading plan once we returned to the competing demands of career, family, friends and other responsibilities. So instead of asking for course syllabi, we asked a group of Harvard faculty members for a list of books that had shaped their thinking and that they believed would contribute most to an individual's understanding and appreciation of the issues before us today and those that will challenge us in the decades ahead.

Our first book regrettably had a number of shortcomings. At

the time of its hasty publication in May 1985, we had wanted to include the reason why each book was recommended and to call upon a broad cross section of faculty members and ideologies. *The Harvard Guide to Influential Books* has given us the opportunity to expand the scope of the book and to reach a larger audience.

We asked each contributor to the *Guide* for the titles of four to six books and the reasons why each book came to mind. We tried to limit our instructions to the participants in the hopes that the responses would be honest and natural. We were looking not for a contrived list of books that made a particular professor look good, but for sincere descriptions of books that truly mattered. We preferred personal reflections, but we also included comments that described the contents of a particular book. We hoped that the combination of personal comment and content is as interesting to the reader as it was to the editors.

We were not looking for a recitation of the classics or a repetition of Western civilization's Great Books. At one point we even considered developing a list of classics that would be "presumed" to have been influential. We even considered restraining the contributors from any discussion of the classics. A few trial interviews quickly reminded us that classics became classics because they have had significant impact on generations of readers. Some have, therefore, been included in the *Guide*.

We sought faculty members distinguished by their original thought and representative of different disciplines. The *Guide* represents 5 percent of the two thousand full-time faculty members associated with Harvard University, from eight graduate schools as well as the college. It includes faculty members at all points in their academic careers, young and old, rising stars and professors emeriti. We wanted our selection of participants to reflect the range of philosophy and ideology that is associated with a large teaching and research university. In addition to diversity of thought we had hoped to reach those faculty members who are known to have a special regard for books and who receive comfort and inspiration from them. Our goals were ambitious, and as the reader will see we were more successful in some faculties than in others.

We have called the professors in the *Guide* "distinguished."
They are distinguished by their contributions—in the classroom, in academic circles, and in their respective fields of
knowledge. They are sometimes distinguished by their reputa-
tions for original thought, by their personal charisma or by
student acclaim for their teaching.

The selection of the participants was a gradual process of
refining our ideas and the suggestions of others. When we asked
others for their opinions we looked for repetition—the same
name suggested by many different sources. We contacted a
large number of people inside and outside the Harvard community. Inside we spoke to alumni, current students, professors
and staff. Outside we spoke with the press, with the public and
with those who do business with Harvard University. We also
asked faculty members from other institutions to suggest Harvard professors whose lists they would most like to see.

About 80 percent of the list was quickly determined. The
names were frequently mentioned—a few unanimously. But
frequency was not our only gauge—we also considered passion.
Sometimes a professor's name was so fervently given that we
were compelled to interview him or her based on the strength
of the urging rather than on the frequency of the mention.

Our interviews were conducted in person, over the phone
and via letters. We asked two simple questions: "What books
have helped to shape your thinking?" and "Why?" As expected,
the reactions to our project varied. Most faculty members were
eager to expand their classrooms, to spend the time and share
a lifetime of experiences with books. There were some who
were too busy and still others who found the exercise too personal, too painful or too pointless. We were most comfortable
with the professors emeriti, and they were the most comfortable with books.

Our interviews generally began with a discussion on the general subject of reading. Specific books would come later—well
into the conversation and often much later when the professors
were by themselves, in their homes surrounded by the books
that they wanted to remember. Many hoped that our project
would encourage reading, particularly among the young. They

feared that the nation's children are not reading, not talking and not interacting, but spending their time, sometimes exclusively, watching TV and listening to music. Many of the contributors to the *Guide* hoped to instill the habit of reading in their own children and grandchildren. For many, it didn't matter what children read as long as they read. Some even looked back with fond memories to their own reading of comic books, particularly the Classic Illustrated Comics. Despite claims to the contrary at the time of their publication, Classic Comics were for many gateways to the classics.

Our questions sparked not only observations about reading but comments on the dynamic relationship between reading and writing. "Once I started writing, I stopped reading," professors would often note, as if reading were exclusive of both original thinking and writing. In a world governed by "publish or perish" requirements, reading would inevitably give way to writing. In one conversation, a quick-witted faculty member suggested that perhaps we should offer tenure to those who *read* a certain number and quality of books rather than to those who *write* them.

There were, however, those who claimed that nothing shapes your own thinking like your own writing. For that matter, each professor's work should be among his or her most influential books. They are not, however, included in this *Guide*. We asked each professor to refrain from listing his own books or those of his colleagues. While their own books are excluded, some did cite the works of their colleagues but with such fervor that there can be no doubt as to the book's importance to them.

For most of the contributors the questions, "What books have influenced your thinking?" and "Why?" appeared much easier to answer than they actually were. Selecting the books was difficult after a lifetime of reading. It was just as difficult for them to describe the reasons for their choices. Almost everyone took longer to think about their choices than they had expected.

Their choices and their reasons are given in the *Guide*. For all faculty members, each book had wide-ranging and often powerful consequences. *Three Soldiers* by John Dos Passos, for example, made William Alfred a pacifist. An early reading of C. E. M. Joad's *Introduction to Modern Political Theory* persuaded Roderick MacFarquhar of the virtues of socialism, while two other books, *Individualism and Economic Order* by Friedrich Hayek and *Socialism* by Ludwig Von Mises, "shook" philosophy professor Robert Nozick out of his then socialist beliefs.

Often books provided direction for the contributors. At eighteen, Nicolaas Bloembergen, now a Nobel Laureate in physics, read Albert Einstein's *Evolution of Physics,* which convinced him "that the study of physics posed some of the most challenging questions to the human mind." Richard Hofstadter's *Anti-Intellectualism in American Life* helped Thomas McCraw to determine his own vocation. Lines from Dante's *Divine Comedy* came to Dante Della-Terza's "rescue in time of perplexities" by giving him "a sense of direction, a certitude." Plato's *Republic* prompted Judith Shklar to ask the question that has preoccupied her as a political theorist since adolescence: "How are we to think about our personal lives and experiences in a world order, which is entirely remote from us, but nevertheless impinges upon us constantly and often incomprehensibly?"

Other books provided understanding. *Art and Reality* by Joyce Cary helped John Dunlop to "understand and to appreciate the necessary gap between intuition and expression, between the privacy of creation and imagination and the attempt to express in concept and in language." In struggling through *Foundations of Quantum Mechanics* by Josef Maria Jauch, Chris Edley, a lawyer-to-be at the time, "gained new stores of patience, humility and, strangely, confidence."

Finally, books provided the contributors with the lighter side of life. D. H. Lawrence's *Lady Chatterley's Lover* gave Myron Fiering "the first hints of the joys of love, and supplemented street talk as the main source of information to satisfy [his] growing curiosity about feeling, loving and sharing."

Compiling the *Guide* was not without its exhilarating challenges and occasionally frustrating moments. It was exhilarating in that the pursuit introduced us to many who had a passion for reading, who spoke of those special books in their lives as many speak of best friends and life's great experiences. The task was challenging in that this book, like any worthy pursuit, entailed much more than we ever imagined. Reaching an elusive group of individuals with extraordinarily demanding schedules was one of our greatest challenges. And it was occasionally frustrating because we had much to learn about Harvard, about its faculty and about writing or editing a book. In the course of our pursuit, we inevitably encountered questions about "elitism" and perpetuating the Harvard mystique in a book restricted exclusively to the opinions and views of Harvard faculty members. Part of the nature of mystique is to be secretive, and part of the nature of elitism is to be exclusive. Our answers to such claims are information, openness and the willingness of the Harvard faculty to share their thinking. They did so with the reservation that what was influential to them may have no bearing or relevance to others.

A book about books by its very nature cannot be elite because it discloses rather than withholds. We hope that this *Guide* will offer what we expect of all books—a means for all to learn and progress regardless of their circumstances.

The book was not logistically easy. The professors were in Cambridge, Massachusetts and the editors were in Washington, D.C. and Oklahoma City, Oklahoma. Commuting to Boston became a regular routine, and long-distance calls became an inevitable part of our lives. In all, however, the experience of the book far exceeded any of our inconveniences.

The project was not without its lighthearted moments. In looking for a certain professor's office in Harvard's Museum of Comparative Zoology, for example, we were told to "turn left at the carnivores and it's the doorway between the giraffes and the camels under the whale." There were also those quiet moments in Widener Library, those historic moments in Robert Coles's office, where President Franklin Delano Roosevelt lived while a student at Harvard, those refreshing moments touring the grounds of Dumbarton Oaks in Washington, D.C., those reverent moments on the glass floors of the Divinity School library and those gracious moments in the homes of the faculty.

For the convenience of the reader, the *Guide* is divided into three major sections; the first section contains each faculty member's submission, arranged alphabetically. Here, each participant is described briefly.

Some clarification is necessary here regarding two pieces of information included in the biographies of the participants that may be unique to Harvard University. First, certain faculty members are identified as being "University Professors." This special category of professorship was created in 1935 for individuals of distinction. University Professors are selected by the university president to honor scholars working on the frontiers of knowledge that extend beyond the conventional limits of departments and specialties. To be named University Professor is Harvard's highest honor. Less than a dozen now carry this distinction, and the majority of them have participated in this book. Second, many of the faculty included in this book were "junior fellows." A junior fellow in the Society of Fellows is a distinction that was created in 1933, by President Abbott Lawrence Lowell. President Lowell founded the society as a counterweight to the rigidity of the Ph.D. system. The fellows endure a rigorous selection process to do independent work for three years. Only eight students per year are selected to join this challenging interdisciplinary program. We included that information in certain biographies to show the reader the diversity of the society's past membership.

The *Guide* includes, in addition to those of faculty members, the thoughts of several librarians. We asked them to join us at the suggestion of many faculty members who have enormous respect for Harvard's librarians and the research capabilities of Harvard's libraries.

We have included, following the biographical sketches, a comment written by the contributor either introducing the books they selected or commenting on reading in general. The commentary on each book is preceded by a standard bibliographic citation, which is either the particular choice of the professor or the most recent, and preferably paperback, edition available (indicated by "Pb"), selected by the editors for the reader's convenience. The date in parentheses following the title is the date of the book's original publication, if different from that of the edition cited.

The second section of the *Guide* is an index of all the books selected by the faculty. It is arranged alphabetically by author with bibliographic information to enable the reader to locate the books in libraries or bookstores. Following each citation, the name or names of the Harvard faculty who mentioned the particular book is given in brackets. By referring to the alphabetical section, the reader can review the comments of a particular faculty member.

The final section of the *Guide* provides an opportunity for the reader to complete the thinking that we hope has been stimulated by reading this book. The most often asked question we encountered from colleagues and associates during production of this book was, "Has anyone mentioned such-and-such a book?" This was almost always followed by "I think I know what books I would mention," or "I wonder which books I would mention." We have made room for our readers' reflections because we think from our experience and from the comments of our Harvard participants that actually writing down one's choices can be very valuable to an understanding of the effects of reading on thinking. We have followed the Reader's Reflection page with space for making a Reading Plan. The first version of this book showed us that in many cases readers marked up their copies, checking off books they intended to read. We have added some structure to that process in the hope that a more formal reading plan will increase our readers' commitment to themselves and further encourage reading.

For those who have studied at Harvard, *The Harvard Guide to Influential Books* will, we hope, provide an opportunity to continue their education. For those who have not studied there, the *Guide* will introduce its readers to a group of faculty members who are eager to share their knowledge. More importantly, it will provide an introduction or a reintroduction to a splendid collection of books. It may even prompt some to make time for reading, to shake the seductive routine of work and sleep and embark on a plan to read.

C. M. D.
C. M. D.
K. D. P.

Cambridge, Massachusetts
Oklahoma City, Oklahoma
Washington, D.C.

The Harvard Guide to Influential Books

Daniel Aaron

Daniel Aaron is the Victor S. Thomas Professor of English and American Literature and Language Emeritus at Harvard University and has recently edited The Inman Diary. *He is also president of the Library of America, dedicated to preserving the works of American writers. Professor Aaron has had a lifelong interest in encouraging reading.*

Most of us read promiscuously. Our response to a particular book depends a good deal on when we intersect with it and under what circumstances. In my own case, the books I was required to read usually meant less to me than those whose titles I came across in the pages of other writers or accidentally discovered on my own. Some of the books that deeply engaged me during my adolescence were "trash" to my mentors. It seems too pompous to say that any of the following books played "an important role" in my life. They were important to me for personal reasons.

Edmund Wilson. *Axel's Castle: A Study in the Imaginative Literature of 1870–1930* (1931). New York: W. W. Norton, 1984. (Pb)

This book was very liberating. It was my first extended exposure to the symbolist movement and drew me to Yeats's later poetry, to Joyce's *Ulysses,* to Gertrude Stein's *Three Lives,* and of course to Wilson's collected reviews and essays. Eventually I read everything he wrote, and I still regard him as America's foremost modern man of letters.

James Gibbons Huneker. *Egoists, a Book of Supermen* (1909). New York: AMS Press, 1975.

———. *Iconoclasts, a Book of Dramatists* (1905). Westport, Conn.: Greenwood, 1969.

———. *Ivory, Apes and Peacocks* (1915). Philadelphia: Richard West, 1973.

———. *Unicorns* (1917). New York: AMS Press, 1976.

I came across Huneker's essays in 1929. By that time he was considered a relic of the fin de siècle and was hardly referred to, but to me he was a revelation. He introduced me at a susceptible age to the "poisoned honey" of the continent, to his "soul-wreckers." Thanks to him, I found Nietzsche, Huysmans, Strindberg, Baudelaire, Flaubert. He was more enthusiastic than critical, but I read him at the right time.

George Henry Borrow. *Lavengro.* 3 vols. London: J. Murray, 1851.

I read this novel, a fictionalized autobiography, in my late teens. It tells of a young wanderer-scholar who has mastered the Romany tongue and is befriended by a company of English gypsies. Borrow's racy earthy style and amusing irreverence appealed to me very much. His fascination with languages ("Lavengro" is the gypsy word for "philology") matched my own.

Kenneth Burke. *Permanence and Change* (1935). Indianapolis: Bobbs-Merrill, 1965.

Almost more than any work I can think of, this one helped me to clarify the relation between literature and society, criticism and life. Through Burke I discovered Thorstein Veblen. His discussions of "perspectives by incongruity" and "symbolic action" made me see the uses of history, psychology, sociology, and philosophy in the interpretation of literature. Thereafter Burke became for me our American Coleridge.

Stendhal [Marie Henri Beyle]. *The Red and the Black* (1830). Lloyd C. Parks, trans. New York: New American Library, 1970. (Pb)

I suppose this is my favorite novel along with *Anna Karenina.* I've read it more times than any other novel for reasons never exactly clear to me except that I take undiminished delight in its wit, audacity and stylistic brilliance and its psychological insights. To me, at least, the novel has the perfect plot.

James Ackerman

James Ackerman is the Arthur Kingsley Porter Professor of Fine Arts. His essays and articles are on the history of architecture, critical and historical theory, and the interaction of art and science. His books focus on his long-held fascination with Rome: The Architecture of Michelangelo, Palladio *and* Palladio's Villas. *Recently he has expanded his artistic interests to film:* Looking for Renaissance Rome *(1976) and* Palladio the Architect and His Influence in America *(1980).*

I'm not sure that any of these books (except possibly for Barthes) would have the same impact today that they did when published; they are still worth reading, but they were written in and for another milieu. If all important books retained their value permanently we wouldn't need to produce any new ones.

Roger Fry. *Vision and Design* (1920). New York: Oxford University Press, 1981. (Pb)

I was sixteen when I bought this book of essays on various themes, and I was overwhelmed by my first contact with its subtle and sensitive approach to art. Fry's elegant prose reinforced his message that the essence of art resides not in the reproduction of nature but in form, color, rhythm and other abstract characteristics. Today his idealistic position seems rather old hat, but his writing is still much more engaging and persuasive than that of almost any of our current critics.

Sigfried Giedion. *Space, Time, and Architecture.* Cambridge: Harvard University Press, 1941.

In my post-college years, this book introduced me and my fellow students to modern architecture when hardly any examples of it could be found in America. For Giedion, the new architecture, especially that of Europe, was not only the first great expression since the Baroque period, but was destined to revolutionize the way we live. We swallowed the argument whole and did what we could to crusade for a totally modern environment. Today I see the shortcomings as well as the virtues of Giedion and architectural modernism, but I am offended by the shallow attack on both by some "postmodern" critics.

E. H. Gombrich. *Art and Illusion: A Study in the Psychology of Pictorial Representation* (1960). Princeton: Princeton University Press, 1961. (Pb)

This book fundamentally influenced the way I speak and write about pictures. Gombrich's central argument, which was based on the most advanced research in perception psychology, was that artists cannot see the visual world except in terms of formulas that shape their perceptions, and that to a great extent these formulas are based on their experience of existing works of art. We, in turn, approach their work with our own formulas. The book laid to rest the claim of Ruskin and later criticism that the best painters of nature had learned to look with an "innocent eye," uncontaminated by concepts or knowledge. Gombrich showed how much every effort to project onto a flat surface the "real" world we perceive as we move about and use two eyes is affected by the social environment, by preexisting art and by personal experience.

Percy W. Bridgman. *The Way Things Are* (1959). New York: Viking, 1961.

No intellectual innovation in this century is comparable in its far-reaching impact to that sparked by the discovery in natural science and mathematics that no proposition can claim to have absolute authority; each can be verified only in terms of the operations employed to measure it. This book, by a Nobel Prize–winner in physics, articulating what he calls "operational" reasoning, helped me to see the implications of this concept for the criticism of literature and art. The humanities as well as the sciences had been in the grip of absolute principles and were liberated by their dissolution. Incidentally, nearly all the major humanistic writings of the past generation have been the work of scientists, not humanists.

Roland Barthes. *The Pleasure of the Text.* Richard Miller, trans. New York: Hill & Wang, 1975. (Pb)

This is the only relatively recent book I have included, which proves that the mind becomes less receptive with age. It is a collection of Pascalian *Pensées* which, as the title implies, ruminate on the relaxed and sensuous enjoyment of reading. It was calculated to counteract and balance the excessive sophistication and Puritanism of modern criticism. Since Barthes, as one of the fathers of structuralist/semiotic interpretation, exerted a powerful influence on the making of that criticism, one of the pleasures of *Pleasure* is in its sly subversiveness. Because a major enjoyment in the reading of this or of almost any well-crafted text is in the quality of the language, much is lost in translation.

S. James Adelstein

S. James Adelstein prepared himself for his career by studying science at M.I.T. and medicine at Harvard. His profession has developed both educational pursuits, with clinical research in nuclear medicine and scientific research in radiation biophysics. He has been a member of the Harvard Medical Faculty since 1960 in the Departments of Anatomy, Medicine and Radiology. Currently, he serves as dean of Academic Programs.

Despite doubters, reading has been a good way to prepare for the last five centuries.

Claude Bernard. *An Introduction to the Study of Experimental Medicine* (1865). H. C. Greene, trans. New York: Dover, 1957. (Pb)

For the general reader it marks a watershed in the intellectual history of medicine from an empirical, somewhat mystical vocation to a profession based on scientific reality and experimentally verifiable phenomena. Personally it provided me with the conviction, on historical grounds, that medicine is an exciting field for scientific inquiry.

Hans Zinsser. *As I Remember Him: The Biography of R. S.* Boston: Little, Brown, 1940.

Most embryonic physicians are caught up in the crusades against infectious disease at one time or another (Sinclair Lewis must have known it when he wrote *Arrowsmith*). What a delight to have a sprightly and irreverent biography that deals not only with an important life in bacteriology and epidemiology but with a broader academic world as well. When I entered Harvard Medical School, I thought all professors would have the wit of Dr. Zinsser; some did not.

J. Robert Oppenheimer. *Science and the Common Understanding.* New York: Simon & Schuster, 1954.

The discoveries and applications of physical science have had a profound effect on thought and action in the twentieth century, but those of us not educated in modern physics have had to rely on others to convey the essence of this intellectual revolution. Oppenheimer does it very well in this series of Reith Lectures given in 1953; to his explanation he adds considerable philosophic reflection, of the kind that has made him one of the more enigmatic scientists of our time. A year after these lectures were published, I temporarily broke off the study of medicine to learn more physics.

Norbert Wiener. *The Human Use of Human Beings: Cybernetics and Society* (1950). New York: Avon, 1967.

Computers and robotics are now so commonplace that we think of them as standard household and factory items. Along with technical developments that made them possible there developed a profound theory on information and control. This book is a milestone in the documentation and translation of that theory for the educated but nonspecialized reader. Professor Wiener was my instructor in one undergraduate course on mathematics. He made me understand something about mathematical insight; his book is insightful too.

Ève Curie. *Madame Curie* (1937). Vincent Sheean, trans. New York: Doubleday, Doran, 1938.

A true scientific heroine. Mme. Curie's struggles, tragedies and triumphs are well known. Her daughter, Ève, tells the story with sensitivity and the proper attention to detail. From this book I learned much about scientific tutelage, the promise of radioactivity in the service of medicine and the struggle of women for equality and recognition.

William Alfred

William Alfred is the Abbott Laurence Lowell Professor of the Humanities at Harvard. A native of New York City, he is a noted playwright (Hogan's Goat), *translator (Modern Library* Beowulf) *and teacher. Besides his achievements in the classroom, he continues to produce screenplays and scripts for television and the theater.*

These books might prepare their readers for the challenges of the twenty-first century by prompting them to ask questions of the fictions they indulge themselves in, along these lines:

1. Since changes inevitably alter life and our way of dealing with it, so threatening any fixed order we may aspire to that we grow desperate or enraged, can no way be found to assess the perils of that desperation and rage by assessing the fictions in which those feelings are expressed?

2. Does private rage avalanche into international catastrophe?

If that be the case, can no means be found to divert that rage from racist, religious, national or political objects to those elements in our nature which in the nobly furious words of Conor Cruse O'Brien "make us more eager to die for the good of mankind than to live and work for it"?

John Dos Passos. *Three Soldiers* (1921). Boston: Houghton Mifflin, 1964. (Pb)

I saw the Lew Ayres–Lewis Wohlheim movie version of Erich Maria Remarque's *All Quiet on the Western Front* when I was eight or nine, and remembering it still at sixteen, took *Three Soldiers* out of the library. Reading it made me a pacifist.

Evelyn Waugh. *Vile Bodies* (1930). Boston: Little, Brown, 1977. (Pb)

In the pinched, sad thirties, I became an addict of P. G. Wodehouse through reading his novels serialized in the *Satur-*

day Evening Post, which at a nickel a copy even I could afford. Someone told me Evelyn Waugh was funnier; and I read *Vile Bodies.* Funnier the book was; but I was as troubled as amused by such passages as:

> "Adam darling, what's the matter?"
> "I don't know. . . . Nina, do you ever feel that things can't go on much longer?"
> "What do you mean by things—us or everything?"
> "Everything."

Those, taken together with the book's ending, in 1930, on a battlefield during World War II gave me a bleak pause. Wodehouse's irrepressibly cheerful Noel Coward fox-trot had turned into Ravel's "La Valse" under Waugh's manic baton.

Thomas Mann. *The Magic Mountain* (1924). H. T. Lowe-Porter, trans. New York: Random House, 1969. (Pb)

I read Mann's ironic diagnosis of the diseases which brought imperial Europe down in Harry Slochower's unforgettable course at Brooklyn College. I had just returned, my pacifism even more confirmed, from service in the war in the Pacific. I was particularly struck by the way Mann built toward the bloody delirium of his last chapter by dramatizing the growing anger of his characters at private unfulfillment and the fright and disappointment that accompanies the death of an accepted order.

Elizabeth Bowen. *The House in Paris* (1935). New York: Avon, 1979. (Pb)

Years later, advising a tutorial student on a thesis, I reread *The House in Paris;* and I saw the anger which Mann had anatomized in his male characters embodied in a woman. Appalled by the prospect of a stuffy marriage with a man of her own class, that book's upper-middle-class heroine betrays both her husband-to-be and her best friend by sleeping with her best friend's fiancé. Waking the next morning in a gray hotel room, she assesses that experience in terms of a failed revolution: "People must hope so much when they tear streets up and fight at barricades. But, whoever wins, the streets are laid again and the trams start running again. One hopes too much by destroying things." She must be the first writer who noticed the dangerous fusion of elated hope with destructiveness.

George Orwell. *Coming up for Air* (1940). New York: Harcourt, Brace, 1969. (Pb)

I reread *Coming up for Air* with that same tutorial student when I assigned it to her to widen her sense of the uses of narrative in that period. In the third chapter of that book, its protagonist, a white-collar worker, looks out of his commuters' train at a bomber overhead and thinks, with a calmness that seems part relief, that in two years' time such planes will be blasting everything in sight to kingdom come. I also assigned the letters of Evelyn Waugh from the years preceding and immediately following the First World War that she might notice the reaction of exasperated envy that irascible seismograph of his culture had to those returning from the international massacre.

Graham T. Allison

Graham T. Allison is the dean of Harvard's John F. Kennedy School of Government. He is also the Don K. Price Professor of Politics, having served as a professor at Harvard since 1972.

Professor Allison's teaching and research concentrate on political analysis, American foreign policy, and ethics and public policy. His works include Hawks, Doves, and Owls: An Agenda for Avoiding Nuclear War *and* Essence of Decision: Explaining the Cuban Missile Crisis.

A North Carolinian educated at Harvard and Oxford, Dean Allison is a director of the Council on Foreign Relations, special adviser to Secretary of Defense Caspar Weinberger, and a consultant to various government agencies.

Raymond Aron. *Peace and War: A Theory of International Relations* (1962). Richard Howard and Annette Baker Fox, trans. Garden City, N.Y.: Doubleday, 1966.

A magisterial overview of the stuff of international relations.

Winston S. Churchill. *History of the English-Speaking Peoples* (1956–58). 4 vols. New York: Dodd-Mead, 1983. (Pb)

A simple, stirring account of the progress of modern civilization spearheaded by "the English speaking peoples."

Winston S. Churchill. *The Second World War,* Volume I: *The Gathering Storm* (1948). Boston: Houghton Mifflin, 1983.

An insider's account of the West's failure to prevent the most avoidable world war.

Thomas C. Schelling. *The Strategy of Conflict.* Cambridge: Harvard University Press, 1960. (Pb)

The heart of the logic of both conflict and conflict resolution.

Frans De Waal. *Chimpanzee Politics: Power and Sex Among Apes.* Janet Milnes, trans. New York: Harper & Row, 1983. (Pb)

Insightful analysis of our closest relatives—with whom we share more genes than horses do with zebras.

Kenneth Andrews

Kenneth Andrews is the Donald K. David Professor of Business Administration at the Harvard Business School and until recently was editor and publisher of the Harvard Business Review. *His field is business policy and his principal book is* The Concept of Corporate Strategy.

The classics I have identified will be as relevant to the recurring problems of achieving results in organizations and of making leadership effective that will characterize the twenty-first century as they are to those of the present day. The ideas are timeless; their power and application are virtually unlimited.

Chester I. Barnard. *The Functions of the Executive* (1938). Thirtieth anniversary ed. Cambridge: Harvard University Press, 1968. (Pb)

As I said in the introduction to the thirtieth anniversary edition, this is the most thought-provoking book on organization and management ever written by a practicing executive. The combination of intellect and experience is such that his conceptual approach to organization and management has not been made obsolete. He applies systematic thought and a generous exposure to responsibility in explaining the necessity to achieve results through cooperation.

Mary Parker Follett. *Dynamic Administration* (1940). Henry C. Metcalf and L. Urwick, eds. London: Pitman, 1973.

Follett examines the importance in a democratic society and in business organization of the effort to achieve an integration of all points of view and to find in conflict a way to a higher-order solution that is more satisfactory to those who participate in it than would be dominance of their original point of view. Her paper on constructive conflict and the superiority of integration over domination and of compromise as ways of dealing with it has influenced all the work I have done in trying to understand purposeful management.

George C. Homans. *The Human Group* (1950). London: Routledge and Kegan Paul, 1975.

This book was my introduction to the possibility that the human group can be understood as a functioning entity. Here, some of the consequences of the Western Electric experiments are applied to current understanding of human organization.

William James. *Pragmatism* (1907). Cambridge: Harvard University Press, 1978. (Pb)

Pragmatism is the quintessential American philosophy and an integral part of the intellectual history from which the other books that I have found influential have emerged. Though denigrated by those who misunderstand the essential nobility of James's conviction that emotion and action can transform the world and that truth can be found in experience, this book is a monument to the effort to make ideas influential and transform them into action. That reality consists of human experience shaped by purpose is a central truth of great importance to leaders of business and other kinds of organizations.

F. J. Roethlisberger and **William J. Dickson.** *Management and the Worker* (1934). Cambridge: Harvard University Press, 1946.

This is the definitive account of the Western Electric experiments at the Hawthorne Works which transformed the study of business administration and, in effect, originated the study of what was once called "human relations" and is now designated "organization behavior." Perverse interpretation of this research and its finding as exploitation of workers does not obscure its classic importance in the understanding of human organization.

Abraham Zaleznik. *Human Dilemmas of Leadership.* New York: Harper & Row, 1966.

This is the central volume in Zaleznik's successful application of psychoanalysis to the study of human behavior and organizations. It has informed my still partial understanding of problems of power, authority, and dependency, and their implications for leadership.

Clarissa Atkinson

Clarissa Atkinson is Professor of the History of Christianity at the Harvard Divinity School. Her field is the history of the family as it intersects with the history of Christianity, particularly during late medieval and early modern Europe. Her next book will look back at the Christian ideology of motherhood. She has written Mystic and Pilgrim: The Book of the World of Margery Kempe *(1983) and* Immaculate and Powerful: The Female in Sacred Image and Social Reality *(1985), coedited with Margaret Miles and Constance Hall Buchanan.*

I hope these books will encourage people to think about the past in ways that are helpful in preparing for the future.

Margery Kempe. *The Book of Margery Kempe.* Hope Emily Allen and Sanford Brown Meech, eds. London: Oxford University Press, 1940.

Hope Emily Allen edited this fifteenth-century spiritual autobiography by a woman of King's Lynn who was a mystic, a housewife and a pilgrim. Margery Kempe's own story is wonderful, but when I first saw it with Allen's notes (written in the 1930s), what impressed me was Allen's sense of the existence of a women's history distinct from and connected to "history" (that is, to men's history). Allen was not able to finish the work on Margery Kempe, unfortunately, but she was a pioneer in the perception of feminine experience.

William Strunk, Jr. and **E. B. White.** *The Elements of Style* (1959). New York: Macmillan, 1979. (Pb)

As far as I know, this is the only book on writing that can be read for pleasure, so that its wisdom is absorbed with delight. Strunk and White make you want to write well: to be verbose, or to use jargon, would be to disappoint your friends. What's more, E. B. White practiced what he preached, which fosters the comforting illusion that we can learn to write like him if we follow these "simple" rules.

Virginia Woolf. *A Room of One's Own* (1929). New York: Harcourt Brace Jovanovich, 1981. (Pb)

In pointing to some of the connections between the poverty of women's institutions and the poverty of women's history, Woolf illuminates questions that we have not yet managed to resolve, and creates a new character—Shakespeare's sister—to live in our collective imagination. This brilliant, angry, inspiring work, despite (or perhaps because of) its blindness to the injustices of class, prompts us to look for our own blind spots.

Edward H. Carr. *What Is History?* (1961). New York: Random House, 1967. (Pb)

I read this book at about the time that I started to prepare to be a professional historian—that is, when I entered graduate school. Carr's images of the historian's selection of "facts" were so vivid and persuasive that I finally grasped the point that there is no such thing as a history that is out there, waiting for us to discover it. National, class, ethnic and gender groups constructed their own visions of the past, and have always done so. This may no longer be news, but it was news to me then, and Carr's is still the best brief explanation of the subjectivity of historical interpretation.

Joan Kelly. *Women, History, and Theory.* Chicago: University of Chicago Press, 1984.

Joan Kelly's reflections on the way in which women's history has changed "history" broke new ground for students of society and culture. I had known and worked with each of these individual essays, but their cumulative effect in book form is more than the sum of its parts: this is a body of interpretation that alters the ways in which we understand the past.

Bernard Bailyn

Bernard Bailyn, whose historical work centers on the history of the colonies, the American Revolution and the Anglo-American world in the preindustrial era, is the Adams University Professor at Harvard University and director of the Charles Warren Center for Studies in American History. He has written extensively in his field and was awarded the Pulitzer Prize in 1968 for The Ideological Origin of the American Revolution. *He has taught at Harvard since 1949.*

Wonderful books to read:

David Thomson. *Woodbrook* (1974). New York: Irish Book Center, 1981. (Pb)

A profoundly moving memoir of a young English historian's love affair with Ireland and with his young Irish tutee. It is a perfect merging of personal experience and historical awareness, beautifully written. It explains the Anglo-Irish tragedy better than any book I know, and shows history to be a living force.

Thomas Mann. *Doctor Faustus: The Life of the German Composer, Adrian Leverkühn, as Told by a Friend* (1947). H. T. Lowe-Porter, trans. New York: Random House, 1971.

A brilliant commentary, in fictional form, on German culture—its great achievements and deadly disease. Beyond all the learning and speculation in the book, it is wonderfully inventive, simply as fiction.

Ernest Jones. *The Life and Work of Sigmund Freud* (1953–57). 3 vols. New York: Basic Books, 1961. (Pb)

I read this as something of a morality tale of the heroic achievements of one of the most creative minds in the history of Western culture. It is told as a triumph of sheer genius and creativity over all sorts of adversity. And it happens to be true.

William Faulkner. *Absalom! Absalom!* (1936). New York: Random House, 1972. (Pb)

This dark, multigenerational saga of Southern life, woven in an elaborate narrative structure, swept me along by its wildly imaginative storytelling. And then I discovered that there are real historical models for most of the major figures, especially the mysterious Colonel Sutpen. It is soaring fiction and weirdly perceptive history at the same time.

William Trevor. *The Stories of William Trevor.* New York: Penguin, 1983. (Pb)

These are the best contemporary short stories I know: deadly bullets, all of them, piercing some sensitive area of common experience.

Virginia Woolf. *The Letters of Virginia Woolf.* Nigel Nicolson, ed. 6 vols. New York: Harcourt Brace Jovanovich, 1975–80.

The sheer verbal skill in these dashed-off letters is superb —and they are marvelously perceptive and penetrating. So are her *Diaries.*

Walter Jackson Bate

Walter Jackson Bate is the Kingsley Porter University Professor at Harvard and a distinguished scholar of eighteenth- and nineteenth-century English literature. Among his many books are From Classic to Romantic *(1946),* The Burden of the Past *(1969) and two biographies,* John Keats *(1964) and* Samuel Johnson *(1977), each of which won the Pulitzer Prize for biography.*

Great books are the most valuable means of deepening us as "experiencing natures"; and it is only as experiencing natures that we can prepare for new challenges.

Benjamin P. Thomas. *Abraham Lincoln* (1952). New York: Knopf, 1974. (Pb)

The most succinct of the many biographies of one of humanity's greatest heroes.

The Bible. King James version (1611).

Often called the "noblest monument of English prose," the King James version is interwoven with the texture of our speech, and remains a supreme beacon for the spiritual and moral life of mankind.

James Boswell. *The Life of Samuel Johnson* (1791). New York: Random House, 1964. (Pb)

The most fascinating of all biographies, and one of universal appeal because its subject shared so deeply almost every aspect of the experience we all share.

Werner W. Jaeger. *Paideia: The Ideals of Greek Culture* (1934). Gilbert Highet, trans. New York: Oxford University Press, 1965. (Pb)

A profound study of what permitted a small people to create the basis of Western culture.

Alfred North Whitehead. *Science and the Modern World* (1925). New York: Free Press, 1967. (Pb)

Unrivaled in showing what, from the ancient world to the twentieth century, permitted and encouraged the giant adventures of the mind that have formed our world.

William Shakespeare. *Shakespeare: Complete Works* (1592–1611). Alfred Harbage, ed. Baltimore: Penguin, 1969.

The most searching example in literature of the interplay of human action presented in language no other writer has equaled.

Daniel Bell

Daniel Bell is the Henry Ford II Professor of Social Science at Harvard. Besides writing articles and books in his field of sociology, he cofounded The Public Interest, *is on the Board of Editors of* Daedalus, *and is a contributing editor of the* Partisan Review. *He is a trustee of the Institute for Advanced Study in Princeton, New Jersey and a member of the National Research Council's Board on Telecommunications and Computers. His most recent book is* The Deficit: How Big? How Long? How Dangerous? *written with Lester Thurow, to be followed by a book funded by the National Science Foundation on the new technology.*

Mortimer J. Adler, ed. *The Great Ideas: A Syntopicon of Great Books of the Western World* (1952). Chicago: Encyclopedia Britannica, 1955. (Vols. 2 and 3 of *Great Books of the Western World.*)

Alan L. Bullock, ed. *The Harper Dictionary of Modern Thought.* New York: Harper & Row, 1977.

My list would be constantly changing with new books being added all the time. Readers need to understand that no book stands by itself. It is part of a continuing dialogue with its predecessors. Each book is a part of a river of books. Books are embedded in a historical context; Aristotle's *Metaphysics* cannot be understood without an understanding of the pre-Socratics, for example. You need to lead from one book to another—maybe using Mortimer Adler's *Syntopicon.* You don't have to go back and read everyone that came before. Then you would be a part of an infinite regress. You have to start somewhere. The point is to be aware that reading and ideas do not arise *de nova.* There is an element of history behind all reading—that continuing dialogue again. Any intelligent reader has to keep in mind the question, What was it about previous answers and writings that was unsatisfactory and insufficient and gave rise to the new formulation?

In picking books you cannot be a magpie picking one Aristotle, one Shakespeare. First, the reader must ask, What are the relevant questions? and then, What books address themselves to those questions? If it's a question about the nature of justice then proceed from Aristotle to John Rawls. Readers should have a sense of purpose for reading *and* they need to know how to relate one book to another. Readers need to know ways of reading—how to trace out an idea by following its threads.

My own earliest reading was boy books—Nick Carter detectives. But they got me into the habit of reading. My own experience of life on the Lower East Side of New York drew on one thematic and problematic definition that shaped my entire life. My father died early and my mother was a factory worker. I was surrounded by slums, garbage scows, Hooverville. It was the "why" and the "does it have to be this way" that led me and my reading to the socialist movement, and on to my profession of sociology.

The answer to your question is more complex, rich and variegated than the notion that somewhere there is a set of books that impressed you. It is too simplistic an approach. Maybe we should be urging people toward favorite encyclopedias as a beginning point. A good one is Alan Bullock's *Harper Dictionary of Modern Thought*.

Nicolaas Bloembergen

Nicolaas Bloembergen is professor of physics in the Applied Sciences Division and Harvard's Gerhard Gade University Professor. He was born and educated in the Netherlands and joined the Harvard faculty in 1949. In 1981, Professor Bloembergen received the Nobel Prize in Physics.

Albert Einstein and **Leopold Infeld.** *Physik als Abenteuer der Erkenntnis* (*The Evolution of Physics,* 1938). Simon & Schuster, 1967. (Pb)

This book I read at the age of eighteen. It convinced me that the study of physics poses some of the most challenging questions to the human mind. I have not been disappointed in pursuing physics as a lifetime career. The book was published at the same time in the English language with the less informative title *The Evolution of Physics.*

Philip Morrison, Phylis Morrison, Charles Eames, and **Ray Eames.** *Powers of Ten.* New York: W. H. Freeman, 1982.

Nowadays, there are many excellent books introducing the high school and college student to the human quest in science and technology. If I had been born fifty years later, I am sure this charmingly illustrated book would have alerted my mind to the challenges of science. This book is the first in the series of the Scientific American Library. Many of these volumes could be recommended.

Erich Maria Remarque. *All Quiet on the Western Front* (1928). New York: Fawcett Book Group, 1979. (Pb)

In the 1930s this book opened my eyes to the senselessness of trench warfare in World War I, and the accompanying degradation of the human spirit. The same theme can, of course, be found in many other more recent books, including Norman Mailer's *The Naked and the Dead,* based on episodes from World War II. It is a sad commentary on the human condition, that each generation produces books of this nature.

William Bossert

William Bossert is an esteemed population biologist with current research interests in computer applications in medicine, the management of marine fisheries and evolutionary biology. He is the David B. Arnold Professor of Science at Harvard and was formerly a junior fellow in the Society of Fellows. Former students and his peers praise his pioneering efforts on behalf of Harvard students to bring the University into the computer age. He is also consistently described as an excellent teacher.

Albert G. Ingalls, ed. *Amateur Telescope Making* (1926). 3 vols. New York: Munn, 1945.

Shikubu Murasaki. *The Tale of Genji* (ca. A.D. 1000). Edward G. Seidensticker, trans. New York: Random House, 1985. (Pb)

The Scientific American.

An illness kept me in bed and away from school most of one year when I was very young. I read voraciously, since I could do little else. My diet included all of the classics in English literature from Shakespeare to Damon Runyon. The result of this overdose was not entirely positive. I have read very little fiction since then, except for a few works forced on me by their popularity in dinner conversation or required during my undergraduate education. Most everything in these two categories proved very unsatisfying, with a few exceptions such as *The Lord of the Rings* in the former category and one remarkable work in the latter. That work was *The Tale of Genji* by Lady Murasaki, which I read in the fine translation by Arthur Waley. Despite its age, nearly a thousand years, this work is as fresh as a well-written novella from Brazilian television. I had always longed for the day that I would have sufficient fluency in a foreign language to be able to think in that language. *The Tale of Genji* achieved something greater than that for me. It lead me to fantasize in a foreign culture. After reading the book I daydreamed of piercing through the court intrigue and scheming to glimpse at the harem that Lady Murasaki so vividly portrayed. Because of it I can never feel distant from another culture despite superficial barriers of language, custom and manner.

Most of the nonfiction I read now is of a technical nature and not likely of interest to a general audience. I would like to mention, however, a regular reading experience that is important to me and should be more widely read in this country. That is the monthly journal *Scientific American.* The journal contains articles on every branch of science, with special concern for the latest developments in molecular biology and particle physics. Since its beginning over a hundred years ago, *Scientific American* has kept its readers abreast of the latest science in articles prepared in a first-rate tutorial style. The publishers have always been concerned to make the societal implications of scientific developments clear to the reader. For example, the regular articles on military technology since World War II have been the best available information on that subject. The question of the accessibility of *Scientific American* articles to a general audience has been debated. I concede that if a new reader to the journal attacked a recent article on grand unification theories in modern physics without the preparation of reading previous articles on this subject in the journal in recent years, not much would be learned. If the general question of accessibility of *Scientific American,* however, is correctly answered in the negative then I am very disappointed in the intellectual state of our society. There are few societal decisions that I would willingly trust to leaders who could not read *Scientific American.*

Finally, I must add that I am very fond of the *Amateur Telescope Making* handbook in three volumes, which was spawned in the pages of *Scientific American.* I don't believe that there is any group of hobbyists as fond of talking and writing about their hobby as amateur telescope-makers. The prose of these volumes, which is often Victorian in style, conveys a sense of the importance of this hobby in the lives of the authors that is quite seductive. If anyone is looking for a hobby I recommend that they read these volumes, and they will, as did I, start grinding pieces of glass together.

Alan Brinkley

Alan Brinkley is the Dunwalke Associate Professor of American History at Harvard, specializing in twentieth-century American history. His attention focuses on the Depression, the New Deal, and the American South. His work Voices of Protest: Huey Long, Father Coughlin, and the Great Depression *won the American Book Award in 1982. He will soon publish* The Transformation of New Deal Liberalism.

William Faulkner. *Absalom! Absalom!* (1936). New York: Random House, 1972. (Pb)

When I try to think of books that have given me particular pleasure and that have affected me in particularly important ways, I think first of William Faulkner's *Absalom! Absalom!* (1936), which I have always considered one of the greatest of all American novels, a work I've read and reread with constantly increasing admiration. Long before I became a historian, I loved this book for its remarkable depth and complexity and its enormous passion and excitement. Eventually, however, I came to see in this novel some compelling justifications for my own interest in the past. It succeeds better than any work I know in revealing how history can operate as a living force in the lives of men and women.

Robert Penn Warren. *All the King's Men* (1946). New York: Harcourt Brace Jovanovich, 1982.

For many of the same reasons, I'm greatly attached to Robert Penn Warren's *All the King's Men.* It's a novel principally concerned with individuals and their pasts; and it too reveals how history defines (and often burdens) us in dealing with the present. But it's also a novel about politics, and few works of literature convey as clearly the elemental forces that politics can at times unleash.

Mark Twain. *The Adventures of Huckleberry Finn* (1884). New
York: Harper & Row, 1984. (Pb)

For somewhat different reasons, I think of *Huckleberry
Finn,* the greatest of Twain's works and in my opinion the
greatest American literary achievement of its, and perhaps any,
era. *Huckleberry Finn* reveals more about nineteenth-century
America than any work I know. And yet it also displays a moral
sensibility that resonates clearly with the values and beliefs of
our own era.

George F. Kennan. *Memoirs* (1967). 2 vols. New York: Pantheon, 1983.

George Kennan's *Memoirs,* especially the first volume
(1925–1950), have always seemed to me a work of special importance. It's an account of an indisputably important public
life, and yet it reveals as well the private world of a man of
enormous sensitivity and reflectiveness. I know of few pictures
of the public world so deftly and contemplatively drawn.

Richard Hofstadter. *The Age of Reform: From Bryan to F.D.R.*
New York: Knopf, 1955.

Richard Hofstadter's *The Age of Reform* is a work with
which I for the most part profoundly disagree. But it has also
always been a model to me of literate, bold, and imaginative
historical inquiry. It's a reminder to professional historians of
how scholarship can move beyond the narrow, specialized
bounds we impose on ourselves and make itself of interest and
importance to a larger world.

Graham Swift. *Waterland: A Novel* (1983). New York: Simon &
Schuster, 1984.

Among very recent works, I'm particularly fond of *Waterland,* a novel by a young English writer named Graham Swift.
Like *Absalom! Absalom!* and *All the King's Men, Waterland* is

not only a "story," but a "history," an exploration of how families struggle with the burdens of their own pasts. It's also a
wonderfully entertaining and absorbing mystery of great sophistication and complexity.

Robert Brustein

Robert Brustein is artistic director of the acclaimed American Repertory Theater Company in Cambridge, director of the Loeb Drama Center and professor of English at Harvard University. As one of the leaders of the American resident theater movement, he is known for his enormous support of innovative work and his ability to galvanize other creative people. He is theater critic for the New Republic.

Anton Chekhov. *Plays and Letters* (1884–1904). New York: W. W. Norton, 1977. (Pb)

The best example—after Shakespeare—of how an artist can express himself truthfully and still retain the full measure of his humanity.

Lionel Trilling. *The Liberal Imagination* (1950). New York: Harcourt Brace Jovanovich, 1979.

At the same time a great collection of essays on literature and society, and a demonstration of the continuing tension between liberalism and art.

William Butler Yeats. *The Poems of W. B. Yeats* (1887–1939). Richard Finneran, ed. New York: Macmillan, 1962. (Pb)

The master modern poet, finding language for every human emotion from the pangs of unrequited love to the ache of old age.

Henrik Ibsen. *Complete Major Prose and Plays* (ca. 1880s). Rolf Fjelde, trans. New York: New American Library, n.d. (Pb)

———. *Speeches and New Letters* (ca. 1880s). Arne Kildal, trans. Brooklyn: Haskell, 1972.

No better record of the adversarial relationship between the artist and the state.

James Joyce. *Ulysses* (1918–20). New York: Random House, 1976. (Pb)

All of English literature in one book—compressed and mythologized through the language and vision of a unique modern artist.

Friedrich Nietzsche. *Philosophy and Truth* (1870s). Daniel Breazeale, ed. and trans. Atlantic Highlands, N.J.: Humanities Press, 1979.

A revolutionary series of treatises on the transvaluation of all inherited values.

Constance H. Buchanan

Constance Buchanan is director of Women's Studies in Religion at the Harvard Divinity School. For the past decade, Constance Buchanan has been engaged in developing and directing a Harvard center for research on religion, gender and culture.

These books are about the normative dimension of human life and thought, and about diversity. They are, in particular, concerned with how we might be more self-conscious and self-critical, examining too often the unacknowledged values and assumptions that shape what we see and do.

Geoffrey Chaucer. *The Canterbury Tales* (ca. 1390). New York: Penguin, 1951. (Pb)

The Canterbury Tales is like a verbal Brueghel—a huge canvas depicting medieval English society vividly and in rich detail. What appears to be a simple tale of religious pilgrimage is really a study of the human condition, particularly the meaning of goodness or holiness in human life. Both, Chaucer tells us, are seldom what or where human beings expect them to be. His stinging social criticism warns that human piety and claims for righteousness are often in individuals and institutions the occasion for human folly and corruption. Combining as it does a deep empathy for the foolishness as well as for the dignity of human beings, Chaucer's social criticism imparted to me at an early age the value of observing, respecting, criticizing, and always seeing the humor of our humanity.

Michael Walzer. *The Revolution of the Saints: A Study in the Origins of Radical Politics* (1965). Cambridge: Harvard University Press, 1982. (Pb)

Walzer has a rare gift for understanding how individuals are oriented and motivated by religious ideas and how these ideas interact with social, economic and political realities.

Whereas many scholars assume religion has to do with another world, Walzer understands it as a way of seeing and responding to this world. This study of the Puritan saints is a tremendously skillful exploration of how in seventeenth-century England religion provided the tools for reconceptualizing and reconstructing established social and political arrangements. All too often, modern biases against religion prevent us from seeing what is obviously true historically and around the modern world—religion is a powerful force in public life.

Virginia Woolf. *Three Guineas* (1928). New York: Harcourt, Brace & World, 1963. (Pb)

In *Three Guineas,* Virginia Woolf deftly examined the relationship between gender and social values in education and the professions, and the implications of this relationship for both individuals and society as a whole. In doing so, she anticipated a central insight of contemporary analysis of gender, society and culture: that gender and value are deeply intertwined in a culture and in the social arrangements cultural patterns shape. She also saw that the historical exclusion of women from education and the professions—from public power—has given them "freedom from unreal loyalties" and a distinctive moral voice. This freedom and distinctive moral perspective, she argued, if women can self-consciously sustain both as they gain access to power, will be an important resource for transforming the basic value structure of contemporary society and the orientation of that structure toward war.

Margaret R. Miles. *Image as Insight: Visual Understanding in Western Christianity and Secular Culture.* Boston: Beacon, 1985.

This is one of those rare books that productively criticizes basic, too frequently unacknowledged assumptions in our ways of thinking about the past. *Image as Insight* lets us see that our approach to understanding historical and contemporary reality is fundamentally skewed by reliance on verbal texts. Arguing that the full task of historical understanding requires as well interpretation of visual images, and of images and texts in relation to one another, Miles proposes a hermeneutics for interpreting the visual as historical evidence. She demonstrates how this will alter our knowledge and conception of human reality. Both have been restricted by traditional methods of historical interpretation which have led us to reconstruct the past as the history largely of an unrepresentative, small elite of skilled, male language users and actors—as the history of the modern subjective consciousness.

Jeanne S. Chall

Jeanne S. Chall is professor of education and director of the Harvard Reading Laboratory. Her most widely known books include: Learning to Read: The Great Debate; *the* Dale–Chall Formula for Predicting Readability; *and* Stages of Reading Development. *A fellow of the American Psychological Association and a member of the National Academy of Education, she has served on the board of directors of the National Society for the Study of Education and the International Reading Association, and has been president of the Reading Hall of Fame. She is regarded as Harvard's "expert on reading."*

The first three works influenced directly my choice of career and early research and scholarship. The next two influenced, broadly, my approach to analysis of issues. And the last two represent more recent influences on my thinking.

Irving Lorge. "Predicting Reading Difficulty of Selections for Children." *Elementary English Review,* Volume 16 (October 1939), 229–33.

This article was the first I read on readability, and in a real sense it changed my life. Soon after reading it, I decided to go to graduate school to become an educational psychologist and researcher. The article presented the first easy-to-use readability formula based on a synthesis and refinement of earlier research and the author's original ideas—and it did it so clearly, simply and effectively. The ideas and the analysis are still as fresh and compelling today as they were when first written more than forty years ago.

Edgar Dale. *The Higher Literacy: Selections from the Writings of Dr. Edgar Dale.* Champaign: University of Illinois Film Center, 1982.

Edgar Dale's writings on readability, vocabulary and the mass media have also had a strong and lasting influence on me. His writings have also served as models of clarity and grace.

George K. Zipf. *The Psycho-Biology of Language* (1935). Cambridge, Mass.: M.I.T. Press, 1965.

I do not recall how I happened to read George K. Zipf's *The Psycho-Biology of Language.* But I thought of it as a personal discovery. Based on a different body of theory and evidence than the one with which I was familiar, he documented that in all languages one could find an inverse relationship between word frequency and word length. This gave me a convincing explanation as to why readability research had consistently found word length and frequency of usage predictive of difficulty. Zipf provided the bigger explanation—that the more the words are used, the shorter they become, and the more meanings they tend to have.

Ruth F. Benedict. *Patterns of Culture* (1934). Boston: Houghton Mifflin, 1961.

I read *Patterns of Culture,* in paperback, when it had long been accepted as a classic work, to be read by all concerned with the human condition. It was, for me, a great awakening— a view of society and of the individual through a new lens. Societies could be viewed in broad patterns of values and behaviors that influence what individuals do and value. Thus, behavior that is considered abnormal in one society may be accepted and even honored in other societies. I have read and reread it entirely and in part many times. I was influenced, first, by its ideas. I have also been influenced by its methods and have used the idea of contrasting patterns in my research and analysis of educational issues.

David Riesman, with **Reuel Denny** and **Nathan Glazer.** *The Lonely Crowd* (1950). New Haven: Yale University Press, 1973. (Pb)

The Lonely Crowd had a similar influence on me. What I admired, and still admire in the book, is the broad sweep of the analysis—historical, social, psychological—of the change in the American character. Similar to *Patterns of Culture,* I found both books beautifully written.

Jean Piaget. *Structuralism* (1968). Chaninah Maschler, ed. and trans. New York: Basic Books, 1970.

J. B. Carroll. "Developmental Parameters of Reading Comprehension" (1974). In J. T. Guthrie, ed., *Cognition, Curriculum, and Comprehension.* Newark, Del.: International Reading Association, 1977. (Pb)

I have had an almost lifelong friendship with the works of Jean Piaget. It became more intense when, in the early 1970s, I was working on a model of reading development and a friend gave me a copy of his *Structuralism.* This started me on a ten-year study of the development of reading. Toward the last phases of my work, I was encouraged further by the model of John Carroll.

Henry James. *The Wings of the Dove* (1902). New York: Penguin, 1974. (Pb)

My first introduction to Henry James was through a friend who shared with me a copy of *The Americans.* From then, until about a decade ago, I was always reading or rereading some Henry James. What made him so compelling? Perhaps it was his complexities—of character, incidents and style. I think they offered me an escape from my own work in which I strive for clarity, simplicity and directness. I have also learned much about the psychology of reading from Henry James. When I first started reading James, I found his sentences almost impossible. They became quite readable with exposure and practice.

Hale Champion

Hale Champion continues his many-faceted Harvard career, now as executive dean of the John F. Kennedy School of Government and faculty chairman of the Senior Executive Fellows Program. He began his career as a reporter. In 1958 he joined Governor Edmund Brown of California as press secretary and then became director of finance. He served as undersecretary of the Department of Health, Education and Welfare in Washington, D.C. from 1977 to 1979.

The challenge of every century (and I hope the twenty-first will not be wholly different) is to keep humanity's ever-increasing capacity for self-destruction within bounds, and to shape political behavior and governance to that end. Our one best hope is to understand the human condition better and give it an appropriate politics.

Anthony Powell. *A Dance to the Music of Time* (1962–75). 12 vols. Boston: Little, Brown, 1976.

This is the life of a modern man in urban society (London), his sensibility, his relationships, his experience and his reflections over most of the same decades in which I lived. It has, for me, all the values of comparative studies. It is also wonderful reading.

James MacGregor Burns. *Roosevelt: The Lion and the Fox* (1956). New York: Harcourt, Brace, 1963. (Pb)

This may not be the most scholarly Roosevelt (FDR) biography, but it came early and strongly shaped my sense of the intersections of politics and governing at a time that both became permanently part of my emotional life.

Herman Melville. *The Confidence-Man; His Masquerade* (1857). Herschel Park, ed. New York: W. W. Norton, 1971. (Pb)

Most Melville authorities will tell you that this is one of his worst books; and, indeed, I suppose I would not miss *Moby Dick* for it. But its black humor is that of the spirit of American political life, outrageous, surrealistic, and full of promises, false and true, kept and unkept, often not even intended. It is the torturous truth about that side of the American political character that produced Andrew Jackson, Lyndon Johnson, Warren G. Harding, Ronald Reagan, and thousands of others.

Leo Tolstoy. *War and Peace* (1865–69). Louise Maude and Aylmer Maude, trans. George Gibian, ed. New York: W. W. Norton, 1966.

In my view, the most memorable statement of the relationship between men and history, between individuals and events, in all fiction. This is passionate objectivity.

Richard E. Neustadt. *Presidential Power* (1960). New York: Wiley, 1980. (Pb)

This is the revised version: the first edition was the first time political science ever really spoke to me with a sure sense of both large societal purpose and the nuances of institutional responses.

Alexander Hamilton, John Jay, and **James Madison.** *The Federalist* [*Papers*] (1788). Benjamin F. Wright, ed. Cambridge: Harvard University Press, 1961.

Most of our intergovernmental literature is a kind of shifting Sargasso Sea not worth ploughing through. There aren't better insights or more ingenious polemics anywhere than in these originals.

Alfred D. Chandler

Alfred Chandler is the Straus Professor of Business History at the Harvard Business School. He is the author of numerous works, including Strategy and Structure: Chapters in the History of the American Industrial Enterprise *(1962) and* The Visible Hand: The Managerial Revolution in Modern Business *(1977). For many, he is considered to be the dean of the organizational school of historians. His forthcoming work, a cross-national study, is tentatively titled* Scale and Scope.

Max Weber. *The Theory of Social and Economic Organization* (1922). A. M. Henderson and Talcott Parsons, trans. New York: Free Press, 1947. (Pb)

————. *From Max Weber: Essays in Sociology* (1946). H. H. Gerth and C. Wright Mills, eds. and trans. New York: Oxford University Press, 1979. (Pb)

These are the two best translations of the works of Max Weber, one of the world's most influential social scientists. When I read these as an embryonic historian, they opened up a new world. From a vast array of historical data Weber developed concepts—bureaucracy, charismatic, idea types and many others—that are still central in analyzing the recent experiences of modern man.

Ralph Henry Gabriel. *The Course of American Democratic Thought* (1940). New York: Ronald Press, 1956.

A masterpiece of synthesis, this study reviews changing American attitudes and values from the early nineteenth century to World War II, by focusing on what Gabriel calls the "American democratic faith." It provides an impressively coherent overview of the development of ideas of such American writers, philosophers, and political thinkers as Emerson, Thoreau, Melville, Whitman, Calhoun, Summner, Royce, Henry

Adams and others, as the nation transformed itself from a rural, agrarian westerly-moving entity to an industrial, urban world power.

Stephen K. Bailey. *Congress Makes a Law: The Story Behind the Employment Act of 1946* (1950). Westport, Conn.: Greenwood Press, 1980.

This is still the most illuminating book that I have read on the American legislative process. It begins by reviewing the economic and political situations and the ideological attitudes and values that led to the gestation of this legislation and then follows the bill along a torturous course from committees, through the Senate and House and then to the final compromises in conference committee. Few studies illustrate more clearly and precisely the interactions of ideas and attitudes and of procedures and traditions, as well as the impact of perceived needs and opportunities and individual personalities, on the definition of a piece of legislation that helped to reshape the role of government in the American economy.

Thomas C. Cochran. *Railroad Leaders, 1845–1890: The Business Mind in Action.* Cambridge: Harvard University Press, 1953.

This is one of the finest pieces of economic and social history written in the past generation. It does more than tell a story. It provides a systematic understanding of the ideas and actions of a discreet and most influential group, the presidents of major American railroads from 1840 to 1890. By carefully reviewing the working correspondence of sixty senior executives, it reveals the views of the men who created the nation's first big business on finance, ownership and control, administration, strategies of growth, technological innovation, labor relations, public opinion and the role of government. There is no better introduction to the implications of the rise of modern managerial enterprise than this book.

Theodore Roosevelt. *The Letters of Theodore Roosevelt.* Elting
   E. Morison, ed. 8 vols. Cambridge: Harvard University
   Press, 1951–54.

Carefully selected and annotated, these letters are, like
those of the railroad presidents, operating documents used to
direct and carry out the multifaceted business of the presidency. There are also letters to family, friends and a wide variety of acquaintances in prominent positions throughout the
world. T. R. was a man of energy, enthusiasm and convictions
who wrote what he meant. So these letters reveal much about
the nature of the man and the nature of the presidency. They
are particularly valuable in showing a wide variety of complex
matters that an active president like T. R. had to handle in a
single day. Again, like the letters of the railroad presidents, such
letters are basic sources of information with which historians
must work.

Mary V. Chatfield

Mary V. Chatfield has been the head librarian at the Baker Library of the Harvard Business School for eight years. Her association with the Harvard community began as an undergraduate at Radcliffe College. She earned her M.B.A. at the Business School while continuing her duties as head librarian. She tries to read one book a week.

God, democracy, and food should prepare anyone for any century.

The Book of Common Prayer (1549). New York: Oxford University Press, 1928.

As a daily or occasional guide to behavior or as a source of comfort and guidance, it is without peer. The beauty of the language alone is sufficient reason for a nonbeliever to read it.

Alexander Hamilton, John Jay, and **James Madison.** *The Federalist [Papers]* (1788). Benjamin F. Wright, ed. Cambridge: Harvard University Press, 1961.

An ever-current and germane discussion of the rewards of a democratic form of government and the difficulties encountered in implementing it.

H. H. Munro. *The Short Stories of Saki* (1894–1916). New York: Doubleday, 1976.

Reminds you that life is complex as are people. Justice is frequently meted out when it is least expected, and a sense of humor leavens almost all situations.

Barbara Pym. *Excellent Women* (1952). New York: Harper & Row, 1980. (Pb)

———. *Quartet in Autumn* (1977). New York: Harper & Row, 1980. (Pb)

The daily life of ordinary people is as rich and varied as that of any exotic tribe, but the discovery of this richness requires careful study.

Any good cookbook.

The most soothing of all reading. The rational is still achievable in the most chaotic of worlds.

Judith Martin. *Miss Manners' Guide to Excruciatingly Correct Behavior* (1982). New York: Warner, 1983. (Pb)

For guidance, sustenance and correction.

C. Roland Christensen

C. Roland Christensen is Harvard's Robert Walmsley University Professor. He is the first member of the Harvard Business School faculty to receive this honor. At the Business School he is known by peers and students as the father of the case method, although he attributes the distinction to the ancient Greeks. He is well known for his association with boards of directors as a member, as a course topic and as a field of research. He has a passionate interest in business policy.

Here are the books—all old, dog-eared, reread and reread, little (no big fat volumes), most committed to memory—of my five-inch bookshelf. But they miss the greatest influence on this educator—Miss Adams, a seventh-grade teacher in Iowa City, Iowa. She introduced me to poetry, where the ultimate wisdom —the philosophy of life—is found. The first step in the development of an anthology was our study of "Miniver Cheevey" by Edwin Arlington Robinson. It is still exciting fifty-four years after that original encounter.

Edward H. Carr. *What Is History?* (1961). New York: Random House, 1967. (Pb)

Carr's little book has a magnificent message—to live we must understand our historical roots. Carr gives us a way of understanding the past so as to predict the future.

Jean Rostand. *Can Man Be Modified?* (1956). Jonathan Griffin, trans. New York: Basic Books, 1959.

Rostand, a biologist, views man in a very human way, examines how science is impacting that basic humanness and then teases us with what he/she will be in future centuries.

Mark Spade [Nigel Balchin]. *How to Run a Bassoon Factory, or Business Explained* (1934). Boston: Houghton Mifflin, 1936.

Spade tickles the mind; with tongue in cheek, he describes business so that one laughs—even roars—at his chosen vocation.

Edwin Way Teale, ed. *The Insect World of J. Henri Fabre* (1949). New York: Harper & Row, 1981.

Fabre looks at the smallest and lowest—insects—and shows us their great abilities—even wisdom. A constant reminder to look at the ordinary to see the extraordinary.

William I. Beveridge. *The Art of Scientific Investigation* (1951). New York: Random House, 1960. (Pb)

For the investigator, this little book is a gold mine of reflection and practical suggestion. He brings the power of scientific discipline to bear on everyday life.

Adolph A. Berle, Jr. *Power Without Property; A New Development in American Political Economy.* New York: Harcourt, Brace, 1959.

The book raises fundamental questions about modern business organization and ownership. It outlines the quiet revolution which has changed the power bases of our industrial society.

Robert Coles

Robert Coles is a research psychiatrist for the Harvard University Health Services, as well as professor of psychiatry and medical humanities at the Harvard Medical School. Since 1963, he has served as a consultant to the Southern Regional Council on "Psychiatric Aspects of Desegregation in the South." Among his thirty-five books are Children of Crisis *(in five volumes) and* Erik H. Erikson: The Growth of His Work. *In May 1981, Dr. Coles received a grant from the John D. and Catherine MacArthur Foundation. He is now working in countries such as Northern Ireland and South Africa on the question of political socialization, studying the way children of various nations obtain their political convictions and moral values.*

The Bible.

I keep the Bible on my desk, and go back again and again to the Psalms, to certain passages in Isaiah and Jeremiah, to Matthew and Luke, to passages in St. Paul's letters—Corinthians, Romans.

George Eliot. *Middlemarch* (1871–72). New York: Bantam, 1985. (Pb)

George Eliot's *Middlemarch* has been a companion since college days. I've read it three times—at different times in my life. I teach it at Harvard College and Harvard Medical School. Its moral power is compelling; it makes one stop and think about what this life's purposes ought to be.

Walker Percy. *The Moviegoer* (1961). New York: Avon, 1979. (Pb)

Similarly with Walker Percy's *The Moviegoer,* a wonderfully comic yet intensely serious examination, in the tradition of

Kierkegaard, of this "present age." I use *The Moviegoer,* too, in teaching undergraduates and medical students, and find it quite helpful in a course I teach at the Harvard Business School—an examination of ethical issues through certain novels and short stories.

Georges Bernanos. *The Diary of a Country Priest* (1936). Pamela Morris, trans. New York: Carroll & Graf, 1984. (Pb)

Ignazio Silone. *Bread and Wine* (1937). Harvey Ferguson, Jr., trans. New York: New American Library, 1980. (Pb)

The Diary of a Country Priest by George Bernanos and *Bread and Wine* by Ignazio Silone are long-standing favorites of mine—their evocation of the pastoral (as opposed to the prophetic), a constant help against certain occupational hazards that accompany writing and teaching.

Charles Dickens. *Little Dorrit* (1857). Harvey P. Sucksmith, ed. New York: Oxford University Press, 1982. (Pb)

The later novels of Dickens mean a lot to me—especially *Little Dorrit.* I grew up hearing Dickens read aloud by my parents, and I still go back to him—even teaching certain novels of his which offer glimpses of lawyers and the law at Harvard Law School. His moral energy never fails to get us all going in class.

Leo Tolstoy. *The Death of Ivan Ilych* (1886). Aylmer Maude, trans. New York: New American Library, 1960. (Pb)

Finally, there is *The Death of Ivan Ilych* by Tolstoy—a powerfully wrought, ever-so-affecting reminder of what moral matters we had best try to settle before we take leave.

John Williams Collins III

John Collins is the librarian of the Graduate School of Education at Harvard. His professional interests include bibliographic instruction, information access, and database searching.

Apart from individual titles in particular disciplines, books such as *A Guide to Reference Books,* 9th ed. (1976), which open the doors to information access and the printed word at large, will provide readers with the tools and skills necessary to find the information that will enable them to meet the challenges of the twenty-first century.

Graham T. Allison. *Essence of Decision: Explaining the Cuban Missile Crisis.* Boston: Little, Brown, 1971. (Pb)

For its insight into the decision-making process.

Jack Kerouac. *On the Road* (1957). New York: Penguin, 1979. (Pb)

For its depiction of an era and a life-style.

Percy Bysshe Shelley. *The Complete Poetical Works* (1813–21). New York: Oxford University Press, 1974.

For the beauty of the poems.

Philip Gaskell. *A New Introduction to Bibliography.* New York: Oxford University Press, 1972.

Offers an opportunity to gain an understanding and appreciation of the books as a material object.

Eugene Paul Sheehy. *A Guide to Reference Books.* 9th ed., 2d suppl. Chicago: American Library Association, 1982. (Pb)

Because it provides access to reference books basic to research.

Richard N. Cooper

Richard Cooper is the Boas Professor of International Economics at Harvard's Graduate School of Arts and Sciences. From 1963 to 1977, he was professor of economics and provost at Yale University. He served as undersecretary of state for economic affairs from 1977 to 1981.

The accumulated wisdom of others can give direction to action, provide tools for analysis and thought, and warn of dangers to a productive, tolerant and humane society. These books help in that.

Arthur M. Schlesinger, Jr. *The Vital Center: The Politics of Freedom* (1949). London: Deutsch, 1970.

Eric Hoffer. *The True Believer: Thoughts on the Nature of Mass Movements* (1951). New York: Harper & Row, 1966. (Pb)

Karl R. Popper. *The Open Society and Its Enemies* (1945). 2 vols. Princeton: Princeton University Press, 1966.

Sir John W. Wheeler-Bennet. *The Nemesis of Power: The German Army in Politics, 1918–1945* (1953). New York: St. Martin's, 1964.

These four books impressed on me the danger to civilized society of persons with an intolerance of dissent from their own agenda for society, and the importance of continued vigilance to keep them from gaining and exercising power. Schlesinger's book addresses the dangers of political extremism both on the right and on the left; Hoffer describes the psychology of what he calls a true believer; Popper traces the philosophical history of political authoritarianism since Plato; and Wheeler-Bennett offers a detailed history of how Adolf Hitler out-maneuvered the senior German Officer Corps in his successful pursuit of absolute power.

Robert L. Heilbroner. *The Great Ascent: The Struggle for Economic Development in Our Time.* New York: Harper & Row, 1963.

William H. McNeill. *Plagues and Peoples* (1976). Garden City, N.Y.: Doubleday, 1977. (Pb)

These two books indicate as well as any that history is much more than kings and generals. Famine and disease have played a much greater role in mankind's misery, and reducing the prevalence of both is a worthy, even noble, vocation.

Paul A. Samuelson. *Economics* (1953). New York: McGraw-Hill, 1980.

Roy F. Harrod. *The Life of John Maynard Keynes* (1951). New York: W. W. Norton, 1983. (Pb)

These two books suggested to me that economics is a subject worth studying.

I have identified books that were formative to my own thinking, so most of them were read long ago. They are still worth reading, though some of them will sound dated to younger minds. I read fewer books now, and more articles, which get more rapidly to the point. For instance, I benefited greatly from John Rawls's *A Theory of Justice* (1971), but I benefited even more from Kenneth Arrow's sympathetic yet critical review of it in the *Journal of Philosophy.* The core argument of Robert Axelrod's important book *The Evolution of Cooperation* (1984) can be found more succinctly stated in a 1981 article in the *American Political Science Review.*

Clare Dalton

Clare Dalton is an assistant professor of law at Harvard Law School, where she teaches contracts and legal history. Her special interests are legal and feminist theory. With her husband she is raising two sons for the future.

My initial response to this invitation was to think about reading that might help others toward the future world I like to imagine us living in. Then I considered the different possibility of reading that would be valuable to people of the future, whether or not they lived in *that* world. Finally, however, it seemed to me that the list, on either interpretation, should be the same. However those people of the future turn out, they would benefit from knowing what some of their forebears thought about, and aspired to, back in the latter part of the twentieth century.

The piece of my reading that I am taking this opportunity to share has to do with women—how some, by the 1980s, had begun to reconceive themselves, and bring themselves, reconceived, into a dialogue with men about how they should together conceive of the world.

G. W. F. Hegel. "The Independence and Dependence of Self-Consciousness: Master and Slave." Chapter IV.A. of *Die Phänomenologie des Geistes* (*The Phenomenology of Spirit,* 1807). Hamburg: Felix Meiner, 1952; New York: Oxford University Press, 1977. (Pb)

This is Hegel's classic account of the individual's unavoidable dependence on others for recognition. From this perspective, independence or autonomy, usually understood as separation from others, is in fact achieved only through connection with others—through dependence. In our own time object-relations psychology, with its emphasis on "mirroring" as a key to identity formation, contains the same core insight. But the starkness of Hegel's account, and its reminder of our potential domination of those who depend on us for recognition, gives it added force.

Margaret S. Mahler, Fred Pine, and **Anni Bergman.** *The Psychological Birth of the Human Infant: Symbiosis and Individuation.* New York: Basic Books, 1975.

Working within object-relations theory, Margaret Mahler describes children as struggling to reconcile their longing for independence and autonomy with an equally strong longing for fusion with and surrender to mother. She describes the child's tendency to grandiosity or omnipotence (denial of mother's otherness) and suggests that psychological wholeness depends on the child's developing an appropriate sense of mother as separate. Her work provides an account of the central struggle of childhood that is quite different from Freud's. It also suggests that the master/slave dynamic intuited by Hegel is in fact the very psychological dynamic through which our individual identities are forged.

Dorothy Dinnerstein. *The Mermaid and the Minotaur: Sexual Arrangements and Human Malaise.* New York: Harper & Row, 1976. (Pb)

Dorothy Dinnerstein shares Margaret Mahler's understanding that separation-from-mother is the key to later individual development. But she argues that our society systematically subverts that possibility, leaving men and women differently situated, but allied in a residual (subconscious) hatred and fear of mother, and of women. She suggests the consequences of this malaise for relations between men and women, and for the society at large. She urges a radical sharing of parenthood, which would present children with the same need to separate from father that they now experience only in relation to mother, as the road to human progress.

Hester Eisenstein and **Alice Jardine,** eds. *The Future of Difference* (1980). New Brunswick, N.J.: Rutgers University Press, 1985. (Pb)

Hester Eisenstein and Alice Jardine's powerful collection of feminist writing begins in the same general territory as Dinnerstein's book—the psychological dynamics that differentiate women from men. The theme of difference is pursued in sections devoted to current French feminism (strongly influenced by the post-structuralism of such writers as Derrida and Lacan) and recent feminist literary criticism. Finally, the book projects the theme of difference out into the world, exploring its potential for social and political transformation.

Suzette Haden Elgin. *Native Tongue.* New York: Donald A. Wollheim, 1984. (Pb)

Suzette Haden Elgin writes a science-fiction novel both grim and inspirational. The society in which it is set reflects a playing out of some of the most dehumanizing tendencies of our own, including the firm relegation of women to a subordinate status in the service of men. But the women, invisibly, are fighting back—through the development of their own language. In its dramatic portrayal of the negative potential of our cultural values, and its celebration of the positive potential of difference, this book makes a fitting postscript to my list of suggested reading for the future.

Dante Della-Terza

Dante Della-Terza is the Irving Babbitt Professor of Comparative Literature at Harvard University. Professor Della-Terza was born in southern Italy, in a town destroyed by the earthquake of 1980. He studied in Pisa, Zurich and Paris and moved to the United States in 1959. He taught at UCLA from 1959 to 1963 and joined the Harvard faculty in 1963. Professor Della-Terza is currently writing about the disappearance of his home town in the earthquake of 1980 and the collective wound it caused.

Readers will identify in the books only the truths they have been able to conquer or preserve by their own efforts. Books say better on our behalf what life teaches us. They are in a sense ourselves.

Dante Alighieri. *The Divine Comedy* (ca. 1307–21). New York: Penguin, 1984. (Pb)

I started reading the poem when I was in high school. Our teachers would ask us to memorize entire cantos. In a sense it was a felicitous coaction since Dante's journey became a part of myself. The lines I learned came to my rescue in time of perplexities by giving me a sense of direction, a certitude.

Giovanni Boccaccio. *The Decameron* (ca. 1348). New York: New American Library, 1982. (Pb)

After the first gloomy pages of the book the reader reaches a landscape of rejuvenation, rebirth and revival. A spark of hope defeats darkness; the world becomes alive again with its doubts and certitudes, its tricks and heroisms, its comic fears and noble behaviors. It teaches the reader how loving and lovable the world can become.

Ludovico Ariosto. *Orlando Furioso* (1532). New York: Oxford University Press, 1983. (Pb)

There is a way to escape relativity through evasive attitudes of selfishness, there is a way to absolve in our dreams the deep sense of our life. Dream becomes a metaphor for life. Ariosto tells with grace and irony a truth about ourselves which is far stronger than the historical setting that produces it. He has been able to fill poetic dreams with experience and wisdom, hope and determination.

Michel de Montaigne. *Selections from the Essays* (1595). Donald M. Frame, ed. and trans. Arlington Heights, Ill.: Harlan Davidson, 1973. (Pb)

When besieged by endless traps man learns how to grasp values, how to outline intellectual and moral commitments which represent a frontier of self-preservation. Seldom has a book been written with such literary skill and such implacable lucidity.

Giovanni Battista Vico. *Autobiography* (1725–28). M. H. Fisch and T. G. Bergin, trans. Ithaca, N.Y.: Cornell University Press, 1963. (Pb)

One learns by reading it how a man deprived of skills that could help him to become prominent in a competitive society can bravely construct an image of the self in which all the deep thoughts, all the world's dreams, are mirrored.

Jeroslav Hasek. *The Good Soldier Svejk and His Fortunes in War* (1922). Cecil Parrott, trans. Cambridge, Mass.: Robert Bentley, 1980.

It is perhaps not a very great book. It gives me, however, a sense of comic relief when I am confronted with the arrogance of the powerful. I owe Hasek many good laughs in gloomy times. I am grateful for it.

Paul M. Doty

Paul M. Doty is Mallinckrodt Professor of Biochemistry. In addition to his work on nucleic acids and gene structure, Mr. Doty has had a long-time interest in arms control, science policy and international affairs. Director emeritus of the Center for Science and International Affairs, he has been a presidential adviser on arms control. He was an early participant in the Pugwash Conferences on World and Scientific Affairs, which first brought U.S. and Soviet scientists together informally to discuss the problems of arms control.

Molecular biology:

Erwin Schrödinger. *What Is Life?* (1946). New York: Cambridge University Press, 1967.

James D. Watson. *The Double Helix* (1968). New York: New American Library, 1969. (Pb)

Bruce Alberts et al. *Molecular Biology of the Cell.* New York: Garland, 1983.

In a very slim volume Schrödinger, a theoretical physicist, focused with remarkable foresight on what the genetic material had to be like. Watson describes his discovery with Crick and Wilkins of the detailed structure of the genetic material, DNA, by recounting his view of it as it occurred in his early twenties. Alberts and five other authors, including Watson, put together an integrated, detailed picture of the molecular basis of life that has flowed from the discovery of the structure of DNA.

The atom, the Russians and ourselves:

Herbert F. York. *Race to Oblivion.* New York: Simon & Schuster, 1970.

Andrei D. Sakharov. *Progress, Coexistence, and Intellectual Freedom* (1968). New York: W. W. Norton, 1970.

Hedrick Smith. *The Russians* (1976). New York: New York Times, 1983.

Strobe Talbott. *Endgame: The Inside Story of SALT II.* New York: Harper & Row, 1979.

In a small volume York captures the insider's view of the way the nuclear arms race developed and reached the "ultimate absurdity" with which we now grapple. Sakharov at an early stage analyzes the dangers inherent in the race and the basis for hopeful outcome. By presenting so clearly the nature of the Russian system Smith shows the difficulties that the two very different societies of the East and the West face in resolving the dilemma they have created. Talbott dissects a major act in this unfolding drama in a way that mirrors the complex interactions of politics and technology so as to convey the essence of the challenge to maintain the chain of human continuity and achievement.

Reaction to challenge:

Leo Tolstoy. *War and Peace* (1865–69). Louise Maude and Aylmer Maude, trans. George Gibian, ed. New York: W. W. Norton, 1966.

Winston S. Churchill. *The Second World War* (1948–53). 6 vols. Boston: Houghton Mifflin, 1983.

Michael Collins. *Carrying the Fire: An Astronaut's Journeys.* New York: Farrar, Straus and Giroux, 1974.

In quite different ways each book displays on a broad canvas three great human adventures. To share in these even vicariously from the safety of an armchair nevertheless enlarges the spirit and the sense of belonging to a tough, resourceful and courageous species.

John T. Dunlop

John Dunlop is the Lamont University Professor at Harvard University. A mediator and arbitrator in labor-management matters, Mr. Dunlop served as the secretary of labor from 1975 to 1976. He was director of the Cost of Living Council during 1973 and 1974, prior to which he was dean of Harvard's Faculty of Arts and Sciences.

The books all deal, I believe, with persistent and continuing issues, with reflection and action, with reflection and expression, and with individual and group relations.

Alfred North Whitehead. *Science and the Modern World* (1925). New York: Free Press, 1967. (Pb)

The lectures consider the aspects of Western culture that have been influenced by the development of modern science. "The mentality of an epoch springs from the view of the world which is, in fact, dominant in the educated sections of the communities." I have often cited Whitehead's emphasis that "the new tinge to modern minds is a vehement and passionate interest in the relation of general principles to irreducible and stubborn facts."

Samuel Eliot Morison. *Admiral of the Ocean Sea: A Life of Christopher Columbus* (1942). Boston: Northeastern University Press, 1983. (Pb)

The detailed account of Columbus's voyages of discovery are inherently interesting, but they also provide a suggestive counterpoint to the opportunities and the problems of other voyages of discovery—in the realm of the mind or in organizational building. The process of discovery is of consuming interest and importance.

Talcott Parsons. *The Structure of Social Action* (1937). New York: Free Press, 1968. (Pb)

The relations of economics to other systems of social analysis and social behavior is a continuing problem of the first magnitude to anyone concerned with the economic aspects of behavior. The comparative study of the thought of Alfred Marshall, Vilfredo Pareto, Emile Durkheim and Max Weber is instructive to this continuing problem of the relations of economics to other social analysis. Modern economists too seldom consider these issues.

Joyce Cary. *Art and Reality: Ways of the Creative Process* (1958). Freeport, N.Y.: Books for Libraries Press, 1970.

This volume has helped me to understand and to appreciate the necessary gap between intuition and expression, between the privacy of creation and imagination and the attempt to express in concept and in language. This is a continuing problem of creativity of ideas or institutions.

Roscoe Pound. *Social Control Through Law* (1942). Hamden, Conn.: Archon, 1968.

Irrespective of this analysis, the problem of social control of individual and group or organizational behavior is a continuing problem of tension in all societies and particularly in Western societies with their values. The secularization of control and its consequences is a persistent concern.

Theodore Reik. *Listening with the Third Ear* (1948). Garden City, N.Y.: Garden City Books, 1951.

In the work of dispute resolution, as well as in common discourse, interpreting what parties say and what they really mean is of fundamental importance. Reflection on this process of distinguishing the two is of continuing significance to reflection and action.

Diana Eck

Diana Eck is a professor of comparative religion and Indian studies at Harvard University. She is the moderator of the World Council of Churches program on "Dialogue with Proper Living Faiths." Her most recent book is Banaras, City of Light *(1982), which followed* Darsan: Seeing the Divine Image in India *(1981).*

The Bhagavad Gītā (ca. A.D. 1). Franklin Edgerton, trans. Cambridge: Harvard University Press, 1944.

The Bhagavad Gītā is a basic resource for understanding the spiritual life of India, and in my reading and rereading of it through the years, it has become a resource for my own life as well. I first read it in the mid-1960s and was put off by the setting: a battlefield, where the warrior Arjuna recoils at the prospect of fighting his cousins, and throws down his weapons. His charioteer Krishna takes him to task for renouncing his duty to fight. It took me some time to see what Hindus have seen here—that this is not a treatise on war, but a treatise on the nature of responsible action. Krishna teaches the *yoga,* or discipline, of action: to act and be involved in the world, without personal or egotistical attachment to the fruits of those actions. It is a scripture that has challenged and engaged Hindus for many centuries and has given rise to generations of interpretation and commentary.

Wilfred Cantwell Smith. *The Meaning and End of Religion* (1962). New York: Harper & Row, 1978. (Pb)

This book completely changed my understanding of "religion." Here Smith argues that the noun "religion," as it is used today in the West, has come to refer to a sphere of activities or beliefs that can somehow be circumscribed and distinguished from other spheres of life, such as politics, economics, or social life. Not only does this miss the point of what it means and has meant to be "religious" in the West, but it seriously misrepresents the nature of human religiousness in the Hindu, Buddhist, or Muslim traditions. In essence, Smith suggests that we drop the word "religion" as a noun, and use the adjective "religious," that quality which conditions *all* the activities of religious people. Of course there are objective facts to be studied in attempting to understand the great, ever-changing cumulative religious traditions of humankind. But as students of these traditions we are challenged, even further, to understand "faith," that is, the engagement and commitment of the people for whom they have been meaningful. In my own work, this has reminded me repeatedly that I am not trying to understand some abstract thing called "Hinduism," but I am trying to understand Hindus and the life, meaning and transcendence that they perceive.

Ananda K. Coomaraswamy. *Yakshas* (1928–31). 2 vols. New Delhi: Munshiram Manoharlal, 1971.

I first read this book when I was doing fieldwork in Banaras, India in 1973. It opened my eyes to an entire ancient Indian world view that was not readily apparent from the study of classical Hindu texts. It had little to do with the renunciation of "this shore" for the "far shore" of liberation, *moksha.* It was focused, rather, on the vibrant life-force deities of "this shore" —the *yakshas,* associated primarily with the generativity of trees, and the *nagas,* associated with rivers and pools. The existence of these ancient deities could be intimated from the classical texts, since the Buddha, Shiva, and Krishna all conquered and subsumed them in their rise to popular prominence. The nature and history of these deities, however, was clearer from art-historical sources. Coomaraswamy, a great cultural and art historian, helped me come to value the indispensable importance of art and image in the study of religious traditions, especially popular traditions which have been excluded in textual sources. Even more important, he helped me to see the persistence of the *yaksha/naga* deities even in the popular traditions of India today.

M. K. Gandhi. *Gandhi, an Autobiography: The Story of My Experiments with Truth* (1927–29). Mahadev Desai, trans. 2 vols. New York: Dover, 1983. (Pb)

This was my first introduction to Gandhi, and I still think it is the best introduction. Gandhi was a prolific writer; his collected works fill over eighty volumes. Here Gandhi tells his own story, reflecting on his life as a man in his fifties, who had already spent twenty years in South Africa, had worked out his philosophy of nonviolent social change, and had been actively involved for ten years in the freedom struggle in India. Since it was written to be serialized in Gandhi's newspaper, *Young India,* this autobiography has something of a didactic and episodic quality. What I love about this book is that here one encounters a person, with all his foibles and faults, with his views on food and sewing machines, on social justice and political change. Gandhi reveals so much of himself that I can say I met Gandhi here. I argued and quarreled with him, but eventually he won my heart.

Mary Daly. *Beyond God the Father: Toward a Philosophy of Women's Liberation.* Boston: Beacon, 1973.

This is a powerful and important book, not only in feminist theological thinking but in feminist analysis more generally. Daly looks clearly and critically at the patriarchal symbols that have shaped the thought and culture of the West. In this book, Daly begins to move beyond the Christian tradition into a post-Christian feminism. In a sense, she had already made this move when she preached at Harvard's Memorial Chapel in 1971, the first woman to preach at a Sunday service in 336 years. At the end of the sermon, she led a dramatic walkout, inviting the congregation to affirm its faith by "rising and walking out together." Daly's work has had a tremendous impact on women and men, inside and outside the church, for whom the symbol of "God the Father" has been changed forever. When I first heard and read Daly, I had already spent time in India, and the sovereignty of my old familial notion of God the Father had already been questioned by the insights and critiques of Hindu friends and teachers. Daly helped me to see the same key issues of Christian patriarchy and chauvinism from a feminist perspective within my own culture. I too walked out in 1971, but walked back in almost immediately—into a church that, I think, needs to be challenged to a larger and more inclusive theological vision.

Christopher Edley

Professor Edley's primary areas of teaching and research at the Harvard Law School are administrative law and public policy. He is also actively involved in a number of projects related to racial justice and poverty. He served in the Carter administration as assistant director of the White House domestic policy staff responsible for income-maintenance and social-services policy. He joined the Harvard faculty in 1981, and hopes to spend much of his career in the public sector.

Of the genuinely uncertain questions facing the United States, the problem of color and social justice seems to me more urgent and demanding than any, except avoidance of nuclear and environmental catastrophe. Three of these books offer important insights on that problem. But instead of preaching a policy program, they teach a creative sensitivity. *Justice Accused* and *Simple Justice* do this while portraying law and lawyers in works that should be required reading for anyone remotely involved or interested in law.

Robert M. Cover. *Justice Accused: Antislavery and the Judicial Process* (1975). New Haven: Yale University Press, 1984. (Pb)

The project and its execution are deeply important: the tension between the formal demands of the rule of law, and an individual's sense of truer justice. Cover's wonderful exploration of the judicial administration of slavery offers both moving accounts of individuals pressed to apply laws they abhorred, and an enlightening exploration of underlying themes concerning legal positivism, natural justice, and the failings of legal science. *Justice Accused* is only incidentally about a historical subject, because contradictions between law's stated commitment to justice and the realities of oppression are so familiar. Finally, Cover's powerful methodology can serve as a model for examination of contemporary legal and social questions. He has greatly influenced my own views about law and about scholarship.

Richard Kluger. *Simple Justice* (1975). New York: Random House, 1977. (Pb)

This is what "a life in the law" is supposed to be about. Kluger gives a historical account of the litigation battles leading up to the Supreme Court's 1954 decision in *Brown v. Board of Education,* but it reads like a best-selling novel. It's a rich, instructive, and inspiring account of noble lawyering. For me as a black lawyer a generation and a half too young to have been in those battles, it's a compelling exploration of my professional and political roots. Just in telling a story and introducing some genuine heroes, *Simple Justice* speaks mountains of truth.

Malcolm X. *The Autobiography of Malcolm X* (1965). New York: Ballantine Books, 1977.

Even if I had not been a teenager, my first reading of *Malcolm X* would have served as something of a lightning rod, dramatically focusing a variety of impressions, frustrations, angers and hopes. I doubt that it actually had concrete effects on my sense of values or my life goals—too many other forces were at work to isolate any one or two books. But even if it did not change me, this book helped me to know myself and to appreciate better the conditions of Black America.

Josef Maria Jauch. *Foundations of Quantum Mechanics.* Reading, Mass.: Addison-Wesley, 1968.

I offer this book not for itself, but for what it represents. As an undergraduate at Swarthmore College I majored in mathematics (though I always planned on law school). Jauch's was one of several books that brought me face to face with my intellectual limits. I worked for hours to understand half a page, and for weeks to understand just a handful of pages, *feeling* myself stretched to the maximum, yet often falling short. My well-worn excuses (too tired, too busy; unprepared, uncommitted) were unavailable. It was a pure test of a certain kind of ability. The experience of the testing, as much as the results, proved crucial in my constitution. I gained new stores of patience, humility and, strangely, confidence. Mathematics has a pure aesthetic, and is cruelly judgmental when your inadequacies are bared. It may be that not all fields offer such pure tests, but they should be sought out wherever available.

Archie C. Epps

Archie C. Epps, dean of students at Harvard College, is a native of Lake Charles, Louisiana. He came to Harvard as a graduate student in 1958 after he received his A.B. degree from Talladega College in Alabama. He was awarded an S.T.B. by the Harvard Divinity School in 1961. His main intellectual interests are sociology of religion and Afro-American literature and history. He edited the speeches of Malcolm X at Harvard, which were published by William Morrow in 1968 and which included an introductory essay entitled "The Paradoxes of Malcolm X." His forthcoming book, Coping with College: Issues Faced by Students in the 1980s, *will be published in the winter of 1987.*

Each of these books illuminates an area of human thought that seeks to project man beyond the everyday. They were important to me for the special vision of the future they contained.

Robert N. Bellah. *The Broken Covenant: American Civil Religion in a Time of Trial* (1975). Minneapolis, Minn.: Winston Press, 1976. (Pb)

Robert Bellah's seminal work, *The Broken Covenant,* was published just before the bicentennial of this country. It portrays an American people who have interpreted their history as having a religious meaning. They saw themselves a chosen people. Bellah traces the myths that helped shape the American identity and underscores how they were being reexamined in light of the difficulties facing the nation. He shows the interplay between religion and secular myths. He achieves new perspectives on the constant struggle in the republic to reclaim values and a true sense of freedom. This book will whet your appetite for more Bellah, especially *Beyond Belief* and *Habits of the Heart.*

Harry A. Wolfson. *Religious Philosophy* (1961). New York: Atheneum, 1965. (Pb)

These secular essays are vintage Wolfson. A scholar in the ancient tradition, his studies range from Judaism to the patristic Fathers and finally Islamic theology. His work lays the foundation for understanding the common threads and differences in the three religious traditions that arose in the Middle East. Wolfson wrote books on many of the subjects discussed in the essays. This book illuminates the whole corpus of his work and renders him somewhat more accessible to the nonspecialist.

I read *Religious Philosophy* because Professor Wolfson directed my attention to the last piece, a sermonette given in Appleton Chapel, 17 March 1955. It is called "The Professed Atheist and the Verbal Theist," and begins with a quotation from Psalms 14:1: "The fool hath said in his heart, there is no God." Lasting less than six minutes in delivery, Wolfson's sermon summarizes the history of religious philosophy and the misguided efforts to provide secular versions.

W. E. B. DuBois. *The Souls of Black Folk* (1903). New York: New American Library, 1969. (Pb)

This small book introduced me in a detailed way to the richness of black life at the beginning of the twentieth century. Its marriage of a grasp of fact and soaring poetic prose makes it a tour de force that sweeps the reader along and immerses him in the Negro world. It encouraged me to read other books by DuBois who was one of our pioneer sociologists. He must have believed, as did F. R. Leavis, that scholarship should in part serve to produce an educated and informed public, because he wrote for general consumption.

Ralph Ellison. *Shadow and Act* (1964). New York: Random House, 1964. (Pb)

If you want to understand the joy in black life despite suffering, this book will be an invaluable aid. This collection of

essays by the author of *Invisible Man* has been my guidepost
since it was published, in the midst of a debate between Ellison
and Baldwin. Ellison stressed the particularity of black experience but also the way it embodied the universality of mankind.
It contains an important review of Leroi James's *Blues People*
and a discussion of the centrality of black life in the American
experience. It held out the view that it is possible to live beyond
race. Of course, Ellison is a superb craftsman, essayist and con-
versationalist of charm, intelligence and force.

Myron B. Fiering

Myron Fiering is the Gordon McKay Professor of Engineering and Applied Mathematics at Harvard University. A "survivor of the New York public school system," Professor Fiering has taught water resources and decision theory in the Division of Applied Sciences since 1961. He has part-time appointments at the Harvard Medical School and the School of Public Health to continue his research in the fluid mechanics problems associated with burn treatment and his interest in water-borne disease. He occasionally builds model trains.

I listed books that have been most useful in forming my views and biases—in providing the special set of filters through which I view the world. They are neither the most useful professional texts nor the books I have enjoyed the most.

John Von Neumann and **Oskar Morgenstern.** *Theory of Games and Economic Behavior* (1944). Princeton: Princeton University Press, 1980. (Pb)

Theory of Games and Economic Behavior taught me always to analyze situations, conflicts, negotiations—whatever—within a probabilistic framework. A classic, it survives today because of its insights into the ways people perceive and respond to risk, and it has profoundly influenced my personal and professional lives.

Percy W. Bridgman. *Reflections of a Physicist* (1950). Bernard I. Cohen, ed. Salem, N.H.: Ayer, 1980.

Richard Von Mises. *Probability, Statistics, and Truth* (1928). Hilda Geiringer, trans. New York: Dover, 1981.

Reflections of a Physicist and *Probability, Statistics, and Truth* had much the same effect as von Neumann's work—they shaped a lifelong viewpoint not by inculcation of formulas but by gentle nudging.

Anne Frank. *Anne Frank: The Diary of a Young Girl* (1947). New York: Doubleday, 1967. (Pb)

Thucydides. *History of the Peloponnesian War* (ca. 431–404 B.C.). Richard Livingstone, ed. New York: Oxford University Press, 1960. (Pb)

The *Diary* of Anne Frank helped to teach me who I am and whence I come; Thucydides' *History of the Peloponnesian War* helped to teach me who we all are and whence we all come, as well as that history need not be dull.

Mark Twain. *The Adventures of Tom Sawyer* (1876). Berkeley: University of California Press, 1983. (Pb)

Elizabeth Barrett Browning. *Sonnets from the Portuguese* (1850). New York: Crown, 1977.

Twain's *Tom Sawyer* and Browning's *Sonnets* are simply too beautiful for words other than their own; they taught me how fragile are the great works of the mind of man—the *Pietà,* the *Mona Lisa,* the *Moonlight Sonata,* even a great university under siege.

Erskine Caldwell. *God's Little Acre* (1933). New York: New American Library, n.d. (Pb)

D. H. Lawrence. *Lady Chatterley's Lover* (1928). Lawrence Durrell, ed. New York: Bantam, 1983.

Finally, to an adolescent growing through a tightly constrained world, Erskine Caldwell's *God's Little Acre* and Lawrence's *Lady Chatterley's Lover,* my first erotic books, gave the first hints of the joys of love and supplemented street talk as the main source of information to satisfy my growing curiosity about feeling, loving and sharing.

Franklin Ford

Franklin Ford is Harvard's McLean Professor of Ancient and Modern History, respected for his work in modern French and German history. His research interest in the history of murder and tyrannicide culminated in the recent book Political Murder. *He is a former dean of the Faculty of Arts and Sciences.*

My selection, as you will see, is highly personal. They are all favorites of mine, in part because each of them has helped me to think in the present, about the past, with some hope of making more sense of the rest of the time continuum: the part that still stretches ahead.

A fuller understanding of humanity, including its gropings and errors, but also its achievements and flashes of greatness, is what I take to be one of the historian's primary goals. It must also be a goal of anyone who thinks seriously about dangers and opportunities, some of which are already urgent realities while others require imagination to discern even as serious possibilities. My choice of works that seem "historical" in the best, because extended, sense will no doubt surprise some readers; but so may the contents of the works themselves, when seen in that light.

Garrett Mattingly. *The Armada* (1959). Boston: Houghton Mifflin, 1984. (Pb)

Mark Twain. *The Comic Mark Twain Reader.* Charles Neider, ed. Garden City, N.Y.: Doubleday, 1977.

George Otto Trevelyan. *The Early History of Charles James Fox* (1880). New York: AMS Press, 1971.

Max Weber. *From Max Weber: Essays in Sociology* (1946). H. H. Gerth and C. Wright Mills, eds. and trans. New York: Oxford University Press, 1979. (Pb)

Anatole France. *The Gods Will Have Blood (Les dieux ont soif)*

(1912). Frederick Davies, trans. New York: Penguin, 1979. (Pb)

Karl Polanyi. *The Great Transformation* (1944). Boston: Beacon, 1985.

Michael Shaara. *The Killer Angels* (1974). New York: Ballantine, 1975. (Pb)

Sybille Bedford. *A Legacy* (1956). New York: Echo Press, 1976. (Pb)

Felix Gilbert. *Machiavelli and Guicciardini* (1965). New York: W. W. Norton, 1984. (Pb)

T. H. White. *The Once and Future King* (1958). New York: Putnam, 1958.

Thucydides. *History of the Peloponnesian War* (ca. 431–404 B.C.). Richard Livingstone, ed. New York: Oxford University Press, 1960. (Pb)

Robert Nisbet. *Prejudices: A Philosophical Dictionary* (1982). Cambridge: Harvard University Press, 1983.

Howard Frazier

For over twenty-five years, Howard Frazier has educated and enthused medical students at the Harvard Medical School. His subjects include internal medicine and nephrology. In addition, he pursues research issues in personal health care as the director of the Institute for Health Research at the Harvard School of Public Health. His personal health-care routine includes canoeing and camping.

Books both reflect and influence how I look at the world; for that reason I have considered a group of books from early in my life—the decade from age twelve to age twenty-two, when I think I was more open than I am now. I have organized my comments without going back to these books and astonishing myself with my poor memory. To modify Cromwell: "What you have is a portrait of me, painted with warts and all." The decade includes my transition from sheltered suburban Chicago, to enrollment at the University of Chicago at age sixteen, to the South Pacific as an enlisted man in World War II.

Fyodor Dostoevsky. *The Brothers Karamazov* (1915). Andrew MacAndrew, trans. New York: Bantam, 1981. (Pb)

The Brothers Karamazov was my introduction to rationality gone mad. The Grand Inquisitor and Ivan were characters of a rational age and were "rational" men. They set my idea of freedom on its head. I remember being impressed with the cleverness of the Grand Inquisitor's questions, with such plausible arguments for social control. And then, having been led along the argument to the advantages of not being free, how repugnant I found the conclusion. The Grand Inquisitor led me down to a stream from which I couldn't drink. But the conclusions I couldn't accept introduced me to the notion that books were something more than engrossing plots. Thinking sometimes was uncomfortable.

Percy W. Bridgman. *The Logic of Modern Physics* (1927). New York: AMS Press, 1980.

Bridgman's *Logic of Modern Physics* whacked me over the head and knocked out many of my preconceptions about science. Bridgman makes the point that established, codified science depends on well-defined concepts like mass, time and length. But at its edge, science has concepts that are fuzzy and unreliable, and that to avoid ambiguity and make progress at frontiers, science must make use of operational definitions. It was my first exposure to the process of science: the gummy, artistic business of inspired hunches that it really is. He made me more critical of the science I was reading about, more willing to ask questions for which there weren't any pat answers. The notion that Bridgman's physics—the queen of the empirical sciences—proceeded by fits and starts, fumbling, making mistakes, backing up, was a very liberating one when I became a laboratory scientist.

Ruth F. Benedict. *Patterns of Culture* (1934). Boston: Houghton Mifflin, 1961.

Just after I left the affluent, suburban monoculture and moved on to the prideful, turbulent University of Chicago, I read Ruth Benedict's *Patterns of Culture.* That there could be worlds so different from any I knew, that they could even exist, made me a wild cultural relativist. She suggested to me that things that seemed utterly different might, in some sense, be equivalent, and forced me to think about which were better and which were worse, or what meaning "better" and "worse" had. What was the relation between the Grand Inquisitor's case for social control and the variety of Benedict's illustrations of systems that work? How could I choose?

Sophocles. *Antigone* (ca. 440 B.C.). Michael Townsend, trans. New York: Harper & Row, 1962. (Pb)

In my sea bag in the Pacific I made room for two books, a copy of the Greek tragedies and the paperback version of *The*

Pocket Book of Verse. In *Antigone* I had my first introduction
to the notion that good people, serving legitimate ends, might
come into irretrievable conflict with the state, and that they
might be destroyed as a result. After the Grand Inquisitor and
Benedict, I could see better that events might be set in motion
by an individual, basically good, who could then be struck down
by a society that had its own imperatives. It took me beyond
good guys and bad guys to the importance and the price of
standing against the established order.

Morris Edmund Speare, ed. *The Pocket Book of Verse* (1940).
New York: Pocket, 1940.

For an enlisted man, *The Pocket Book of Verse* ideally
suited a life that was full of distractions and interruptions. It
exposed me, in small doses, to language. It opened up the power
of words other than expletives. It went beyond mere direction
to the discipline of making language express something exactly.
It was *The Pocket Book* that led me to Shakespeare and the
Bible, to language that was lovely, carefully crafted, condensed,
precise, masterful.

Henry David Thoreau. *Walden* (1854). New York: Penguin,
1983. (Pb)

Walden I read later, as I observed my contemporaries
rising to what I saw as wealth. It has been important to me. Its
message was to simplify my life, to resist the attractiveness of
the dominant cultural objective of pursuing goods, to resist a
narrow definition of fortune. It gave me the courage to do other
things and to accept the consequences. The first time, I read
Walden against a background of a zillion other books. The
second time, I was older, an academic running around with a
stethoscope in my pocket, part of the pack. Now I occasionally
urge it on others with the hope it will help to reduce the distractions in their lives, that it will convince them their lives won't
end if they don't own it all.

Emanuel A. Friedman

Emanuel Friedman is Professor of Obstetrics and Gynecology at the Harvard Medical School and a practicing physician at Beth Israel Hospital in Boston, Massachusetts. Professor Friedman "rose from humble beginnings," he writes, "in the depression of the 1930s as the son of an impoverished Brooklyn rabbi who sanctioned spirit over ritual, learning for its own sake, and every man's essential role in providing for his less fortunate neighbor."

Nil sine magno labore: This erstwhile motto of Brooklyn College, my alma mater, admonishes that we should try to optimize our natural gifts for personal achievement as well as for the greater good of mankind by applying ourselves with full effort and enthusiasm.

John F. Fulton. *Harvey Cushing: A Biography* (1946). Salem, N.H.: Ayer, 1980.

A convincing biography of one of the fathers of modern medical and surgical precepts who strove for perfection in all he did; his success illustrated the merits of combining focused perseverance with eclectic interests, an example for us all to try to emulate.

Victor Hugo. *Les Misérables* (1862). New York: Penguin, 1982. (Pb)

While this thrilling story gripped me in my formative years with its suspense and adventure, it served to convince me that a worthy cause merited the struggle, win or lose and regardless of the odds.

Charles Darwin. *The Origin of Species* (1859). New York: Penguin, 1982. (Pb)

Reading this, I first began to appreciate that great visions could be derived from fresh perceptions and perspectives about commonplace and properly detailed observations.

Charles Dickens. *David Copperfield* (1850). New York: Advent, 1983. (Pb)

No other book read in my youth gave me the kind of keen insights into the plight of mankind; the pathos of Dickensian London first awakened my social conscience and the idealistic need to contribute and share.

Isaac H. Flack. *Eternal Eve* (1950). London: Hutchinson, 1960.

The compellingly graphic representations of suffering womankind painted here sensitized me in the prefeminist era and motivated my unflagging lifetime interest in obstetrics.

William Strunk, Jr. and **E. B. White.** *The Elements of Style* (1959). New York: Macmillan, 1979. (Pb)

This fabled little guide has served me for decades as an unfailing template for clear communication in both writing and speech, emphasizing the importance of simplicity and directness.

Gerald E. Frug

Gerald Frug teaches contracts, property, administrative law and local government law at the Harvard Law School. He teaches all of them, he writes, in a way that demonstrates why the kinds of books he has mentioned here are essential to understanding law. He has spent almost as much of his professional life as a government administrator as he has as a law teacher. He believes that books of this kind are as important for government officials as they are for lawyers.

These are the six books that have most influenced my thinking.

Jean-Jacques Rousseau. *Social Contract* (1762). Maurice Cranston, trans. New York: Penguin, 1968. (Pb)

This book presents the most readable, passionate account I know of the promise and dangers of democracy, and it offers an essential critique of the narrow meaning we give to the concept of democracy in America today.

Alexis de Tocqueville. *Democracy in America* (1835–40). G. Laurence, trans. New York: Random House, 1981. (Pb)

Like Rousseau, de Tocqueville makes the democratic ideal come alive; his eloquence and insights make the book thrilling to read. De Tocqueville's historical and sociological analysis, like Rousseau's political theory, help the reader get outside the commonplace understandings of democracy prevalent today.

Karl Mannheim. *Ideology and Utopia* (1929). L. Wirth and G. Shils, trans. San Diego: Harcourt Brace Jovanovich, 1985. (Pb)

Mannheim shows us that the way people think about the world is contingent rather than universally shared. He argues that thinking is not a way of getting at the truth about society from the outside; instead, ways of thinking are themselves products of society. The difficulty that Mannheim has in coming to terms with his own thesis at the end of his book adds to the excitement of reading it.

David Shapiro. *Neurotic Styles* (1965). New York: Basic Books, 1965. (Pb)

Shapiro, like Mannheim, describes how different people can understand the world in radically different ways, but Shapiro relies on psychoanalytical rather than sociological insights in his account of the variable nature of thinking. His book makes learning about alternative ways of experiencing the world fun; classifying yourself and your friends in terms of the obsessive-compulsive, hysterical, paranoid and impulsive styles is irresistible.

Norbert Elias. *The History of Manners* (1978). Edmund Jephcott, trans. New York: Pantheon, 1982. (Pb)

Elias provides insight into the historically contingent nature of our own experience of the world through a historical analysis of some of our most mundane experiences: using a fork, blowing one's nose, spitting. Elias's book is not only a fascinating social history but it provides a valuable way to understand how our attitudes toward the world are formed.

Jacques Derrida. *Of Grammatology* (1976). Gayatri C. Spivak, trans. Baltimore: Johns Hopkins University Press, 1977. (Pb)

The books listed above describe how not only democracy but also the normal routines of daily life can be lived in different ways; Derrida's book focuses on the experience of difference itself. Derrida's book is difficult and often puzzling, but he provokes his readers to think about their own ways of thinking in a powerful and insightful way.

John Kenneth Galbraith

John Kenneth Galbraith is the Paul M. Walburg Professor of Economics Emeritus. Galbraith has enjoyed a celebrated life of teaching, public service, writing and thinking. President Truman awarded him the Medal of Freedom. He served as President Kennedy's ambassador to India from 1961 to 1963. A former editor of Fortune *magazine, he has written many books including* The Affluent Society, The New Industrial State *and* The Age of Uncertainty. *His friends say he can frequently be found striding the streets of Cambridge, on his way to the pool.*

I do not urge economics; others will do that. Instead I urge the enjoyments and enlightenment to which the well-seasoned economist and citizen of the future are entitled and which have brought both pleasure and reward to me in the past.

Anthony Trollope.
Barchester Towers (1857). New York: Penguin, 1983. (Pb)
The Last Chronicles of Barset (1867). New York: Penguin, 1981. (Pb)
The Warden (1855). New York: Penguin, 1984. (Pb)

Evelyn Waugh.
Decline and Fall (1928). Boston: Little, Brown, 1977. (Pb)
Scoop (1938). Boston: Little, Brown, 1977. (Pb)

W. Somerset Maugham.
Of Human Bondage (1915). New York: Penguin, 1978. (Pb)
Christmas Holiday (1939). New York: Penguin, 1977. (Pb)

Ring Lardner. *Gullible's Travels* (1917). Chicago: University of Chicago Press, 1965.

Ernest Hemingway. *A Farewell to Arms* (1929). New York: Charles Scribner's Sons, 1982. (Pb)

Norman Mailer. *The Naked and the Dead* (1948). New York: Holt, Rinehart & Winston, 1980. (Pb)

Paul Scott. *The Raj Quartet.*
   The Jewel in the Crown (1966). New York: Avon, 1979. (Pb)
   The Day of the Scorpion (1968). New York: Avon, 1979. (Pb)
   The Towers of Silence (1971). New York: Avon, 1979. (Pb)
   The Division of the Spoils (1975). New York: Avon, 1979. (Pb)

Robertson Davies. *The Deptford Trilogy.* (Pb)
   Fifth Business (1970). New York: Penguin, 1977. (Pb)
   The Manticore (1972). New York: Penguin, 1977. (Pb)
   World of Wonders (1975). New York: Viking, 1977. (Pb)

Carney Gavin

Carney Gavin, a priest in the archdiocese of Boston, has served as curator and associate director of the Harvard Semitic Museum since 1973. Trained in classics at Boston Latin School (founded a year before Harvard), he pursued classical archaeology at Oxford before philosophical and theological studies in the German and Austrian university systems. As a Syro-Palestinian archaeologist, he has been involved in excavations in the Middle East since 1962.

The Bible.

As both a priest and a Syro-Palestinian archaeologist, my involvement with the Bible renders it the paramount book in my life. Its basic message, fascinating puzzles, and its existential significance (as the artifact of our history) have permeated my adult studies and require daily rereadings, retranslations, and analytical explications for me to function usefully in liturgical as well as academic contexts.

Because the Bible actually provides the atmosphere from which I draw breath as well as the excitingly mysterious world which it is my job to explore professionally, the Bible has long ceased to seem to be "a book" for me.

Although my training (in languages, text criticism, and various exegetical disciplines) was largely directed toward *reading* the Bible, its day-by-day utility for me (in bringing good news to Brighton or curating Semitic Museum mummies) together with my life in Bible lands have transformed what I do with its pages (or what its pages do to me) from "reading" in any normal sense. . . .

Beyond permitting time travel, personality encounters and sensory flashbacks, or providing illuminating clues and criteria (for judging present-day piety, wisdom, or pursuits of truth and goodness), "Bible reading" for me means passing back and forth through otherwise impenetrable barriers between the finite and the infinite.

Irrespective of any deference due to realms of mystical contemplation or theological speculation, Bible reading provides me practically with a very handy tool, a two-edged sword, for dealing simultaneously with the abstract and the concrete, the objective and the subjective, the ideal and the real, the immediate and the perennial.

Kristina, Queen of the Swedes, the Goths, and the Vandals. *The Works of Christina, Queen of Sweden* (late seventeenth century). Anonymous English trans. London: Wilson and Durham, 1753.

Usually on my night table, this book never fails to provide a chuckle or to propose a neatly turned truism before I drift off to sleep. The *Pensées* of Queen Kristina of Sweden is an assemblage of over fifteen hundred short sayings, written during the last decade of her life amid Rome's baroque intrigues. Originally, because of Innsbruck's tiny Silver Chapel (hidden way up above the Hafkirche and almost always locked) where Kristina took her life's most decisive step (by becoming a Catholic and thereby relinquishing the Vasa throne), her *Pensées* intrigued me. I, too, had chosen the Silver Chapel for one of life's decisive moments—to celebrate Mass for the first time after ordination. Just as I had no previous idea of that chapel's link with Kristina, I had no suspicion of how much mingled irony and hope, sardonic humor and simplicity of heart, stylistic pretense and true wisdom were to be found in her musings during her final years.

G. K. Chesterton. *The Napoleon of Notting Hill* (1904). New York: Paulist Press, 1978. (Pb)

Tom Palmer. *La grande compagnie de colonisation: Documents of a New Plan* (1937). Worcester, Mass.: Clark University Press, 1981.

Two twentieth-century "Utopian" fantasies have helped my own struggles to make sense of phenomena and theories of Realpolitik as well as of economics. Chesterton's first novel, *The Napoleon of Notting Hill,* was addressed in 1904 to "the human race to which so many of my readers belong." Set in the London of 1984 (amid familiar scenery utterly contrasting with Orwell's projections for that same year) Chesterton's tale of brilliant banners, quixotic but bloody struggles, and bafflingly poetic dialogues focuses on the romance and potential dynamism of little neighborhoods.

This paean to localism—wherein micro-autonomy is proclaimed by each tiny region's glorious gonfalons and the small-group therapy of grassroots governance—was prompted by Chesterton's disgust at the Boer War and Cecil Rhodes's conviction that "the one thing of the future would be the British Empire." Rejecting both H. G. Wells's mechanistic predictions and Tolstoy's Humanitarian Return to Nature, Chesterton suggested that "eighty years after the present date, London is almost exactly like what it is now" except for the radical change that people "had lost faith in revolutions."

Tom Palmer is a pseudonym chosen in 1937 by an extraordinarily wise financial wizard, already then expert in the international metals industry, for *La grande compagnie de colonisation* is written as a scrapbook of the future, with various telegrams, memos, organizational charts, and short notes interspersed with newspaper clippings from *Paris-Soir, La Stampa,* the *Atlantic Monthly,* the *Daily Telegraph,* and the *Luxemburger Zeitung,* from the years 1938 to 1970.

La grande compagnie was written on the eve of World War II, by a foresighted Prussian who had already exiled himself in 1933 from a Germany going mad. In 1938, after recognizing that his appeal simultaneously to self-interest and to idealism was falling upon ears deafened by war drums, the author left Europe to launch five decades of international efforts that were eventually quite successfully parallel to some of La Grande Compagnie's projects.

From several points of view, each book's simple formulas contradict the other's: Palmer's far-flung development projects (however mutually advantageous for both developers and those areas being developed) starkly contrast with Chesterton's neighborhood chauvinism. Dynamically, the solutions represent humanity's centripetal versus centrifugal movements, yet each book gleams with more than a few gems of truth and beauty.

Sheldon Glashow

Sheldon Glashow is the Higgins Professor of Physics at Harvard. His research centers on building models for elementary particles. His Nobel Prize was for his work on the unification of weak and electromagnetic forces. In addition to his thoughtful writings and frequent public television appearances, his course "From Alchemy to Particle Physics" is well known on campus.

Americans love to be told what to do. "You are what you eat!" sells innumerable quack diet books, just as "You are what you read!" brought us the Great Books, the Five-Foot Shelf, and now this colossal act of hubris: the mind-shaping favorites of a hundred professors, annotated. See them astride Plato, Darwin and Freud. Read what they read and be what they be.

I have no list to submit. I care not for this cargo cult. Books are cheap and readily available. To read is the thing, voraciously and eclectically. No guide is needed. Was *Moby Dick* more important to me than the latest Len Deighton thriller, or is browsing through my *Oxford English Dictionary* even more significant? And who should care?

Scientists are often regarded as illiterate oafs, unable to write and unwilling to read, captives of their narrow expertise, deserving candidates for humanists' contempt. Yet, most of us are well-read and can hold our own with historians, literary critics and whatever. Humanists, on the other hand, are often (though not always) scientifically and mathematically inept and proudly so. Our conversations must turn on matters of their concern, not ours. We are disadvantaged because we are compelled by their ignorance to match wits on their territory.

Membership in the community of educated men and women demands competence in science and awareness of its history. Many would dispute this claim. Here, I say, lies one explanation for the decline of American intellectualism. We have strayed from the path set by Franklin and Jefferson, who both admired and appreciated Lavoisier as much as they did Shakespeare.

Nathan Glazer

*Nathan Glazer is professor of education and social struc-
ture at Harvard's Graduate School of Education. His
courses focus on issues in education, ethnicity and American social problems. He is coeditor of* The Public Interest
and has been on the editorial staff of Commentary. *His
most notable works include* Ethnic Dilemmas 1964–1982
(1983); Ethnicity: Theory and Experience, *coedited with
Daniel Patrick Moynihan (1975); and* Beyond the Melting
Pot, *on which Daniel Patrick Moynihan also collaborated.*

Richard Hofstadter. *Academic Freedom in the Age of the College.* New York: Columbia University Press, 1955. (Pb)

Walter P. Metzger. *Academic Freedom in the Age of the University.* New York: Columbia University Press, 1955. (Pb)

These books discuss the kind of issues that are part of the
history of freedom in the United States—academic freedom and
rights. They provide a perspective on how we have developed,
to the point that in America these issues of freedom are no
longer major problems, for we have for the most part settled
them. People have little sense of how the American college and
university came to be, how they developed, how they are organized, and why they play such an important part in American
life. This book will help them, as it did me, to understand them.

Lawrence A. Cremin. *American Education.* 2 vols. to date. New
York: Harper & Row, 1982–. (Pb)

This is a monumental work of scholarship which deals with
key aspects of American life—schools, books and news. Cremin's work explains how we have tried to educate not only in
classrooms but in all sorts of other ways. It gives a unique view
of American history.

Robert E. Klitgaard. *Choosing Elites.* New York: Basic Books,
1985.

Klitgaard's recent book looks at some of the key issues we face in choosing people for scarce positions. It is relevant to every area in which difficult choices must be made. While the book focuses on choices primarily in higher education, it tells us a good deal about problems of minority representation in the professions and in politics.

Donald L. Horowitz. *Ethnic Groups in Conflict.* Berkeley: University of California Press, 1985.

This is a powerful analysis of ethnic conflict in the developing world, where it is a hindrance to development and where there is destruction of people and property on a vast scale. It raises serious and grave issues for every country. The book represents fifteen years of scholarly work and is important reading for an understanding of the problems in the developing world.

E. G. West. *Education and the State.* 2d ed. London: Institute of Economic Affairs, 1970.

Education and the State is one of those books that formed part of the revival of conservative thinking in various spheres of public policy. It raises, in a more convincing way than any other work, the questions, Why should the state educate? How should the state educate? and Should the state have a monopoly on education? West approaches these questions with wonderful scholarship and elegant analytical skills. I can't imagine anyone coming to contemporary issues of education, such as tuition tax credits and vouchers, without reading this book. Any person with an open mind will say, "Here are things I never thought of before."

Stephen J. Gould

Stephen J. Gould is a paleontologist and educator. For seventeen years he has taught geology, biology and the history of science at Harvard, now as the Alexander Agassiz Professor of Zoology. His popular books and monthly column, "This View of Life" in Natural History *magazine have drawn a new generation to science.*

As a kid growing up in New York City, I played stickball and poker instead of doing a lot of reading. I wasn't a nonreader —I read at an average age and an average rate. The passion for reading came later in college.

Charles Darwin. *The Origin of Species* (1859). New York: Penguin, 1982. (Pb)

George G. Simpson. *The Meaning of Evolution* (1949). New Haven: Yale University Press, 1967. (Pb)

Joe Di Maggio. *Lucky to Be a Yankee* (1946). New York: Grosset & Dunlop, 1951.

George Eliot. *Daniel Deronda* (1876). New York: New American Library, 1979. (Pb)

The Bible. King James version (1611). Book of Job.

Oleg Grabar

Oleg Grabar is the Aga Khan Professor of Islamic Art at Harvard with a long-standing interest in Islamic art, architecture and archaeology. His responsibilities on the steering committee of the Aga Khan Award for Architecture take him throughout the world. This year marks the fiftieth and fifty-first Ph.D. theses he has supervised. The Formation of Islamic Art *and* Alhambra *are his best-known books and he is currently completing two more general books on Islamic architecture.*

Alexandre Dumas. *The Three Musketeers* (1844). New York: Penguin, 1982. (Pb)

————. *The Count of Monte Cristo* (1844–45). New York: Bantam, 1981. (Pb)

These are the books I have most often reread since the age of twelve or thirteen for, regardless of their technical imperfections and psychological shallowness, they keep reminding me of the facts that dealing with the past is always talking about people, that imagination is part of the historian's trade, that the past can be fun, and especially that such contemporary terms as "model," "scenario," and "intervention" are nothing but fancy transformations of a novelist's plot to grab a reader's attention.

Ernst H. Kantorowicz. *Frederick the Second* (1927). E. O. Lorimer, trans. New York: Frederick Ungar, 1957.

This book, read when I was an undergraduate, fascinated me with its imagination in reconstructing dramatic events and in weaving complex ideological struggles around an extraordinary individual. The book is inseparable in my mind from other books by the same historian and from my eventual acquaintance with him and the sheer brilliance of his mind and conversation. The book or books are like the imperfect mementos of a man who felt the past as an adventure with a mission. The adventure was people, the mission ordering power.

Earl Baldwin Smith. *Architectural Symbolism of Imperial Rome and the Middle Ages* (1956). New York: Hacker Art Books, 1978.

Here again a flawed book is in fact tied to Smith's teaching and to my growing awareness of the meanings associated with forms and of the possibility of the universal principles of artistic processes and interpretations. Smith's work is inseparable in my mind with several articles written by Richard Krautheimer, André Grabar, Karl Lehman and other more-or-less contemporary historians who, wittingly or not, transferred their own visceral perception of contemporary totalitarianism into an explanation of the past.

Roman Jakobson. "Linguistics and Poetics." In *Style in Language,* Thomas A. Sebeok, ed. Cambridge: Technology Press of M.I.T., 1960.

Another, particularly vibrant introduction to a world in which theoretical models seem almost capable of explaining the realities of art. From this and structuralism it was just a step to semiology, even though nothing has as yet succeeded as well as Jakobson's formulas, because Jakobson felt and knew poetry before he worried about its structure.

Patricia Albjerg Graham

Patricia Albjerg Graham is dean of the Harvard Graduate School of Education and the Charles Warren Professor of the History of Education at Harvard University. She has served as dean of the Radcliffe Institute and vice-president of Radcliffe College. In 1977 she was appointed by President Carter as director of the National Institute of Education, the federal government's educational research agency. She resigned in 1979 to return to Harvard, to her teaching and research activities.

Sigrid Undset. *Kristin Lavransdatter* (1920–22). C. Archer and J. S. Scott, trans. 3 vols. New York: Bantam, 1978. (Pb)

Sigrid Undset's *Kristin Lavransdatter,* which I first read as a young wife and mother, captured my imagination, my ancestry and my hopes for my own future. This long tale of a formidable medieval Norsewoman who fought for her ideals, embodied as they were in her family and political allegiances, enthralled me as I pondered what the twentieth-century equivalent of her life as an American woman would be.

Gunnar Myrdal, with **Richard Sterner** and **Arnold Rose.** *An American Dilemma: The Negro Problem and Modern Democracy* (1944). 2 vols. New York: Harper & Row, 1969. (Pb)

I discovered Gunnar Myrdal's *An American Dilemma* some years after it was originally published. I read it while a graduate student in history of American education at Columbia University. As a resident of Manhattan's Upper West Side I was living for the first time in a racially mixed environment. I found two elements of Myrdal's book fascinating: the analysis of what he called "the Negro Problem" and the response of "modern democracy" to it, and the introduction of a new generation of black scholars and the legitimization of their research on black issues.

Howard Green

Howard Green is a professor of cellular physiology and chairman of the Physiology and Biophysics Department at the Harvard Medical School. He is a medical doctor who is a scientist—an award-winning cell biologist—doing skin research as it relates to skin disorders, including burns.

Hermann Alexander Keyserling. *The Travel Diary of a Philosopher* (1912). J. Holroyd Reece, trans. New York: Harcourt, Brace, 1928.

On the eve of the world's transition to modern times (1912), an aristocrat looked at the declining great civilizations and attempted to extract the significance of what they had created.

Hermann Alexander Keyserling. *The Recovery of Truth* (1927). Paul Fohr, trans. New York: Harper and Brothers, 1929.

In the late 1920s, the same aristocrat put the meaning and eternal problems of human existence (problems of the mind, problems of the soul) into a form assimilable by the thinking man of the twentieth century.

Alexander I. Solzhenitsyn. *The Gulag Archipelago, 1918–1956* (1973). Thomas P. Whitney, trans. New York: Harper & Row, 1985.

The greatest witness to life in the world's most powerful totalitarian state gives his testimony. As he himself wrote, anyone who reads and understands this book can no longer harbor illusions about communism.

Henry James. *The Bostonians* (1886). New York: New American Library, 1984. (Pb)

Apart from its quality as a novel, this book was prophetic:

the author foresaw the disappearance from the world of the masculine spirit and the sentiment of sex.

Fu Shên. *Chapters from a Floating Life* (ca. 1800). Shirley M. Black, trans. New York: Oxford University Press, 1960.

A beautiful and moving story of conjugal love.

Kenneth W. Haskins

Kenneth Haskins serves as both senior lecturer on education and codirector of the Principal's Center at Harvard's School of Education. A trained social worker, Mr. Haskins has had extensive experience in administration and program development in education. He has participated in the development of several national organizations and programs such as the National Black Child Development Institute, and serves on advisory boards of trustees of numerous local science and educational agencies.

W. E. B. DuBois. *Black Reconstruction in America* (1935). New York: Atheneum, 1969. (Pb)

This book describes the attempt to recast the political and economic structures of the United States in a manner that offered hope for a truly advanced society. It further depicts the events leading to the betrayal of the newly freed population's hopes.

John Langston Gwaltney, ed. *Drylongso: A Self-Portrait of Black America* (1980). New York: Random House, 1981. (Pb)

This is a very sensitive presentation of the thinking of those the author considers "ordinary people." The wisdom and sensitivity of black America is demonstrated in what is essentially a political commentary on American race relations.

William Hinton. *Fanshen: A Documentary of Revolution in a Chinese Village.* New York: Random House, 1968. (Pb)

The work of a people attempting to put into practice the dreams of a revolution is portrayed by examining a small village. The process of including the formerly excluded; the struggle to develop mutual respect and self-criticism; the substitution of cooperation for exploration all are sketched in ways that point out the extreme difficulty in transforming ideas into programs.

Albert Memmi. *The Colonizer and the Colonized* (1957). Howard Greenfield, trans. Boston: Beacon, 1966. (Pb)

This work provides a frame of reference for examining current relations between the "haves" and the "have nots." The roles of race and class are delineated as well as the recognition of everyone's contribution to the existence of these relationships.

Milton S. Mayer. *They Thought They Were Free: The Germans, 1933–45* (1955). Chicago: University of Chicago Press, 1966. (Pb)

The title describes the major contributions of this book. An "advanced" nation, in which citizens enjoy their freedom often at the expense of the freedom of others, discovers that it too (or at least a portion of it) is subject to domination and exploitation. Although there are many other instances in our history, this one demonstrates the negative extremes of human behavior.

Hugh Heclo

Hugh Heclo was born in Marion, Ohio, studied and taught at several British universities and received a Ph.D. in political science from Yale University in 1970. He is now a professor of government at Harvard. A former senior fellow at the Brookings Institution in Washington, D.C., Professor Heclo is also a part-time tree farmer and author of three award-winning books in public policy and American politics.

The challenge of the future is always one of trying to make sense of oneself and one's times. Books, even great books, can help only a little bit by showing how other persons in other times have made that effort. Those forearmed in this way may be somewhat less foolish and prideful as they write the novels, plays and social-science interpretations of the next century.

James Fenimore Cooper. *The Leather-stocking Tales* (1823–41). New York: Avon, 1980. (Pb)

A romantic and tragic study of manly character. Beyond their attraction as an adventure tale, these books left me as a teenager with a troubled awareness of the conflict between American "progress" and the living of an honest life.

Alexis de Tocqueville. *Democracy in America* (1835–40). G. Laurence, trans. New York: Random House, 1981. (Pb)

This book threw a new light onto things about this country that I had always taken for granted. Then at the end of the Harper & Row volume, edited by Max Lerner in 1965 or so, one could also read de Tocqueville's notes and earlier materials for what would become *Democracy in America.* One obtained a sense of how a work of penetrating insight evolves rather than happens in a great flash.

G. W. F. Hegel. *Philosophy of Right (Grundlinien der Philoso-*

phie des Rechts, 1821). T. M. Knox, trans. Oxford: Oxford
University Press, 1965.

The *Philosophy of Right* offered an intoxicating excursion
into a self-contained realm of abstract ideas. It seemed to show
how one could penetrate into a deeper reality simply by thinking about ideas, abstractions that moved and unfolded through
time. To realize that Hegel was saying things in German about
dialectics that could not be expressed in English gave one a real
sense of intellectual accomplishment.

Karl Marx. *Das Kapital* (1867). Friedrich Engels, ed. Canton,
Ohio: International, 1984. (Pb)

Volume 1 especially was simply stunning as an exercise in
comprehensive social-historical analysis. Hegel had been
brought down to earth.

Karl Polanyi. *The Great Transformation* (1944). Boston: Beacon, 1985. (Pb)

Another instance of comprehensive historical analysis that
seemed to turn conventional wisdom upside down (free-market
economics as the true social radicalism) and began my enduring
interest in interpreting the modern "welfare state."

Eugene O'Neill. *A Long Day's Journey into Night* (1940) and
A Moon for the Misbegotten (1943). In *Final Acts,* Judith
E. Barlow, ed. Athens, Ga.: University of Georgia Press,
1985.

Having read his earlier plays, I found these last works
expressed many of my own ill-formulated broodings about family life, personal careers and the meaning of it all. Again, it was
Leatherstocking's honest life without the wilderness.

Richard J. Herrenstein

R. J. Herrenstein is the Edgar Pierce Professor of Psychology at Harvard University, where he has primarily done research on human and animal motivational and learning processes. His books include Psychology, I.Q. in the Meritocracy *and* Crime and Human Nature.

These books were important to me—at a particular time and a particular point in my life. They may not be suitable for other times or other people.

Leo Tolstoy. *War and Peace* (1865–69). Louise Maude and Aylmer Maude, trans. George Gibian, ed. New York: W. W. Norton, 1966.

First read when I was about seventeen. Probably the first "great book" I truly enjoyed. It shaped certain views about history.

Charles Darwin. *The Origin of Species* (1859). New York: Penguin, 1982. (Pb)

Important for the obvious reason, plus my own fascination with the way it dealt with the subject of instinct.

John Steinbeck. *The Grapes of Wrath* (1939). New York: Penguin, 1976. (Pb)

I doubt that this would have the impact now that it did when I read it in the 1940s sometime, but it filled me then with a sense of outrage over social and economic injustice.

Franz Kafka. *The Castle* (1926). Willa Muir and Edwin Muir, trans. New York: Random House, 1974. (Pb)

———. *The Trial* (1937). Willa Muir and Edwin Muir, trans. New York: Penguin, 1953. (Pb)

————. *Amerika* (1938). Edwin Muir, trans. New York: New Directions, 1946. (Pb)

These, too, have lost their punch for me, but at the time I read them, they captured the lunacy and futility of individuals struggling with bureaucracies.

Winston S. Churchill. *The Second World War* (1948–53). 6 vols. Boston: Houghton Mifflin, 1983.

This account—especially the early volumes—counteracted to some extent Tolstoy's view of history.

John B. Bury. *The Idea of Progress: An Inquiry into Its Origin and Growth* (1920). Westport, Conn.: Greenwood Press, 1982.

Edmund Wilson. *To the Finland Station* (1940). New York: Farrar, Straus & Giroux, 1972. (Pb)

Wonderful books that tell a good story, and that set a standard for writing on intellectual history.

Howard Hiatt

Howard Hiatt is the former dean of Harvard's School of Public Health and now a professor of medicine at the Harvard Medical School. Earlier in his career he worked on the molecular biology of cancer and was the Department of Medicine chairman at Boston's Beth Israel Hospital. As a professor he now spends his teaching time trying to bring together in the training of physicians some of the public-health issues he worked on while at the School of Public Health.

It is misleading to suggest that the books I mention are crucial—they made a difference. If they had been read at a different time in life they likely would have had a correspondingly different effect.

Paul H. DeKruif. *Microbe Hunters* (1926). New York: Harcourt, Brace, 1966. (Pb)

I read this early in high school, and it whetted my appetite for medicine and science. In retrospect, it is an outrageously romanticized description of important distinguished scientists, written in a familiar style for young and impressionable high-school students. For me it was an important book in my decision to go into medicine as well as in my considering research within medicine.

Hans Zinsser. *Rats, Lice and History: The Biography of Bacillus* (1935). New York: Little, 1984. (Pb)

I read this the summer before college. By then I had settled on a career in medicine. It reinforced my interest in a career in science. It portrayed in a more scholarly fashion the attraction of medical research. More importantly, it made clear that one could combine a deep commitment to medicine and science with a continuing interest in arts, in literature. I was an English major, bound for medical school. That was not too common then, nor is it now.

John Hersey. *Hiroshima* (1946). New York: Bantam, n.d. (Pb)

This book led me to question more than had the irrationality of the nuclear arms race. Six years ago I was asked by a former student who organized it to speak at the first meeting on the medical consequences of nuclear war. It happened while candidates for president in this country were talking about *winning* a nuclear war. I accepted the invitation to open the meeting after re-reading *Hiroshima*. Those who were talking about fighting and winning nuclear war clearly had not read Hersey. They were thinking in preatomic terms. A sustained portion of my time since has been devoted to efforts to portray what the effects of nuclear war would be in medical terms.

James Hodgson

James Hodgson has been associated with the Harvard library system for twenty years. Currently he is the head librarian at the Frances Loeb Library at Harvard's Graduate School of Design, committed to improving the quality and scope of the collection. Prior to joining the Graduate School of Design he managed acquisitions for the Fine Arts Library of Harvard's Fogg Museum.

I would likely recommend any book that enriches the human spirit . . . that is likely to help us keep jolly, sane and, in some way, safe from so many others who will recommend books that champion personal power and profit.

Anthony Powell. *A Dance to the Music of Time* (1962–75). 12 vols. Boston: Little, Brown, 1976.

A *roman fleuve* in twelve parts. Suggests that a life of reflection and observation is to be prized as much as a life of action and that life's meaning is to be found in the accumulation of small events and triumphs (often only dimly perceived) rather than in high moments of bombast and tangible riches.

Mark Twain. *The Adventures of Huckleberry Finn* (1884). New York: Harper & Row, 1984. (Pb)

The essential American novel. Bleaker explorations of the same, uniquely American spirit of risk, adventure and profit— i.e., entrepreneurship—can be found in lesser, but still good books such as *The Godfather,* by Mario Puzo, and *Catch-22,* by Joseph Heller.

Julius Caesar. *The Gallic Wars* (ca. 40 B.C.). Boston: David R. Godine, 1980.

Read as a teenager (and just reread in a modern translation with maps, illustrations and notes published by David Godine) this book introduced me to the remarkable fact that history really did happen!

Richer books, read later and enjoyed more, that similarly reveal the spirit of their times: the journal of Eugène Delacroix; the daybooks of Edward Weston; *Bound for Glory,* by Woody Guthrie.

Antoine de Saint Exupéry. *The Little Prince* (1943). Katherine Woods, trans. New York: Harcourt Brace Jovanovich, 1982.

"Straight ahead of him, nobody can go very far. . . ."

Gregory Bateson. *Steps to an Ecology of Mind* (1972). New York: Ballantine, 1975. (Pb)

Kate Wilhelm. *Where Late the Sweet Birds Sang* (1976). New York: Pocket, 1981. (Pb)

Walter M. Miller, Jr. *A Canticle for Leibowitz* (1959). New York: Bantam, 1976. (Pb)

Two very good science-fiction novels, which suggest that man is not on an inevitable path to perfectability.

Stanley Hoffman

Stanley Hoffman is a professor of government and the C. Douglas Dillon Professor of the Civilization of France at Harvard University. Professor Hoffman has been teaching and writing both about international affairs and about France for thirty years. Educated in France, he came to Harvard as a teacher in 1955.

All of these books (1) deal with the most fundamental choices—often tragic—individuals are called upon to make, particularly as citizens, and (2) are works of art and not merely of instruction.

Jean-Jacques Rousseau. *Social Contract* (1762). Maurice Cranston, trans. New York: Penguin, 1968. (Pb)

The most powerful attempt to reconcile freedom and authority, self-fulfillment and community. It fails, I think—but what an impressive and instructive failure.

Leo Tolstoy. *War and Peace* (1865–69). Louise Maude and Aylmer Maude, trans. George Gibian, ed. New York: W. W. Norton, 1966.

The greatest novel ever written and the most probing attempt to show the effects of war on a diverse group of individuals.

Jean-Baptiste Racine. *Andromaque* (1667). John Cairncross, trans. New York: Penguin, 1976. (Pb)

Love, revenge, lust, motherhood and the aftermath of the Trojan War, in the perfect poetic mix of passion and formality that is Racine's genius.

Roger Martin du Gard. *Les Thibault* (1922–40). New York: Larousse, n.d. (Pb)

Even longer than, albeit not as rich as *War and Peace,* this is another fresco about individuals and war (the First World War) and a humane, wise, compassionate and deeply pessimistic study of lives.

Charles de Gaulle. *The Complete War Memoirs of Charles de Gaulle* (1954–59). J. Griffin and R. Howard, trans. New York: Simon & Schuster, 1964.

The epic story of France's fall and liberation, written by the chief actor in the drama, a leader of genius who was also a magnificent writer.

Raymond Aron. *Peace and War: A Theory of International Relations* (1962). Richard Howard and Annette Baker Fox, trans. Garden City, N.Y.: Doubleday, 1966.

The most comprehensive study of international politics, which tells us both about the limits and about the possibilities of empirical theory and explores the dilemma of ethical action in world affairs.

Gerald Holton

Gerald Holton is the Mallinckrodt Professor of Physics and a professor of the history of science. He has enlivened physics classes at Harvard for forty years. In addition to his well-deserved reputation as a physicist, he is known for his interest and work in arms control and Soviet–American relations. Among his works are Thematic Origins of Scientific Thought *(1973),* The Scientific Imagination *(1978), and* The Advancement of Science and Its Burdens *(1986).*

Mark Twain. *The Adventures of Tom Sawyer* (1876). Berkeley: University of California Press, 1983. (Pb)

Even in German, this and large parts of *Huckleberry Finn* were indestructible, and I read them avidly, as if they showed the way to an escape hatch into an innocent world. A curious view of America emerged from reading Twain, James Fenimore Cooper (Franz Shubert's wish, as he was dying, was for one of his volumes), Karl May's stories of trappers and Indians, and practically all of Zane Grey (during a bout with diphtheria). Of course there were also the American films with those magnetic heroes, Clark Gable, Paul Robeson, James Stewart. . . ."

Homer. *The Iliad* (ca. 800 B.C.). Robert Fitzgerald, trans. New York: Doubleday, 1975. (Pb)

As for many schoolboys in the classical Gymnasium in Vienna—and I can mention here only books from those early years—this was for me the most terrible and unforgettable encounter. It foretold what writing can be at its best, and mankind at its worst. After our forced marches through Caesar's wars, the *Nibelungenlied,* Xenophon's *Anabasis,* the Eddas, and post-Versailles diatribes in our history courses, it became clear that a chief purpose of education was the preparation for war. History would be written by unthinking *ate* and *thumos,* with rarely a moment of rational drawing back, as when Achilles, facing Agamemnon, is made by Athena to sheathe his sword at the last moment.

William Shakespeare. *Romeo and Juliet* (1595). T. J. Spencer, ed. New York: Penguin, 1981. (Pb)

Finally learning English as the last language at sixteen, I came upon a minor production of *Romeo and Juliet,* and have never forgotten the thrill of being transfixed by the poetry of the English language. Perhaps having to recite lines learned by heart from Goethe, Schiller, Heine and Morike had spoiled those for me. Let's put volumes of poetry on our children's shelves!

Ernst Mach. *The Science of Mechanics* (1883). T. J. McCormack, trans. 6th ed. LaSalle, Ill.: Open Court, 1960. (Pb)

Here at last was a book that carefully examined scientific concepts, their historical origins, and their philosophical under-pinnings, often showing that these foundations were badly in need of improvement. So science was not closed after all. Like so many who had been made to believe in textbook science, and in Immanuel Kant's "Thing in Itself," I found here the antidote. I did not know then that Einstein would echo the memory of thousands when he wrote that Mach's "incorruptible skepticism and independence" exerted a profound influence on him as a student.

An encyclopedia.

A big, illustrated, honest, multi-volume encyclopedia. Father kept it in his office, but of course that did nothing to stop me from reading and rereading it, almost volume by volume. So that was how the world was made, what was in it, and how things might work! These "truths" seemed even more fantastic than the inventions of Wilhelm Busch, Grimm's *Tales,* and all the treasured adventure stories of Defoe, Jules Verne and Sven Hedin.

Matina Horner

Matina Horner has been president of Radcliffe College since 1972. Prior to assuming that position, she taught in Harvard's Department of Psychology and Social Relations. In addition to her leadership responsibilities as a college president, she teaches as an associate professor. One of her continuing research interests is the psychology of women.

This is a very tough question—to consider books that have shaped my thinking. I guess the first would have to be the collected works of Emily Dickinson, which I began to read in junior high school.

Emily Dickinson. *The Complete Poems of Emily Dickinson* (mid-nineteenth century). Thomas H. Johnson, ed. Boston: Little, Brown, 1960.

It was the complete poems of Emily Dickinson that made a difference, rather than any one poem, except perhaps for the one that begins "I dwell in possibility." The idea of focusing on possibilities is important to me and I often return to the poem to make this and other points.

Pearl S. Buck. *The Good Earth* (1931). New York: Washington Square Press, 1983. (Pb)

During a recent trip to China, I was reminded of another book from my younger days that also made a lasting impression on me, Pearl Buck's *The Good Earth.* It had a very strong impact on me then which has persisted. Its powerful presentation of some basic cultural differences was a valuable way to be introduced to the importance of seeing and respecting different cultures and values, of accepting cultural differences and of acknowledging the value of other perspectives. Now, back from China, I am tempted to reread it.

Sojourner [Olive Gilbert] Truth. *Narrative of Sojourner Truth* (1878). Salem, N.H.: Ayer, 1968.

Later on, Sojourner Truth's autobiography also made a lasting impression on me. I first read it during the 1960s—as we were beginning to think about women's roles in new ways and feminist views and ideas were being publicly debated. My thinking on these issues began within the supportive environment of a college where expectations for and about women were very high. Sojourner Truth's compelling phrase, "and ain't I a woman," which she used after each description of an activity she did that challenged basic assumptions about women's strength and skills, powerfully captured for me the kind of change being sought in expectations about women, then and now.

Sigmund Freud. *The Interpretation of Dreams* (1900). New York: Avon, 1980. (Pb)

Edward C. Tolman. *Purposive Behavior in Animals and Man* (1967). New York: Irvington, 1967.

Professionally, Freud's collected works, especially his *Interpretation of Dreams,* the first of his works that I read, and Tolman's *Purposive Behavior in Animals and Man,* were very important to the development of my thinking. Both challenged previous assumptions about human and animal motivation and behavior. Freud's depiction of the role of unconscious instincts and impulses in human behavior and Tolman's convincing examples of the ability of animals to learn "what leads to what" and thus to "think" were critical not only to my thinking but to the history of psychology.

Dr. Seuss [Theodor Seuss Geisel]. *The Sneetches, and Other Stories.* New York: Random House, 1961.

I can't resist including Dr. Seuss's *Sneetches,* that wonderful children's book that powerfully shows the foolishness of our

basic need or tendency to divide ourselves into "we" and
"they" and our inability to grasp our fundamental interdependence. Not only have I enjoyed reading it to my children but I
have used it in college classes to make some key points.

Harold Howe II

*Harold Howe is a senior lecturer in administration plan-
ning and social policy at Harvard's Graduate School of
Education. He describes himself not as a professor but as
a retired educator who has found a restful place at Harvard University. He has been a history teacher, a school
principal, a school superintendent (in Scarsdale, New
York), a state education planner (in North Carolina), U.S.
Commissioner of Education, and a foundation official
(vice-president of the Ford Foundation). He has served as
a trustee of Yale, Vassar and the College Board and is now
a trustee of Teachers College at Columbia University. He
has written what he describes as "quite a lot of dull prose"
about education affairs.*

A. E. Housman. *The Collected Poems of A. E. Housman* (1867–
1936). New York: Holt, Rinehart & Winston, 1971. (Pb)

As the world gets more complicated, and it certainly has
during my sixty-seven years, a new resolve is needed to deal
with the unexpected. Housman conveys a somewhat pessimistic
message, which I find sustaining.

Gunnar Myrdal, with **Richard Sterner** and **Arnold Rose.** *An
American Dilemma: The Negro Problem and Modern De-
mocracy* (1944). 2 vols. New York: Harper & Row, 1969.
(Pb)

For understanding the issue of race in the American experience, there is no book to equal this. It has influenced a generation of scholars and the Supreme Court of the United States,
and through them it helped create the civil-rights movement
of the twentieth century. Myrdal recognizes the moral aspects
of the problem and weaves them together with the analysis of
a social scientist to create a magnificent insight. Much of my
time and effort have been spent on racial issues in education,
both schools and colleges, and this book is the bedrock I return

to on the subject. Myrdal's basic view is still relevant. "The
American Negro problem is a problem in the heart of the
American. It is there that the interracial tension has its focus.
It is there that the decisive struggle goes on."

Christopher Fry. *The Lady's Not for Burning* (1949). New York:
Oxford University Press, 1977. (Pb)

A romantic drama in extravagant language, which I read
at least once a year. It helps me to stay young at heart, and it's
just plain fun in its combination of comic and serious themes of
life and death and human foibles ranging from lust to moralistic
bureaucracy. Who else but Christopher Fry would call the
moon, "A circumambulating aphrodisiac divinely subsidized to
provoke the world into a rising birthrate" (p. 67)?

Mark Twain. *The Writings of Mark Twain.* Author's National
Edition. 25 vols. New York: Harper, 1899–1918. (Also
subsequently published letters and other writings by the
same author.)

Twain will carry you from youth through adulthood with
novels, stories, essays and social commentary. Quintessentially
American, he opens our eyes to our peculiarities and to our
ways of life. His warning against the dangers of staying in bed
because so many people die there combines with deep insights
into racial issues in *Huckleberry Finn* to provide an almost
endless cafeteria of delightful reading. For Americans who
want to know who they are and how they got that way, Twain
is center stage.

Rudyard Kipling. *Collected Works* (1886–1932). 22 vols. Garden City, N.Y.: Doubleday, Page, 1927.

I started with the *Just So Stories* ("way down by the great,
grey, green, greasy, Limpopo River"), *The Jungle Book, Kim,*
and *Stalky and Co.;* progressed through *The Barrack Room
Ballads* and other verse where I learned that "the sins that ye

do by two and two, ye must pay for one by one"; and graduated to the endless tales of India, the empire, and British society. Most critics think an interest in Kipling is a sign of a juvenile mind. If so, I plead guilty. But if you haven't read "The Taking of Lungtungpen" (from *Plain Tales from the Hills*) or "The Strange Ride of Marrowbie Jukes" (from *Under the Deodars*), you're missing something.

Omar Khayyam. *Rubaiyat* (early twelfth century). Edward Fitzgerald, trans. Garden City, N.Y.: Doubleday, n.d. (Pb)

A slight strain of perversity in regard to my inheritance as the son of an educator and Presbyterian minister and the grandson of missionaries in nineteenth-century Hawaii probably leads me to the affection I hold for this delightful verse. It punctures pomposity, praises wine, women and song, and gently derides religion. I enjoy it. I have always felt the need to joke about the things I was most serious about. Hence my life spent in education is for me joyfully teased by Omar Khayyam.

Jerome Kagan

Jerome Kagan is a professor of psychology at Harvard's Graduate School of Arts and Sciences. Professor Kagan holds a Ph.D. from Yale University and has written many works, most notably Infancy; The Nature of the Child; *and* Birth to Maturity.

These books should generate a tolerance for others and appreciation of the power of historical contexts to create our deepest assumptions about human nature.

Maurice H. Mandelbaum. *History, Man, and Reason: A Study in Nineteenth-Century Thought.* Baltimore: Johns Hopkins University Press, 1971.

Mandelbaum's analysis of the relation between the European conception of human nature and historical events in the eighteenth and nineteenth centuries helped me to understand why American intellectuals, and especially twentieth-century social scientists, were so strongly committed, until recently, to a belief in the power of the environment and the malleability of human characteristics, as well as resistant to all sentimental arguments that did not rest firmly on reason. The basis for our idealistic view of perfectible children, sculpted by education in home and school to make rationally based moral decisions in times of conflict, becomes an almost inevitable outcome of the blend of egalitarianism, evolutionism, and material science that has dominated thought since the eighteenth century.

Alasdair C. MacIntyre. *After Virtue: A Study in Moral Theory* (1981). Notre Dame, Ind.: University of Notre Dame Press, 1982. (Pb)

After Virtue extends Mandelbaum's conclusions to the domain of ethics by arguing that historical conditions determine many of the moral premises of a society. MacIntyre points out, for example, that our acceptance of the naturalness of individual rights is not a universal, for there is no word or phrase in ancient or medieval languages that refers to an individual's right to a particular resource. This assumption is not made until the close of the Middle Ages. I learned from MacIntyre that a society's views of right and wrong are fragmented survivals of a series of economic and political events that lead the community to treat social facts as moral imperatives. Thus, the role of history is a common theme that unites the books by MacIntyre and Mandelbaum.

Pär Lagerqvist. *The Eternal Smile* (1934). Erik Mesterton et al., trans. New York: Hill and Wang, 1971.

A single sentence in this story by a Swedish novelist captures the idea that MacIntyre was trying to develop. After an interminably long search, a large group of dead people find God and the leader steps forward and asks him what purpose he had in creating human beings. God replies, "I only intended that you need never be content with nothing." After reading that line I saw the meaning of the tree-of-knowledge allegory in Genesis. Human beings are prepared by their nature to believe that there are right and wrong acts, but history and the nature of the society in which persons live will determine more exactly those categories of intention and action that will be treated as moral or immoral.

Ernst E. Mayr. *The Growth of Biological Thought* (1982). Cambridge: Harvard University Press, 1985. (Pb)

Mayr's history of biological thought over the past few centuries helped me see more clearly the relation between categories in biology and those in psychological development. Mayr notes that biology, unlike physics, deals more often with qualitative categories, rather than continua. Thus, biology is a unique science that is not easily reduced to physical concepts. Mayr understands that in biology the most useful categories are those that have been inductively derived from phenomena, rather than posited a priori. I believe that modern psychology is in a phase of development in which it can benefit from the inductive strategy that eighteenth- and nineteenth-century biologists used with such profit. Such a frame is present in Darwin's great insight that evolution should not be viewed as a series of variations on a set of ideal types, but rather as a series of transformations on ancestors.

Jean L. Briggs. *Never in Anger.* Cambridge: Harvard University Press, 1970. (Pb)

The central message in this ethnography of the Eskimo of Hudson Bay is that despite the fact that this culture is characterized by a continual suppression of anger and aggression, none of the systems that are typically associated with denial of anger in Western society occurs among the Eskimo. Thus, this culture provides a refutation of the Freudian hypothesis that repression of anger must lead to symptomatology. The obvious implication is that the validity of the psychoanalytic hypothesis is restricted to certain cultures. It follows, then, that there are no universal outcomes of either the suppression or expression of anger, independent of the social context.

Nicole LeDouarain. *The Neural Crest.* New York: Cambridge University Press, 1983.

This monograph by a distinguished neuroembryologist describes the growth and transformation of the cells that begin as a small necklace around the embryo's spinal column and migrate to their final homes in the central nervous system of the newborn. The main point is that although all the cells are alike originally, they become transformed over their journey into structures that cannot be changed. The different transformations each type of cell undergoes is a function, in part, of the cells that are encountered on the way. This story of the migration of the neural crest cells furnishes a useful metaphor for the psychological growth of a human being, who is also transformed through the contacts he or she has in the life journey.

A salient theme in the six books noted above is that absolutes are hard to find in nature; most laws are constrained by particular contexts. But there must be a small number of universal relations that trace their way back to biology. The final book supplies one of these mechanisms.

Georg Von Békésy. *Sensory Inhibition* (1965). Princeton: Princeton University Press, 1967. (Pb)

This book, which I read as a young psychologist, is the one exception to the relativism contained in the first six volumes. One basic biological mechanism is that brain and mind are constructed to maximize contrasts and to improve the signal-to-noise ratio. The mind rebels against the ambiguity and relativity in nature and tries to create simple, prototypical conceptions. If one idea is a little more salient than another, the mind tends to exaggerate the former and minimize the latter. Hence, there is a biological basis for our attraction to stereotype and to single ideas that mute the gradations that are inherent in nature. As a result, we are seduced into believing in absolutes, when nature contains only families of relations among events.

John Kao

John Kao is a performing musician, psychiatrist, entrepreneur, and business school professor. The road toward these goals has taken many turns: the study of philosophy and social science in college, psychiatry in medical school, and general management in business school. Currently, he teaches and does research on the topics of entrepreneurship and corporate creativity at the Harvard Business School, and "is rewarded by the annual opportunity to teach these topics to M.B.A. students."

As our technological and social milieux change at an increasing rate, our thinking as a species must be anchored by a profound understanding of human behavior and values. Our success in addressing the challenges of the twenty-first century will be influenced by our wisdom and by our ability to blend human skills: intuition, a tolerance for ambiguity and a comfort with paradox combined with the deepest compassion.

A. E. Van Vogt. *The Voyage of the Space Beagle* (1939). New York: Woodhill, 1977.

I first read this book at age eleven, and have reread it several times since. It is an enthralling science fiction, an outerspace version of Darwin's original journey. What particularly captured my attention was Van Vogt's creation of a new science of human behavior. Called "nexialism," it was a sophisticated blend of psychology, medicine and organizational politics which allowed the protagonist to help his parochial colleagues and save their mission from disaster. Seeds of an interest in human behavior, interdisciplinary studies, "underlying knowledge" and iconoclastic people were sown by this book.

Carl G. Jung. *Memories, Dreams, Reflections* (1963). Aniela Jaffé, trans. New York: Random House, 1965. (Pb)

While all of Jung's work had a deep influence on me, I was particularly struck by this work, his autobiography. Jung writes with the excitement of a detective, the skill of an artist, and the flair of a mystic as he develops a new vision of human personality. I was particularly struck by his humanity as a clinician, which led me to follow his path into clinical psychiatry. Jung inspired me as someone who was not afraid to confront the mysteries of life, art, dreams and the unconscious through the "science" of human personality.

Erich Neumann. *The Origins and History of Consciousness* (1949). R. F. C. Hall, trans. New York: Pantheon, 1954. (Pb)

Reading Neumann provided an important complement to my work with Jung. He extended Jungian psychology on a grand scale to show the beauty and logic inherent in a wide range of human experience: dreams, art, mythology, social organization, history, culture.

Joseph Needham, with **Wang Ling.** *Science and Civilisation in China* (1954). Cambridge: Cambridge University Press, 1985.

Joseph Needham is a particular hero of mine for his erudition and intellectual scope. *Science and Civilization in China* presents a vast panorama of the emergence of scientific and technological thinking in China over three millennia, no mean achievement by any standard. Needham approaches his subject as a historian, sinologist, natural scientist, sociologist, philosopher. The result is a delicious and enormous banquet.

Lao Tsu. *Tao Te Ching.* Witter Bynner, trans. New York: Putnam, 1944.

Any work that can capture science, philosophy and human nature in eighty stanzas of verse deserves special comment. The *Tao Te Ching* has been a bedside companion of mine for many years. Its relevance is never-ending; always surprising. For example, when I studied psychology it was a valued text on human behavior. As an organizational specialist, I learned a great deal from it about politics and leadership. I use it as a favorite present to friends who are entrepreneurs and senior managers. The book says it all.

Gordon D. Kaufman

Gordon Kaufman is a professor of theology at the Harvard Divinity School. As a Mennonite conscientious objector in World War II, and thus as a member of a cognitive minority in a time of intense emotion, Professor Kaufman early became aware (a) of the relativity and plurality of all human convictions about right and truth, and (b) of the great power of religion in human affairs, and also its extremely problematic character. Most of his intellectual life, he writes, has been devoted to attempting to understand and address these issues, and the following books have been important in pursuing that quest.

These books explore fundamental questions about human nature and the nature of truth, about the role of religion in human affairs and the meaning that faith in God can have today; they have been particularly important to me in my struggle with the significance of modern cultural and religious pluralism, a problem that can only become increasingly urgent as we move into the twenty-first century.

Immanuel Kant. *Critique of Pure Reason* (1781). New York: St. Martin's, 1969. (Pb)

———. *Critique of Practical Reason* (1788). Lewis Beck, trans. New York: Garland, 1977.

I read the first *Critique* in its entirety at age eighteen, and have done so probably about twelve times since. Kant's "Copernican revolution" taught me (a) that what we call "knowledge" is no simple matter of "external objects" leaving their imprint on the mind, but is rather a complex process of interaction between subject and object; and (b) that all intellect, morality and religion are grounded on the creativity and freedom of the human agent. These positions have helped to provide a philosophical basis for my views on the social and historical relativity

of all knowledge and also on the function and importance of
religious symbols.

George H. Mead. *Mind, Self and Society from the Standpoint
of a Social Behaviorist* (1934). Charles W. Morris, ed. Chicago: University of Chicago Press, 1967. (Pb)

My understanding of the social and personal relativity of
all human thought and practice was especially influenced by
Mead's theory of selfhood and mind as social and linguistic
through and through, rather than fundamentally individualistic
and rationalistic. I first encountered Mead at about age twenty-
three, and his ideas have provided a reference point for virtually all my subsequent reflection on human nature.

Ludwig Feuerbach. *The Essence of Christianity* (1841). E. Graham Waring and F. W. Strothmann, eds. New York: Frederick Ungar, 1975. (Pb)

Feuerbach's claim that all theology is actually disguised
anthropology, that all religion is really a projection of human
subjectivity and feelings onto a cosmic screen, is the fountain-
head of much modern interpretation of religion. This view has
usually been understood as essentially destructive of religion
and theology, but it has provided me with fundamental insights
without which I would not have been able to develop my own
reconception of theology as essentially "imaginative construction."

H. Richard Niebuhr. *The Meaning of Revelation* (1941). New
York: Macmillan, 1967. (Pb)

————. *Radical Monotheism and Western Culture.* New York:
Harper & Row, 1960. (Pb)

Niebuhr, through articulating a thoroughly sociohistorical
conception of selfhood (influenced by Mead), showed that, precisely because all our experience and thinking is historically and
culturally relative, both selves and societies need systems of

value and meaning to orient themselves in the world; faith in God has special significance because of the sort of orientation it can provide. Niebuhr thus showed me both that theology is still important in our modern pluralistic world and how theology can best be done today. Of all my teachers he probably influenced me the most.

R. G. Collingwood. *The Idea of History* (1946). T. M. Knox, ed. New York: Oxford University Press, 1956. (Pb)

———. *An Essay on Metaphysics* (1940). Lanham, Md.: University Press of America, 1984. (Pb)

I wrote my doctoral dissertation on "The Problem of Relativism and the Possibility of Metaphysics," and Collingwood (along with Wilhelm Dilthey and Paul Tillich) was a principal resource. Collingwood helped me to understand both that all our thinking is inescapably historical and that all history is the work of human imagination. With his conception of "absolute presuppositions" he helped me see what metaphysics and theology can be in a historicist world.

Karl Barth. *The Epistle to the Romans* (1918). Edward C. Hoskyns, trans. 6th ed. New York: Oxford University Press, 1968. (Pb)

Barth's greatest book, powerfully showing how human religiousness—especially Christian religiousness—instead of relating to God in fact turns us away from God, showed me that the *theological* critique of religion is actually more profound and devastating than any secular critique, for it can take up into itself all the insights of a Feuerbach and a Marx, a Nietzsche and a Freud, and go beyond them. Theology, thus, has an autonomy and a unique significance of its own, and it need not be constrained by any specific commitments to religiosity.

Henry N. Wieman. *The Source of Human Good* (1946). Carbondale, Ill.: Southern Illinois University Press, 1964. (Pb)

This book, read for the first time shortly after its publication, enabled me to understand from very early on that the importance of the idea of God is to be seen principally in terms of the functions it performs in human life and thought (rather than in terms of its putative "meaning"); and those functions may well be more effectively performed in the contemporary world by a conception utilizing metaphors like "creative event" rather than the more traditional personalistic and political metaphors of "father," "lord," and "king." These insights of Wieman have become increasingly important for my recent work.

John V. Kelleher

John Kelleher is about to retire as professor of Irish studies at Harvard University, where he is acting chairman of the Celtic Department. His connection with Harvard began in 1940 as a member of the Society of Fellows—in his words, "to paraphrase an old joke: the first in the field and the first to leave it."

I wrote sketches for recommended readings several times, but they were in lame prose and besides I was put off by the realization that it wasn't particular books but individual authors that had significantly influenced me. I hope the resulting compromises may be of use.

Seán O'Faoláin. *The Finest Stories.* Boston: Little, Brown, 1957.

I put down this title because I must record my debt to O'Faoláin and because he is best known here for his short stories, but I could as properly cite his biographies of Irish figures, or his editorials in *The Bell* (1939–45), or his many studies of the Irish people and the nation they have been creating. He is supremely the writer as citizen. I know of none so sensitively perceptive and sane.

James Joyce. *Ulysses* (1918–20). New York: Random House, 1976. (Pb)

For years I wondered why the book continued to appeal despite the steadily rising barrier of interpretation that surrounds it. Finally it dawned on me that *Ulysses* is about the only upbeat masterpiece of this century—and immensely funny too. In its own artfully tangled way it records the heartening adventures of people of quiet courage.

John Millington Synge. *The Playboy of the Western World* (1907). New York: Barnes & Noble, 1968.

I think Synge was the greatest of all modern Irish writers. His work is all of a piece, rammed with vitality, and, for all of Synge's own iron reserve, it has extraordinary emotional range. In this play he also shows that he is a wonderful comic writer —probably the more so for his basic sense of tragedy.

Eoin MacNeill. *Celtic Ireland* (1921). Dublin: University Press of Ireland, 1981.

Again one title to indicate my debt to a man's entire work. MacNeill would be happy to know that much of what he wrote is now outdated. He was that rare type, a great innovative scholar quite without vanity. Almost alone he transformed the study of early Irish history from apology or polemic to true historiography, and did that happily.

Maria Edgeworth. *Castle Rackrent* (1800). New York: Oxford University Press, 1982. (Pb)

An extraordinarily seminal work by a woman of genius. It is not only the first true Irish novel, but the first regional novel, immensely admired in its day and imitated everywhere. Raised in England, brought to Ireland as a young girl, she somehow learned more about Ireland, present and past, than I am sure she was aware of knowing. The result is a work of vivid realism.

William Butler Yeats. *The Poems of W. B. Yeats* (1887–1939). Richard Finneran, ed. New York: Macmillan, 1962. (Pb)

I cite the latest and most complete edition. Yeats parlayed the damnedest combination of natural gifts, spasmodic learning, native shrewdness, indomitable dedication, some willful half-beliefs, and a few deep insights—parlayed these into memorable, powerful poetry. Useful poetry, too, that sticks to the ribs.

Duncan Kennedy

Duncan Kennedy is a professor of law at the Harvard Law School. He teaches contracts, torts, property, the history of legal thought and housing law and policy. Two of his works are Legal Education and the Reproduction of Hierarchy *(1983) and* The Structure of Blackstone's Commentaries *(1979). He is a founding member of the Conference on Critical Legal Studies.*

What attracts me to these books may be the effort to come to grips with large, frightening facts of inequality, oppression, alienation, while at the same time exploring the slippery, self-contradictory nature of the self as it tangles and disentangles itself in the world of others, without giving up on survival by speculation, collective struggle and self-doubt.

G. W. F. Hegel. *The Phenomenology of Mind (Die Phänomenologie des Geistes,* 1807). J. B. Baillie, ed. and trans. New York: Harper & Row, 1967. (Pb)

An attempt to put everything together before anything was clear, revolutionary and romantic but also a classical integration. I tried to read it three times with no success, finally made it through with a friend in tiny chunks. More than worth the pain.

Karl Marx. *Das Kapital,* vol. 1, *The Process of Capital Production* (1867). Friedrich Engels, ed. Canton, Ohio: International, 1984. (Pb)

After Book 1 (impossibly obscure) it's more like *Middlemarch* or Balzac than my picture of orthodox Marxism. This is the book you're not supposed to read and that you know is all wrong before you start. But it's not much about economic determinism or materialism or state control of everything. Instead it's how the powerful got their power and what they did with it.

Sigmund Freud. *A General Introduction to Psychoanalysis* (1909, 2d ed. 1920). New York: Boni & Liveright, 1977. (Pb)

As with Marx, it's not the tight, totalitarian theories the disciples have spun that count here. It's the unconscious, there all the time but never there until you trick it into sight, the self permanently destabilized.

Marcel Proust. *Remembrance of Things Past* (1913–27). 3 vols. C. Scott Moncrieff and Terence Kilmartin, trans. New York: Random House, 1982. (Pb)

The more perfectly you grasp what you and I are like and how we fit in, the more it seems our next and contradictory selves wait around the corner in a world turned upside down. Again you have to get through a slow opening, toward bliss.

Virginia Woolf. *To the Lighthouse* (1927). New York: Harcourt, Brace, 1964. (Pb)

This is my favorite book, an intensely loving, utterly critical revelation of marriage and family life, men, women and children. It gets at the amazingly complex but ephemeral ideas and emotions that are there every second in everyone without ever telling you anything straight out.

Jean-Paul Sartre. *Critique of Dialectical Reason* (1960). New York: Schocken, 1983.

As with the *Phenomenology,* everything is here, but now after we know we can know nothing in the way Marx and Freud wanted to know everything. The vindication of Proust and James and Virginia Woolf, also transcendence of what's passive in their work, without their pure genius.

Francis Keppel

Francis Keppel is a senior lecturer on education at Harvard's Graduate School of Education. He was dean of the Education School from 1948 to 1962 and U.S. Commissioner of Education from 1962 to 1966. He later served as chairman of the General Learning Corporation (1966–74) and is now chairman of Appropriate Technology International. His teaching focuses on state and federal policies affecting education, with special interest in federal programs in compensatory education, student financial aid and desegregation and educational boards, including the Lincoln Center for the Performing Arts in New York.

These books may help the reader to avoid being surprised, and surprise often leads to bad judgment.

The Bible (Both the King James version and recent translations).

Even apart from matters of personal belief, the Bible is indispensable to an understanding of the history of the West. Without it, literature and art lose some of their meaning, and the visual arts particularly have been a central part of my life.

Werner W. Jaeger. *Paideia: The Ideals of Greek Culture* (1934). Gilbert Highet, trans. New York: Oxford University Press, 1965. (Pb)

Jaeger's conclusion that society itself is the major force in educating the young formed my thinking when I started a lifelong career in education after World War II.

Alexander Hamilton, John Jay, and **James Madison.** *The Federalist [Papers]* (1788). Benjamin F. Wright, ed. Cambridge: Harvard University Press, 1961.

For any citizen of the United States, and particularly one with strong interests in public affairs, *The Federalist [Papers]* helps to explain our mixture of optimism for social progress and realism about man's weakness.

Lawrence A. Cremin. *American Education.* 2 vols. to date. New York: Harper & Row, 1982–. (Pb)

This massive and magisterial account, stretching from colonial to modern times, puts schools and colleges into context. It is for me a successor to Jaeger, and its annotated bibliography is incomparable.

James B. Conant. *Education in a Divided World* (1948). New York: Greenwood Press, 1969.

Almost forty years later, Conant's analysis stands up well, and brings back to a devoted admirer a man of remarkable honesty and moral courage.

New York Times, daily and Sunday (1948 to date).

Candor compels me to report that I have probably spent more time reading the *Times* than reading books. But it is the best continuing set of unbound volumes on paper that I know about the times of my own life and about future possibilities.

Winthrop Knowlton

Winthrop Knowlton is the director of the Center for Business and Government of Harvard's John F. Kennedy School of Government. Mr. Knowlton, former chief executive officer of Harper & Row, Publishers, is the Henry R. Luce Professor of Ethics, Business and Public Policy at the Kennedy School.

The books I have selected deal with the nature of tyranny and freedom and with scientific and cultural change (how they come about and what they bring in their wake). None of them falls readily into a single category such as "economics" or "ethics." Four of the six are about individuals. Their heroism provides insight into problems that endure across centuries and inspiration about how best to lead one's life in the face of those challenges.

Maria Dermoût. *The Ten Thousand Things* (1958). E. M. Beekman, ed., Hans Koning, trans. Amherst: University of Massachusetts Press, 1983.

Freeman J. Dyson. *Disturbing the Universe: A Life in Science* (1979). New York: Harper & Row, 1981. (Pb)

Friedrich August von Hayek. *The Constitution of Liberty* (1960). Chicago: Regnery, 1972.

Joseph A. Schumpeter. *Capitalism, Socialism, and Democracy* (1942). New York: Harper & Row, 1983.

André Schwarz-Bart. *The Last of the Just* (1959). Stephen Becker, trans. Cambridge, Mass.: Richard Bentley, 1981.

Alexander I. Solzhenitsyn. *One Day in the Life of Ivan Denisovich* (1962). Ralph Parker, trans. Alexandria, Va.: Time–Life Books, 1981.

Martin A. Linsky

Martin Linsky, a lecturer in public policy at Harvard's John F. Kennedy School of Government and a former Massachusetts state representative and newspaper editor, specializes in teaching and research in the areas of the press and legislatures. His most recent work is Impact: How the Press Affects Federal Policy Making *(1986).*

Plato. *The Republic* (370–360 B.C.). James Adam, ed. 2 vols. New York: Cambridge University Press, 1963.

I read Plato's *Republic* in a seminar the second semester of my sophomore year at college. It taught me that there are some important questions to ask, that just because there are questions it doesn't mean that there are answers, and that even if there are, the questions and the questioning might be more important anyway.

Walter Lippmann. *Public Opinion* (1922). New York: Free Press, 1965. (Pb)

No one before Walter Lippmann or since has understood as well the dilemmas in a free society which arise out of the complex relationships among the governors, the governed and the mass media. When I finished *Public Opinion,* I knew that somehow it would be with me the rest of my life, and so it has.

James D. Barber. *The Lawmakers: Recruitment and Adaptation to Legislative Life* (1965). Westport, Conn.: Greenwood Press, 1980.

As a legislator, I was always frustrated by the gap between my own view of the integrity and inherent worth of the legislative process and what I perceived to be the conventional wisdom about how awful legislatures were. *The Lawmakers,* which Barber wrote originally as his Ph.D. thesis at Yale, was the first book I found that tried to understand legislators and legislatures on their own terms as they really are, rather than as they might be in some theoretical world conjured up by academics or good-government types. Barber listened to what legislators had to say. Even though the book was published back in 1965, it still is unique in illuminating my favorite part of government.

Henry Beetle Hough. *Country Editor* (1940). Greenwich, Conn.: Chatham, 1974. (Pb)

Country Editor made me realize that one could live an intense, engaged professional life and a calm, secure private life at the same time. I'm not sure that I really believed it was possible before, and the book has become a kind of guidepost for maintaining the balance.

Richard Harris. *Freedom Spent.* Boston: Little, Brown, 1976 (out of print). Appeared in *The New Yorker,* 17 and 24 June 1974; 18 August 1975; 3, 10 and 17 November 1975; and 5, 12 and 19 April 1976.

Freedom Spent is important to me for two reasons: first, it is the most powerful reaffirmation of the values inherent in the Bill of Rights that I have ever read. Second, it is brilliant writing and reporting—my own model of great journalism, where the author drives you to the conclusion not by rhetoric or exhortation, but by the power of the reporting, the facts and the narrative.

David M. Livingston

David Livingston is a professor of medicine at the Harvard Medical School—molecular biology is his field. He teaches, runs a laboratory and does active clinical medicine. His special interest is oncko genes, their products and how the latter function. He wrote an op-ed piece for the New York Times *on the irksome vacuous noise broadcast over airplane loudspeakers. Additional op-ed pieces he writes may follow.*

William Thackeray. *Vanity Fair* (1847–48). John Sutherland, ed. New York: Oxford University Press, 1983. (Pb)

This poignant story left me with the indelible impression that privilege and success are not necessarily eternal even for the brightest and/or the most well-intended people. It also exposed me, early on, to the possibility that there might be unfortunate consequences to taking those who are apparently dependent or less fortunate for granted.

Charles Dickens. *A Tale of Two Cities* (1859). New York: Bantam, 1981. (Pb)

I remember feeling that I could nearly palpate the passion of the murderous French anti-Royalists and, for the first time, appreciate the possibility that chronic oppression could break down the barriers which normally block the expression of uncivilized instincts.

John Steinbeck. *In Dubious Battle* (orig. *Dubious Battle in California,* 1936). New York: Penguin, 1979. (Pb)

One's cynical views of what activates the passions of many people need not be all-consuming, for there are "ordinary" individuals who are not weird, whose daily behavior is based largely on moral principles, and who are, therefore, worth emulating.

Paul H. DeKruif. *Microbe Hunters* (1926). New York: Harcourt, Brace, 1966. (Pb)

I didn't decide to become a physician or scientist immediately after finishing this book. However, it provided me with my first taste of the excitement associated with a scientific hunt.

Ford Madox Ford. *The Good Soldier* (1915). New York: Random House, 1951. (Pb)

The practiced arts of civility among educated people are an important manifestation of the gentle nature of the human spirit. However, from this novel I became more aware than ever that they can also be used as cover by those whose morality has been eroded by passion.

David Halberstam. *The Best and the Brightest* (1972). New York: Penguin, 1983. (Pb)

This book gave me my clearest appreciation yet for the enormity of the powers held by senior American foreign-policy makers. It also showed how easily the thin line between responsible and irresponsible use of these powers could be crossed in the interest of serving narrow logic.

George C. Lodge

George Lodge has been a member of the Harvard Business School faculty since 1961, after service in the Eisenhower and Kennedy administrations. He is the author of six books discussing labor unions, change in Latin America, ideology and social change and ideological transition. He continues to research, write about and teach issues regarding ideology and social change. His books include U.S. Competitiveness in the World Economy, *edited with Bruce R. Scott, and a forthcoming work with Ezra Vogel on comparative ideology.*

I have found these books especially useful in understanding both the obstacles to change in various communities and the means of overcoming those obstacles. Whatever the twenty-first century brings it will certainly include change.

F. S. C. Northrop. *The Meeting of East and West.* New York: Oxbow, 1979. (Pb)

Northrop showed me how to perceive the effects of religious, scientific, philosophical and other traditions in the practices of nations. He was particularly helpful to me in my early efforts to develop the concept of ideology for the integrated study of national systems.

Louis Hartz. *The Liberal Tradition in America.* New York: Harcourt, Brace, 1962. (Pb)

From Hartz I learned of the pervasive influence of John Locke in the development of government and business in the United States.

Samuel P. Huntington. *Political Order in Changing Societies* (1968). New Haven: Yale University Press, 1969. (Pb)

Here is a beautifully clear analysis of the historical roots of different nations and of how those roots flowered into various institutional forms and behavior.

Crawford B. MacPherson. *The Political Theory of Possessive Individualism: Hobbes to Locke.* Oxford: Oxford University Press, 1962. (Pb)

This book was especially helpful in its analysis of how Locke overcame his original constraints on the rights to and the uses of property. It helps to explain contemporary arguments about the purposes of the corporation.

Thomas S. Kuhn. *The Structure of Scientific Revolutions* (1962). Chicago: University of Chicago Press, 1970. (Pb)

Kuhn's use of the notion of a "paradigm" helped me to develop a comparable one of ideology, and to explore its uses in understanding the environment of business.

Karl Mannheim. *Ideology and Utopia* (1929). L. Wirth and G. Shils, trans. San Diego: Harcourt Brace Jovanovich, 1985. (Pb)

This book gave me a definition of ideology and a way to use it in the systemic analysis of communities which has been most useful in my thinking and teaching about the roles and relationships of government, business and labor.

Albert Lord

Albert Lord is the Arthur Kingsley Porter Professor of Slavic and Comparative Literature, Emeritus and honorary curator of the Milman Parry Collection in the Harvard College Library. Though no longer a classroom teacher, he continues to research and contribute to his field. He devotes much of his time now to the study of Yugoslavian epic song.

I do not claim originality, only truth, in the first two, and possibly the third, but I expect I am unique in the fourth.

The Bible. King James version (1611).

The book that had the most influence on me from my earliest years has been the Bible. I was brought up on it; as a boy and a young man I learned to quote many passages from it. The fact that many parts of the Bible originated in oral tradition also drew me to a study of the Bible from the point of view of oral literature and lore.

William Shakespeare. *Shakespeare: Complete Works* (1592–1611). Alfred Hasbage, ed. Baltimore: Penguin, 1969.

When I was in high school I read several of Shakespeare's plays and was required to memorize many lines from them. Passages from *Hamlet, Macbeth, Julius Caesar, The Merchant of Venice,* and *As You Like It* have stayed with me through the years, and together with the Bible have formed the backbone of my literary sensibilities. I audited Kittredge's last class in Shakespeare and added several passages from *Othello* to my repertory at that time. In my early teaching in the humanities I taught as well some of the history plays.

Homer. *The Iliad* (ca. 800 B.C.). Robert Fitzgerald, trans. New York: Doubleday, 1975. (Pb)

―――. *The Odyssey* (ca. 800 B.C.). Robert Fitzgerald, trans. Franklin Center, Penn.: Franklin Library, 1976.

The Writings of Milman Parry.

If the first book, the Bible, belonged to my family period and the second came from high-school days, both lasting on into adult life, the third stems from my college years at Harvard in the early 1930s. It was here that my fascination for the Homeric poems began, and no books have had a more profound effect on my life than they. They have been at the heart of most of my scholarly activity. They are associated with the name of my primary teacher in Homer and oral-traditional literature, Milman Parry, and his writings have their place here together with the *Iliad* and the *Odyssey*.

Oral-traditional epic poetry.

Homer and Parry led to listening to epic singers in Yugoslavia and to reading a large body of oral-traditional epic poetry, mostly in Serbo-Croatian and Bulgarian. Although these are not "books" in the conventional sense, they are literary expressions and sometimes, like Homer, they find their way into book form. One in particular, "The Wedding of Smailagic Meho" by Avdo Medjedovic, which I translated into English and published, has had considerable influence on my life, not only in itself, but also in respect to all that it represents. It is in essence the initiatory experiences of a young hero, his marriage, and his succeeding to his father's station in life. Such Van Gennep tales from *Rites of Passage,* whatever form they may take, have been of importance to me in my own life.

The Epic of Gilgamesh (seventh century B.C.). R. Campbell Thompson, ed. New York: AMS Press, 1981.

This holds true of the next book, the *Epic of Gilgamesh,* with its account of acceptance of mortality and its ultimate emphasis on the life of achievement and of family values. It, too, in my experience is also important as representative of several works from the ancient Near East, such as *Enuma Elish* and the Baal epic. These works are basically mythic and as such deal with fundamental problems of life. And with them, I seem to have returned to the place of my beginning.

Roderick MacFarquhar

Roderick MacFarquhar has been a print, radio and TV journalist (1955–67), editor of The China Quarterly *(1959–68) and member of the British Parliament (1974–79). He is now professor of government in Harvard's Department of Government.*

Some—but not all—of the following books are classics which will last. Each individual and generation has their own signposts. But taken together, my books underline the urgency of getting our act together so that we actually reach the twenty-first century, while the Fairbank volume indicates the nature of a nation that will be increasingly important on the world scene after A.D. 2000.

C. E. M. Joad. *Introduction to Modern Political Theory* (1924). Oxford: Oxford University Press, 1953.

C. E. M. Joad's *Introduction to Modern Political Theory* was published by Oxford University Press in 1924 in "The World's Manuals" series. I borrowed it from my father when I was sixteen and found myself quickly persuaded of the virtues of socialism (and leaning toward guild socialism), which I suspect may have been Joad's objective. Although Britons were already beginning to complain at the shortages and the controls the Labour government had to introduce in the difficult postwar years, socialism simply seemed fairer than the prewar system, and more likely to free Britain of the shackles of the class system. I eventually joined the Labour party, became a Labour member of Parliament, and only left the party for the Social Democrats after its post-1979 swing toward the Marxist left.

Emery Reves. *The Anatomy of Peace* (1945). Magnolia, Mass.: Peter Smith, 1969.

I read Emery Reves's *Anatomy of Peace* when I was seventeen and became a lifelong convert to the ideal of world government as the only sure way to avert international warfare. It seemed to me that the Europeans, who had invented the modern nation-state and used it as the vehicle of wars that had spread far outside their continent, had a special responsibility in striving to end the nation-state era. I became an activist in British organizations set up to persuade our countrymen to participate in the emerging European institutions, the ultimate objective of which was to prevent any further European wars.

Arthur Koestler. *Darkness at Noon* (1940). Daphne Hardy, trans. New York: Bantam, 1970. (Pb)

Arthur Koestler's *Darkness at Noon* inoculated me and a whole generation of Oxford students (who had not lived through the Moscow purges of the 1930s) against any illusions about Soviet communism.

W. Olaf Stapledon. *Last and First Men* (1930). Boston: Gregg, 1976.

Olaf Stapledon's *Last and First Men,* which was one of the first science-fiction works I read, predicted the first world state being formed after a Sino–American war and then collapsing in an energy crisis, leading to the disappearance of the "first men," us. It made me realize that if one thinks in a long enough perspective (in his case millions of years), the disappearance of civilization as we know it was far from unthinkable.

William G. Golding. *Lord of the Flies* (1954). New York: Putnam, 1978.

Robert Jungk. *Brighter Than a Thousand Suns* (1954). James Cleugh, trans. New York: Harcourt, Brace, 1970. (Pb)

I was reminded vividly of Stapledon's grim vision a decade later when reading *Lord of the Flies* by William Golding and *Brighter Than a Thousand Suns* by Robert Jungk, a sobering read for a summer holiday. Golding pointed to a darkness of the soul buried within us, Jungk to the human frailties of the scientists who are our guides in the nuclear era. These books underlined for me the urgency of seeking disarmament agreements between the superpowers.

John K. Fairbank. *The United States and China* (1958). 4th ed. Cambridge: Harvard University Press, 1983. (Pb)

John Fairbank's *United States and China* was my first window on the magnificence of Chinese civilization and its modern fate. I think it remains the best short introduction to the subject for student and general reader alike.

John E. Mack

John E. Mack, M.D. is a child and adult psychoanalyst and is a professor of psychiatry at The Cambridge Hospital, Harvard Medical School. He has been devoted to the development of community-based mental health services and to the application of psychoanalytic insights to biographical studies and to a variety of social and political issues, most recently in relation to the nuclear arms race and the U.S.–Soviet relationship. In 1977 he was awarded the Pulitzer Prize for his biography: A Prince of Our Disorder: The Life of T. E. Lawrence.

All of these books speak to the importance of self-awareness and the transformations that can follow from it. Survival, and the realization of our possibilities in the coming century, may depend on a new level of awareness and of responsibility for both the darker side and the loving and creative dimensions of the human spirit.

Childhood stories.

It is much later, if ever, that we discover why a particular story of childhood has had such a powerful impact.

Carlo Lorenzini. *Adventures of Pinocchio* (1882–83). New York: Penguin, 1974. (Pb)

Pinocchio, in addition to being a spine-tingling adventure story, demonstrated that there was hope that an incorrigible small boy might, in the end, turn out all right and be properly appreciated by his parents.

L. Frank Baum. *The Wizard of Oz* (1900). New York: Penguin, 1983. (Pb)

This story, which at first reading I experienced largely as the triumph of good over evil, contained, I learned much later, another important idea: it is unnecessary to look elsewhere for what we think we lack. The potential for courage, love and even intelligence ("brains") lies within ourselves. This proved to be a valuable message for someone who would one day be committed as a psychotherapist trying to enable other people to discover the possibilities within themselves.

W. Somerset Maugham. *Of Human Bondage* (1915). New York: Penguin, 1978. (Pb)

This novel about the torments of misdirected love revealed to me how prone we are to form irrational attachments which hold us in their grip, even while we know that our sense of self—life itself—is being undermined.

Sigmund Freud. *The Interpretation of Dreams* (1900). New York: Avon, 1980. (Pb)

The vast world of irrational behavior and unconscious impulse, feeling and motivation was opened up to me through Freud's writings.

T. E. Lawrence. *Seven Pillars of Wisdom* (1919). New York: Penguin, 1976. (Pb)

I had not believed that a military leader would speak so frankly of the less attractive dimensions of his motivation. This gave me hope that we might some day understand and master the human proclivity to indulge in war making and war following.

Fyodor Dostoevsky. *Notes from Underground* (1864). Jessie Coulson, ed. and trans. New York: Penguin, 1972. (Pb)

These obsessional ruminations of a prisoner impressed me with the extremes of self-doubt and their paralyzing effect. The world of inner conflict and its determining power were vividly revealed.

Nadezhda Mandel'shtam. *Hope Against Hope* (1970). Max Hayward, trans. New York: Atheneum, 1976.

Written in the mid-1960s in the Soviet Union, this is the remarkable testimony of a Russian widow who has preserved the memory and the writings of her poet husband, Osip Mandel'shtam, one of Stalin's countless victims. Through the painful detail—only everyday detail can really illuminate the monstrousness of totalitarian regimes—there emerges an optimistic voice of hope and possibility, evidence that a better human spirit may yet prevail in our blighted century.

Harvey C. Mansfield, Jr.

Harvey Mansfield has been a professor of government at Harvard University for twenty-six years. His research area is political philosophy. His writings flow from Burke, to Machiavelli, to The Spirit of Liberalism. *He is working on a study of executive power.*

These five books reflect the central importance of politics in my life. Or else, one could say, they reflect the central importance of politics, recognized or not, in anyone's life. Whatever draws us away from politics—play, artistry, poetry, thought—at the same time draws on politics to supply the conditions of peace and harmony that such detachment requires.

Plato. *The Republic* (370–360 B.C.). James Adam, ed. 2 vols. New York: Cambridge University Press, 1963.

This problem of attachment–detachment in politics is shown best and most beautifully in Plato's *Republic,* where the human condition is put in the image of prisoners in a cave. The cave is our politics, and the prisoners' chains represent enthrallment to the delusions by which we live. We can, some of us, some of the time, escape from them, but we always have to come back to them.

Aristotle. *Nicomachean Ethics* (ca. 350 B.C.). New York: Oxford University Press, 1980. (Pb)

Aristotle's *Nicomachean Ethics* is the first book on moral virtue and still the best. Not a book on theories of morality, it describes the actual virtues of the moral person. Read today, it seems strangely familiar—we expect it to be obsolete and irrelevant, but do not find it so.

Niccolò Machiavelli. *The Prince* (1513). Peter E. Bondanella and Mark Musa, trans. New York: Oxford University Press, 1984.

Machiavelli's *Prince* gives the clarion call that began the modern age. It tells us to take as our standard the way things actually are done, not the way we wish or profess them to be done. *The Prince* is the greatest book ever written on politics, when politics is understood as devoted solely to winning over an opponent.

Leo Strauss. *Natural Right and History* (1950). Chicago: University of Chicago Press, 1965. (Pb)

Leo Strauss's *Natural Right and History* makes the cause for reading these old books seriously—as if they might be true. He shows that the two grand obstacles to doing so, our beliefs in science and in history, lead us to the necessity that we recover philosophy in its original sense.

Alexander I. Solzhenitsyn. *The Gulag Archipelago, 1918–1956* (1973). Thomas P. Whitney, trans. New York: Harper & Row, 1985. (Pb)

Alexander Solzhenitsyn's *Gulag Archipelago* is the most powerful book of our time. Its accusation against the Soviet Union will outlast that regime and will dog it until its dying days. Its message of freedom sounds the call of honor and sacrifice that attends any notable effort on behalf of freedom, and that is largely missing in the peace-loving West today.

Ernest R. May

Ernest May is a Texan, educated in California, who has been a professor of history at Harvard since the 1950s. A former dean of Harvard College, he is currently the Charles Warren Professor of History and teaches at the Kennedy School of Government. He is author, coauthor and editor of works on the history of the United States, modern international relations and the uses of history for decision making.

My choices offer the reader the opportunity to extend his own range of experience five hundred years back and across a variety of political systems.

William H. Prescott. *History of the Conquest of Mexico* (1839). Abridgment, Gardiner C. Harvey, ed. Chicago: University of Chicago Press, 1966. (Pb)

Prescott's account of Cortez' expedition is the first history I read that held me as much in thrall as any novel. He made me *see* that almost incredible adventure.

Harold G. Nicolson. *Peacemaking 1919* (1933). New York: Grosset & Dunlap, 1965.

Part reminiscence, part history, part spleen, part analysis, this is the best case study of an international conference ever written in English. It still helps me understand better how outcomes in negotiation can be affected by factors of personality, temperament, age, comparative fatigue, staging, and the like, which do not necessarily surface in documentary records.

Eckart Kehr. *Schlachtflottenbau und Partei-Politik 1894–1901.* Berlin: E. Ebering, 1930.

This monograph on the German naval building program of 1898–1902 is justifiably renowned among historians of Germany and of international relations. It is a finely crafted analysis of how domestic parliamentary politics influenced a national policy supposedly "above politics." I read it as a graduate student, and it has continuously influenced my own research and teaching—much of which has dealt with the same theme, played in a number of other settings.

Paul F. Lazarsfeld and **Elihu Katz.** *Personal Influence: The Part Played by People in the Flow of Mass Communications* (1955). New York: Free Press, 1964. (Pb)

This pioneering study of the ways "opinion leaders" shape public opinion was to me enormously enlightening. No other book has helped me so much to understand democratic processes.

Richard E. Neustadt. *Alliance Politics.* New York: Columbia University Press, 1970. (Pb)

For my mind, this study of the Suez and "Skybolt" crises of 1956 and 1962 plays counterpoint to Eckart Kehr's. It explores the ways court and organizational politics influence outcomes consciously (and conscientiously) designed to be "nonpolitical."

Bernard Bailyn. *The Ideological Origins of the American Revolution* (1965). Cambridge: Harvard University Press, 1967. (Pb)

This book argues compellingly that Americans and Englishmen of the 1770s saw issues differently in part because they had different histories in their heads. They read differently the lessons of the English seventeenth-century revolution which was their common heritage, and they respected different authorities and traditions. As so graphically developed by Bailyn, the example of the American Revolution has helped to keep in my own mind—I hope—awareness not only of the varieties of perception possible among seemingly similar individuals but also of what a German philosopher labeled (with uncharacteristic elegance) the *Gleichzeitigkeit der Ungleichzeitigkeiten*—the contemporaneous existence of things noncontemporaneous.

Colin McArdle

Colin McArdle is an assistant professor of radiology at the Harvard Medical School and practices medicine at Beth Israel Hospital in Boston. He was educated in Britain and maintains that he "came over for a year and stayed." He writes that his education was in no way superior but his accent seems to help in this country.

There is a distinct danger that with every year devoted to the medical profession, a doctor will become less and less literate.

Charles Dickens. *Bleak House* (1853). New York: Bantam, 1983. (Pb)

I was forced to read this book at the age of fourteen and have never read another Dickens novel since. This is a warning to overzealous teachers. Fortunately, I was not forced to read Austen or Eliot at this time.

Thomas Pynchon. *The Crying of Lot 49* (1966). New York: Bantam, 1968. (Pb)

I was encouraged to read this book by a somewhat pedantic English scholar. It was, he attested, a significant work, a masterpiece. I struggled through a mishmash of pretentious symbolism and concluded that it was a load of nonsense. It was the literary equivalent of the emperor's new clothes. At that point, I experienced a great sense of freedom, for previously I had stood in awe and silence before all those incomprehensible books and films that seemed to flourish in the 1960s and beyond. Now I was liberated.

P.S. Included in this group are Godard, Resnais, Fowles and many others.

P. G. Wodehouse. *Leave It to Psmith* (1923). New York: Random House, 1975. (Pb)

The first of many Wodehouse books I read. The earliest books are his best. His somewhat wry and incongruous descriptions are continuously amusing. I have consciously tried to adapt his techniques to the lectures I give. I am not as successful as he but I get the occasional laugh.

George Eliot. *Middlemarch* (1871–72). New York: Bantam, 1985. (Pb)

A magnificent monumental novel—the greatest in the English language. I remember the reluctance with which I put the book down and the apprehension I felt as I picked it up again as I anticipated some further disaster befalling one of my favored characters. It may not have altered my life but it certainly enriched it.

George Eliot. *The Mill on the Floss* (1860). New York: Penguin, 1980. (Pb)

Actually it was a dead heat between this book, the *Radiology Journal* and *Sports Illustrated.* The radiology journals I read because I need to know what is happening in my chosen profession. They consist of usually rather dull treatises which can be loosely divided into fiction, nonfiction and loosely based on fact. Occasionally, something really exciting appears. A knowledge of *Sports Illustrated* allows one to communicate endlessly with other males (except Harvard professors). It is regarded as trash by most women. *The Mill on the Floss* gets the nod because of the first book describing Maggie Tulliver's childhood. Pure magic.

Jane Austen. *Pride and Prejudice* (1813). Tony Tanner, ed. New York: Penguin, 1972. (Pb)

Any book I have read over seven times must have had some influence, though I am at a loss to think how exactly this has occurred. It is the most perfectly written book in the English language that I know and Elizabeth Bennet the most perfect woman against whom all others pale.

Thomas K. McCraw

Thomas McCraw was educated in Mississippi and Wisconsin. He taught history at the University of Texas from 1970 to 1976, then went to the Harvard Business School. There, he teaches courses in business–government relations and writes books and articles that take cross-disciplinary and cross-national approaches to this same broad subject. His most recent book, Prophets of Regulation, *was awarded the Pulitzer Prize for History in 1985.*

Obviously, the list I have presented below is a very personal one. My advice to any student, of any age, is to read widely but selectively, discovering for yourself the books that resonate with your own experiences and aspirations. For the twenty-first century, some of these books obviously have not yet been written. Some actually may have to be done not by others but by you yourself.

David E. Lilienthal. *TVA: Democracy on the March* (1954). Westport, Conn.: Greenwood, 1977.

Written by a New Deal technocrat, this book represented a wartime effort to demonstrate that American democracy could be as "efficient" as Fascism. For that reason, Lilienthal oversold his subject and drifted into the realm of propaganda. Even so, when I read the book, I realized for the first time that I myself had grown up in the midst of a genuine American epic. My father, an engineer with the Tennessee Valley Authority from 1933 until 1971, had been wholly dedicated to his many TVA projects and had become a master of the difficult art of managing giant construction works. He had done this at the personal cost of spending his life in an endless series of small towns in Appalachia—a cost shared by the rest of the family. Lilienthal's book, flawed though it is, made me understand that the sacrifices endured by our own family, and many like us, had been well worth the cost. When I became a historian, I wrote two small books on the TVA myself: partly to redress the imbalance created by Lilienthal's own volume, and partly to explore the complex subject of business–government relations in modern America.

Richard Hofstadter. *Anti-Intellectualism in American Life* (1963). New York: Random House, 1966. (Pb)

Though not the best of Hofstadter's many influential books, this one helped me determine my own vocation. I read and reread it as a young naval officer contemplating careers in law, medicine or college teaching in history or literature. Hofstadter's approach in this book, though condescending and off-putting, demonstrated for me that one could be a historian without losing touch with literature: that, indeed, any such separation would be nothing less than stupid, because it would tend to separate ideas from behavior and individuals from historical movements.

David M. Potter. *People of Plenty: Economic Abundance and the American Character.* Chicago: University of Chicago Press, 1954. (Pb)

In this brief, highly interpretive book, Potter attempts to synthesize the meaning of America around the theme of comparative affluence. Although his quantitative data are now obsolete, his book will endure, for several reasons. First, Potter insisted on a cross-disciplinary approach. He became one of the first important historians to draw systematically on other social sciences such as sociology and anthropology, in addition to economics and political science. Second, *People of Plenty* is an explicitly cross-national study. Potter broke the traditional mold of histories focused solely on the United States, and tried to place American culture in its broader world context. In the process, he drew brilliantly not only on other disciplines, but also on foreign commentaries concerning the American character, such as the great work of de Tocqueville. Overall, the book provides a model of open-minded wisdom and bold but unpretentious interpretation.

Walker Percy. *The Last Gentleman* (1966). New York: Avon, 1978. (Pb)

——. *The Moviegoer* (1961). New York: Avon, 1979. (Pb)

These two books, together with several subsequent ones by Percy, represent attempts to express modern philosophy through the literary form of the novel. Such a fusion, long a central aspect of European culture, has remained under-developed in the United States. Percy himself came to it only in middle age, after a noncareer as a dilettante and physician who declined to practice medicine. Influenced by Kierkegaard, Heidegger, and the French existentialists of the 1940s, Percy immersed himself simultaneously in an odd amalgam of European literature and American popular culture. For many years, he experimented with different literary forms, until finally he developed, through his novels, a poignant, powerfully affecting way of articulating the central paradoxes of modern life: that affluence, for those who have achieved it, does not necessarily lead to a more satisfying emotional condition; that the impact of science on humanistic values has proved of little help and considerable harm; and that the very nature and purpose of man remain as elusive and mysterious now as they were in premodern times.

Alfred D. Chandler, Jr. *Strategy and Structure.* Cambridge, Mass.: M.I.T. Press, 1962. (Pb)

More than any other single work, this one shows how certain types of corporations grew to giant size, then diversified their product lines, all the while remaining under the control of a new class of salaried managers. The book is made up of four careful case studies, followed by a much larger sample, of which Chandler asks a series of simple but penetrating questions. In carrying off this ingenious inquiry, the author framed a model of comparative organizational evolution that, in turn, has profoundly influenced research and teaching in many disciplines: history, sociology, economics, and business administration.

Chandler himself is the greatest scholar with whom I have worked (for more than a decade now), and his influence continues to exert itself not only through the "organizational school" of historians, of which he is the dean, but equally in his own great books written after *Strategy and Structure*. These include *The Visible Hand* and a forthcoming cross-national study tentatively titled *Scale and Scope*.

Robert H. Bork. *The Antitrust Paradox: A Policy at War with Itself* (1978). New York: Basic Books, 1980. (Pb)

Although I found myself offended by Bork's arrogant neoconservative viewpoint, his powerful argument jelled much of my thinking about the historical ironies of antitrust. As I have now begun to suggest in my own books, antitrust policy in America, though quite often as misguided as Bork asserts, frequently produced unintended but therapeutic effects that made American business more efficient: not through any replication of the Smithian model of perfect competition—the presumed theory behind antitrust—but instead by forcing American corporations to innovate organizationally, as a means of avoiding illegal cartelization. In this way, antitrust actually helped to turn certain American companies into the world's most efficient economic organizations between 1880 and 1960. During and after the 1960s, the advent of global competition made the story a good deal more complex, and this is the focus of my own current work.

Elizabeth McKinsey

Elizabeth McKinsey is both an associate professor of English and American literature at Harvard and the director of the Mary Ingraham Bunting Institute at Radcliffe College. She is the author of The Western Experiment: New England Transcendentalists in the Ohio Valley *and* Niagara Falls: Icon of the American Sublime.

Central to American literature, all these books enrich our understanding of our cultural and psychic heritage—our myths, assumptions, preoccupations and conflicts. By broadening our historic imagination and sympathy, they can help us face squarely the issues of human and political relations—between the sexes, among racial and ethnic groups, and among nations —that will continue to be critical as we move into the twenty-first century.

Perry Miller, ed. *Margaret Fuller: American Romantic. A Selection from Her Writing and Correspondence* (1963). Gloucester, Mass.: Peter Smith, Pubs., 1969.

When I first read Margaret Fuller (transcendentalist; friend of Emerson, Thoreau, and Hawthorne; one of this country's first and most accomplished literary critics) in college, I kept coming back to her. It took several years to realize why: a brilliant, powerful, passionate, sensitive person, she embodied the split between intellect and femininity that I had been socialized to feel. As a powerful expressive spirit, her works provide both a window on nineteenth-century American culture and a mirror of our own attitudes toward gender, society and achievement.

Herman Melville. *Moby Dick* (1851). Berkeley: University of California Press, 1983. (Pb)

Unquestionably the "biggest" book in American literature, *Moby Dick* wrestles with all the huge metaphysical questions—religious, epistemological, ontological, aesthetic—at the same time that it depicts in minute detail the U.S. whaling industry and through it examines questions of democracy and leadership. All its layers of meaning cohere in Melville's powerfully written masterpiece.

Mark Twain. *The Adventures of Huckleberry Finn* (1884). New York: Harper & Row, 1984. (Pb)

When Hemingway contended that all modern literature began with *Huck Finn,* he was thinking of its vernacular language, its antiromantic realism and episodic structure. The language is wonderful—and funny—and very evocative historically. Perhaps I especially like this one because I'm from Missouri.

William Faulkner. *Absalom! Absalom!* (1936). New York: Random House, 1972. (Pb)

Faulkner is arguably our greatest American writer, and this is his magnum opus. The saga of Sutpen and his family, and Quentin Compson's attempt to come to terms with it, embody all the tensions in Southern and indeed American history—race, sex, regionalism, the individual and community, etc.—as well as basic epistemological questions. A powerful, epic work.

Eudora Welty. *Thirteen Stories.* New York: Harcourt, Brace & World, 1965. (Pb)

These perfect gems evoke a particular Southern rural culture—the "sense of place" that Welty has said is so important to her work—at the same time that they reveal mythic, universal human themes and longings. Welty's mastery of language, storytelling, power and form is infused with an extraordinary warmth and humor. Here is a shrewd and realistic but affirmative vision.

Zora Neale Hurston. *Their Eyes Were Watching God* (1937). Urbana: University of Illinois Press, 1978.

Janice's self-knowledge, tenacity and humor, as well as her story, make her one of the more memorable characters in American fiction. A window on a very particular time and place and social segment of American culture—the rural black South in the 1920s and 1930s—*Their Eyes* is also beautifully written. In its zest for life and love and its iconoclasm it is an earlier version of (and direct source for) Alice Walker's *The Color Purple*.

Margaret R. Miles

Margaret Miles is a professor of historical theology at the Harvard Divinity School. She is the author of many works, most notably Augustine on the Body *(1979);* Fullness of Life: Historical Foundations for a New Asceticism *(1981);* Image as Insight: Visual Understanding in Western Christianity and Secular Culture *(1985); and coeditor with Clarissa W. Atkinson and Constance Hall Buchanan of* Immaculate and Powerful: The Female in Sacred Image and Social Reality *(1985).*

The books I chose all challenge settled impressions of the "natural" inevitability of North American life-styles, assumptions, language and social practices. They expose the extent to which all of these are constructions requiring examination and reevaluation in the face of the issues of social injustice, the nuclear world and the crisis of meaning as we approach the twenty-first century.

St. Augustine. *The Confessions* (ca. A.D. 400). Rex Warner, trans. New York: Penguin, 1961. (Pb)

This book provided my first intimation of the massive conditioning of social, sexual and religious attitudes by the culture of one's birth. I also got from it both Augustine's sense that destructive aspects of one's conditioning *can* be changed, and his realistic respect for the difficulty of change—the stability of the social neuroses.

Jonathan Schell. *The Fate of the Earth.* New York: Avon, 1982. (Pb)

Schell's description of the possibility and results of nuclear war emphasizes the necessity of rapid and fundamental social change if the attitudes and ideology that have brought us to the nuclear world are not to lead to the destruction of human life and of the planet that is our home.

Mary Daly. *Gyn/Ecology: The Metaethics of Radical Feminism*
(1978). Boston: Beacon, 1979. (Pb)

Daly here gives a vivid analysis of sexism, using cross-
cultural examples to demonstrate the victimization of women's
bodies and psyches by patriarchal cultures. She also draws an
alternative: women bonding in communities of support and
empowerment.

Nancy Chodorow. *The Reproduction of Mothering: Psychoanalysis and the Sociology of Gender.* Berkeley: University
of California Press, 1978.

Chodorow analyzes the complex conditioning for motherhood in Western culture, destroying the myth of biological
naturalness. An important book for laying the foundation for
egalitarian parenting.

Michel Foucault. *Discipline and Punish: The Birth of a Prison.*
New York: Random House, 1979. (Pb)

A powerful historical description of Foucault's thesis that
it is not primarily submissive mentalities but docile bodies that
social and political power seek to achieve; the book asks how
bodies are subtly or unsubtly coerced, and for what/whose
ends.

Roland Barthes. *The Pleasure of the Text.* Richard Miller, trans.
New York: Hill & Wang, 1975. (Pb)

"Pleasure is a critical principle," writes Barthes, "interpretation is passion." This book has been inspirational to me in its
insistence that the task of interpretation requires a dialectic
between the passion of the interpreter and the pleasure of the
text.

D. Quinn Mills

D. Quinn Mills is the principal faculty member at the Harvard Business School keeping the study of labor relations alive. The impact of economic and managerial systems on people has been his continuing professional interest. He is noted for maintaining a strong emphasis on the general management aspects of people relationships, tying case research and discussion to the problems of operating-line executives, and avoiding the functional perspectives and responsibilities of personnel managers.

A member of the Harvard Business School faculty since 1976, he is the author of ten books and was appointed the Albert J. Weatherhead Professor of Business Administration in 1978.

Winston S. Churchill. *The Second World War,* Volume I: *The Gathering Storm* (1948). Boston: Houghton Mifflin, 1983.

I was twelve years old and living in Houston, Texas when an aunt gave me a copy of the first volume of Winston Churchill's six-volume history of the Second World War, entitled *The Gathering Storm.* I read the book and found it fascinating. It opened to me the wide world of nonfiction literature. It permitted me to learn about great events as they were viewed by participants, including authors like Churchill who possessed insightful and powerful personalities. Reading Churchill also gave me a respect for our language and for rhetoric—cadences, the crashing thunder of strong words, the rhythmic sequence of sentences. In a short time I had read the remaining five volumes of the series and went on to histories composed by other authors.

William Faulkner. *Intruder in the Dust* (1948). New York: Random House, 1967. (Pb)

———. *The Sound and the Fury* (1929). New York: Random House, 1967. (Pb)

During high school I lived in Memphis, Tennessee. Perhaps because I had moved to Memphis and found the attitudes and opinions of my classmates somewhat different from my own, I began to read in search of explanations of what it meant to be a person from the deep South in the United States. William Faulkner's writings revealed to me the complexity of the Southern tradition—of guilt, revenge and repentance. The most powerful of the books was *The Sound and the Fury,* but the line I most remember came from a less well-known novel entitled *Intruder in the Dust.* "Some things you must always be unable to bear," Faulkner wrote; "injustice, prejudice, and despair . . . not for kudos and not for cash, just refuse to bear them."

Another Southern writer taught me a lesson I've benefited from enormously over my lifetime, a lesson about tolerance. "Nothing human disgusts me," wrote Tennessee Williams in *Night of the Iguana,* "unless it is unkind or violent."

William James. *The Varieties of Religious Experience* (1902). New York: Penguin, 1982. (Pb)

College was for me as for many young people a time of questioning and doubts. I had been raised in a Protestant church but during college became profoundly uncertain about the significance of religious faith. Was religion a positive or a negative influence in mankind's experience?

At this time I happened upon William James's *The Varieties of Religious Experience.* From James's book I learned how hazardous it is to generalize about something as complex as religion. This insight reopened to me the search for a religious faith with which I was comfortable. But James also helped me to avoid easy generalizations and conclusions in other complex areas of human life.

The Bible.

Dietrich Bonhoeffer. *The Cost of Discipleship* (1948). R. H. Fuller, trans. Magnolia, Mass.: Peter Smith, 1983.

In the years since I have read widely in Eastern religious works, and in the writings of the ancient Western world. Marcus Aurelius particularly impressed me. I recall one of his observations about self-restraint: "be careful that you do not feel toward the inhuman as they feel toward men." I also read extensively in the mainstream of Christian writings. I was particularly influenced by Dietrich Bonhoeffer's *The Cost of Discipleship,* since the author later gave his life in the struggle within Germany against the Hitler regime.

I have also nibbled at the Bible continually for many years, especially enjoying comparing different translations. The Bible remains the central form of transmission of the Western heritage, and is the foundation of our moral standards—to my mind far more important than laws. The biblical text that returns most often to my mind is from the Book of Micah: "He has showed you, oh man, what is good—and what does the Lord require of you but to do justice, to love mercy and to walk humbly with your God?" I have over many years rendered many decisions in arbitration hearings, and these words have never been far from my thoughts as I pondered what decision to make.

Milovan Djilas. *The New Class: An Analysis of the Communist System* (1957). San Diego: Harcourt Brace Jovanovich, 1982.

George Orwell. *1984* (1949). New York: Signet, 1984. (Pb)

In graduate school I studied economics and political science. There is implicit, and sometimes explicit for that matter, criticism of our economic and political systems in much that is written in those disciplines. Two books that definitely shaped my perspective were Milovan Djilas's study of Stalinist communism, *The New Class,* and George Orwell's *1984.* The two books constituted a vision of a totalitarian hell, created in this century by people who spoke publicly of their commitment to the improvement of human life. These books helped me to preserve a deep appreciation for our own society, without, I hope, causing me intentionally to ignore its limitations. In particular, I recognized again the value of individual human freedom which Western society affords its members.

Isaac Bashevis Singer. *Stories for Children.* New York: Farrar, Straus, & Giroux, 1984.

Years later I became a parent. One of the greatest joys parenting offers is to try to see the world as children see it. I read the classics of children's literature, and enjoyed them more than I did the first time. Also I discovered Isaac Bashevis Singer's *Stories for Children.* It was helpful to me in my own writing to see that simplicity of theme and treatment could contain great depth of understanding of the human character and of human institutions. In particular I was influenced by Singer's comment at the end of *Stories* that today the only serious literature is that written for children. Popular adult literature is lost in sensationalism and the effort to shock.

Margaret Murie and **Olaus Murie.** *Wapiti Wilderness: The Life of Olaus and Margaret Murie in Jackson Hole, Wyoming* (1966). Jackson Hole, Wyo.: Teton Bookshop, n.d. (Pb)

Now in middle age, I think about what things are of great value in life, and what I should try to experience in the time left to me. I am more aware than ever before of the natural richness of this continent. Recently I have been much impressed by the account that Margaret and Olaus Murie left of their years working for the Forest Service in the Tetons *(Wapiti Wilderness)*. Olaus was a founder of the Wilderness Society, which today attempts to preserve what remains of the American wilderness from unreasonable development. Partly under the influence of their book I am putting aside more of my time for trips into the natural wilderness. This is also, I think, an important spiritual dimension in life.

Martha Minow

Martha Minow is a professor of law at Harvard Law School. A former law clerk to Justice Thurgood Marshall, Professor Minow is also a member of the faculty of the Doing Justice Program at Brandeis University and a member of the board of directors of the American Bar Foundation. Her primary interests and her best-known courses are "Children and the Law" and "Family Law."

I asked myself, what books on my shelf are so worn from rereading—or missing from the shelf altogether because I keep insisting that someone else read them? The list is too long, but here are some that come immediately to mind.

Robert M. Cover. *Justice Accused: Antislavery and the Judicial Process* (1975). New Haven: Yale University Press, 1984. (Pb)

It asks, why did judges who opposed slavery nonetheless enforce the laws governing slavery before the Civil War? Its answers move through debates about whether law is natural or socially constructed, through biography and analyses of the interplay between personality and social role, into psychology and the persistent human desire to avoid personal choice and responsibility, and through the power of language in expressing and shaping what people think is possible.

Isaac Bashevis Singer. *In My Father's Court* (1966). New York: Fawcett, 1979. (Pb)

A memoir of the author's childhood days in the home where his father, as rabbi, heard disputes and struggled for resolutions amid the daily lives of his community in Warsaw. The disputes become windows into the virtues and vices of individuals, the traumas solved by arbitrary rules, and the traumas created by them.

Adrienne Rich. *The Dream of a Common Language: Poems.*
New York: W. W. Norton, 1978. (Pb)

A collection of poems that explore the difficulties of speaking about women's experiences and, in so doing, create the possibility of saying things that haven't before been said.

Hester Eisenstein and **Alice Jardine,** eds. *The Future of Difference* (1980). New Brunswick, N.J.: Rutgers University Press, 1985. (Pb)

A collection of essays that connects the contemporary women's movement with scholarly work. In these connections, breathtaking precision in analysis and careful explosions of disciplinary boundaries appear and reappear. The sustained offering of insights uses and at the same time challenges psychoanalytic thought about the formation of the self and gender identity, epistemological debates over the impossibility of objectivity, and current inquiries into literary analysis and political theory. Audre Lorde's essay, "Poetry Is Not a Luxury," shows so powerfully how there are only new ways of making old ideas, and yet the future of our words, and ourselves, depends on our "need to dream, to move our spirits most deeply and directly and through promise."

Ludwig Wittgenstein. *Philosophische Untersuchungen* (*Philosophical Investigations,* 1953). G. E. Anscome, trans. Frankfurt: Suhrkamp, 1967.

How amazing to find out that a philosopher could have a voice, a playful, personal voice; that reading philosophy could feel like a fun and puzzling conversation; and that things look differently after reading? listening? arguing? with this book.

Norton Juster. *The Phantom Tollbooth.* New York: Epstein & Carroll, 1961. (Pb)

A children's book about the meaning of life, it takes puns seriously so that language and experience both become fresh, and it reminds us that we might well be able to do things that people say could never be done.

Sarah Lawrence Lightfoot. *Worlds Apart: Relationships Between Families and Schools.* New York: Basic Books, 1978. (Pb)

Subtle, vivid depictions of the lives of children, teachers and families that mutually implicate each other even through their separations, boundaries and conflicts. The book gently incorporates insights from social theory while exposing the workings of power, cultural and racial differences, and personal hopes and pain. It makes possible knowledge about what we don't see by exposing what others don't see about us in the gaps between classrooms and homes, and, indeed, the gaps between all the places we may dwell.

John D. Montgomery

John Montgomery is a professor of public administration at Harvard's John F. Kennedy School of Government. Professor Montgomery is currently interested in research dealing with developing countries, their agricultural productivity, entrepreneurial behavior and central government support to urban development as well as U.S. foreign policies and international politics.

P. G. Wodehouse. *Money for Nothing* (1928). London: Barrie & Jenkins, 1976.

Wodehouse demonstrates how to write.

J. S. Bach. *The Goldberg Variations* (1747). R. K. Kirkpatrick, ed. New York: Schirmer, 1938.

Bach enriches the soul; Kirkpatrick develops the techniques for giving the soul expression.

Thomas Mann. *Joseph and His Brothers* (1933–43). H. T. Lowe-Porter, trans. 4 vols. New York: Knopf, 1948.

Mann provides the philosophical insights into human experience in their most palatable form.

Thorstein B. Veblen. *Theory of the Leisure Class* (1899). New York: Penguin, 1979. (Pb)

Veblen shows the outer reaches of hypocrisy.

Samuel P. Huntington. *Political Order in Changing Societies* (1968). New Haven: Yale University Press, 1969. (Pb)

Huntington presents the most reasonably packaged definition of development.

Mark Moore

Mark Moore is the Guggenheim Professor of Criminal Justice Policy and Management. He is also faculty chairman of the Executive Programs at the Kennedy School of Government. His policy interests lie in the area of crime and the criminal justice system—the design of police strategies and the use of deceptive and coercive investigative methods. He is the author of Buy and Bust: The Effective Regulation of an Illicit Market in Heroin.

There are two kinds of people in the world: those who live off of institutions, and those who build the capacity of institutions to perform and develop the talents of other individuals. These books are designed to equip one to become the second kind of individual.

Aristotle. *The Politics* (ca. 335 B.C.). Carnes Lord, trans. Chicago: University of Chicago Press, 1984.

This is the classic statement of why men form institutions and the benefits they derive from them. It includes the heretical idea that one of the purposes of institutions is to encourage virtue among those who live within them.

Thomas S. Kuhn. *The Structure of Scientific Revolutions* (1962). Chicago: University of Chicago Press, 1970. (Pb)

This book establishes the social basis of all knowledge and understanding of the world. It pays tribute to scientific "revolutionaries" who insist on seeing the world differently and reveals the crushing power of "normal" science. But it reminds us that, in the end, even science is a social and political process.

Robert M. Pirsig. *Zen and the Art of Motorcycle Maintenance* (1974). New York: Morrow, 1979. (Pb)

This book brilliantly evokes the intellectual and personal challenges of seeking to integrate "technical" and "aesthetic" intuitions in the pursuit of understanding what "quality" is all about.

Richard E. Neustadt. *Presidential Power* (1960). New York: Wiley, 1980. (Pb)

This book is important primarily as a text in "public" management—as potentially useful to state welfare commissioners as to presidents. It is also a model of both method and style for all those who would write about public management.

Richard E. Neustadt

Richard E. Neustadt is the Lucius N. Littauer Professor of Public Policy at Harvard's Kennedy School of Government and formerly a professor of government at Columbia University. He is a foremost scholar on the American presidency, having served on the White House staff under President Truman and as consultant to Presidents Kennedy and Johnson on various problems of organization and operation, both domestic and international. His writings include: The Epidemic that Never Was *(with Harvey Fineberg),* Alliance Politics, Presidential Power, *and his most recent work,* Thinking in Time, *coauthored with Ernest May.*

Whatever their relationship to governance, whether doing it or subjects of it, readers need to understand the essence of the thing as it has seemed to be up to their time.

Niccolò Machiavelli. *The Prince* (1513). Peter E. Bondanella and Mark Musa, trans. New York: Oxford University Press, 1984.

A plea, in the form of a guide, for maximizing political power on sixteenth-century Tuscan terms by an Italian patriot out of office, wishing he were in, concerned for strength to rally the Italian city-states against the dangers of French domination. His realistic acceptance of the evil in political means *and* its inevitability, indeed indispensability, in striving for heroic ends has shocked critics of politics for five hundred years, yet gain the book its status as what Isaiah Berlin called the first work of modern political science.

Max Weber. *From Max Weber: Essays in Sociology* (1946). H. H. Gerth and C. Wright Mills, eds. and trans. New York: Oxford University Press, 1979. (Pb)

Particularly the essay on "Politics as a Vocation": a moving characterization of the ethical dilemma of the human being called to exercise political power over other humans . . . a Machiavellian dilemma, the Prince being human too, not divine. Weber distinguishes "living for" politics, the calling, from living off it, a mere job. A commensurate "ethic of responsibility" is distinguished from ethics for private life; their ultimate convergence is portrayed with tragic feeling.

Alexander Hamilton, John Jay, and **James Madison.** *The Federalist* [*Papers*] (1788). Benjamin F. Wright, ed. Cambridge: Harvard University Press, 1961. (Pb)

Papers rationalizing and justifying the U.S. Constitution of 1787 (to influence debates over ratification), these constitute collectively a profound assessment of the nature, uses, needs for, dangers in, correctives to—and, by implication, ineradicable dilemmas of—human governance in secular societies legitimized by popular sovereignty.

Henry Adams. *The Education of Henry Adams* (1907). Ernest Samuels, ed. Boston: Houghton Mifflin, 1973. (Pb)

A rich, knotty, idiosyncratic evocation of what time, as it speeds up with the industrial and scientific revolutions, does to values, attitudes, institutions and elites in nineteenth- and early twentieth-century America, and to the terms and conditions of employment on which political power can be held, and by whom —all from the standpoint of a specially invested historian, grandson of the sixth, great-grandson of the second U.S. president.

David B. Truman. *The Governmental Process* (1951). New York: Knopf, 1968.

An indispensable clarification of the roles of potential and organized interests in American public life—and by extension in any political system—taking off from insights in "Federalist 10." Multiple membership in overlapping and competing interest groups, and attitudes amounting to rules of the game, keep citizens from splitting into wholly separate groups and groups from splitting into wholly separate governments.

William Shakespeare. *Henry IV, parts 1 and 2* and *Henry V* (1596–99). Arthur Quiller-Couch et al., eds. New York: Cambridge University Press, 1965. (Pb)

The terms and conditions of employment for kings and crown princes (whether monarchical or not)—pleasures and pains, uncertainties and fears, pains and frustrations included—couched in sixteenth-century terms but evocative of twentieth-century counterparts. Personal, intellectual, moral and managerial dilemmas associated with the wielding of supreme political authority, or waiting in the wings for it, are strikingly portrayed.

Richard R. Niebuhr

Richard Niebuhr has been teaching theology and the history of modern religious thought at the Harvard Divinity School since 1956. Because of his strong interest in undergraduate education, he was named chairman of the Committee on Study of Religion when the undergraduate concentration was first established at Harvard in 1973–74. Besides his well-known book on Friedrich Schleiermacher, he recently delivered and published a series of lectures in Japan on Samuel Taylor Coleridge, William James and Jonathan Edwards. He also enjoys photography, particularly in Wyoming.

I have been a teacher of theology at the Harvard Divinity School for thirty years. The list of books I have chosen today for this guide would likely have been different ten years ago and would probably be different five years hence. Some of the titles represent specific works that have affected my thinking deeply and some represent authors more than the contents of a single book. I believe these books assist in the one indispensable duty of obtaining self-knowledge.

Benedict Spinoza. *Ethics* (1675). New York: Scribner's, 1930.

Benedict Spinoza's *Ethics,* which I laboriously read at eighteen or nineteen in a student edition, introduced me to philosophy as a way of living. Spinoza still defines for me "ethics" in its fullest and most proper sense.

Jonathan Edwards. *A Treatise Concerning Religious Affections* (1746). New York: Baker, 1982. (Pb)

Stylistically, this is the finest of Edwards's works and probably of all American theology. In this and in many of his other writings I value his acuity in observation of the soul as well as of the natural world, his passionateness, lyricism, and rigor of thought. I first read Edwards at the age of twenty-three in a nineteenth-century edition and have been returning to him ever since.

Samuel Taylor Coleridge. *Aids to Reflection* (1825). James Marsh and H. N. Coleridge, eds. Burlington: Chauncey Goodrich, 1840.

————. *Biographia literaria* (1817). J. Shawcross, ed. London: Oxford University Press, 1962.

————. *The Poetical Works* (1796–1819). New York: Oxford University Press, 1969.

Coleridge the poet, critic, philosopher and theologian taught me that words are "living powers" and that our duty is "self-superintendence"—the attaining of distinctness of consciousness. In addition to his poetry, Coleridge's *Biographia literaria* and *Aids to Reflection* have been unfailing socratic interlocutors.

William James. *Pragmatism* (1907). Cambridge: Harvard University Press, 1975. (Pb)

Everything James wrote, from his *Principles of Psychology* to *Radical Empiricism,* remains fresh and provocative. James is my antidote to all forms of reductionism and dogmatism.

Herman Melville. *Moby Dick* (1851). Berkeley: University of California Press, 1983. (Pb)

I can give no single reason for the abiding grasp this book, which I first read at the age of twenty-five, has on me. Ahab says, "Gifted with the high perception, I lack the low enjoying power; damned, most subtly and most malignantly! damned in the midst of Paradise!" Melville is one of the few authors who has brought forth an authentic American myth.

James Agee and **Walker Evans.** *Let Us Now Praise Famous Men* (1941). New York: Ballantine, 1974. (Pb)

This book is the only successful marriage of photographs and text I know and belongs to no genre. Its descriptive power (three tenant families in Alabama, 1936) is unsurpassed in exhibiting "the cruel radiance of what is."

Robert Nozick

Robert Nozick is the author of Anarchy, State and Utopia *(1974), which received a National Book Award, and* Philosophical Explanations *(1981), which received the Ralph Waldo Emerson Award of Phi Beta Kappa. He has recently been considering "the best things in life" in preparation for a book of the same name. This third book "examines what's important about life: happiness, the self, sexuality, love, intellectual creativity and wisdom." Previously chairman of the Harvard University Philosophy Department, he is now the Arthur Kingsley Porter Professor of Philosophy at Harvard.*

The earliest very powerful impact of the printed word that I can remember was from the classic comics I read as a child. How I dwelled on *Moby Dick, The Last of the Mohicans, Les Misérables, The Hunchback of Notre Dame,* and *The Adventures of Robin Hood!* If the dialogue and descriptive prose were skimpy, this was more than made up for by the narrative force and the vivid pictures.

John Stuart Mill. *On Liberty* (1854). Elizabeth Rappaport, ed. Indianapolis: Hackett, 1978. (Pb)

To judge by the number of times I recall quoting it in high school, Mill's *On Liberty* impressed me greatly; it combined a position I found congenial, the careful marshaling of reasons and also great rhetorical force—hence the ease of quoting.

Plato. *The Republic* (370–360 B.C.). James Adam, ed. 2 vols. New York: Cambridge University Press, 1963.

I didn't fully recognize it at the time, I think, but Plato's *Republic* (along with some early dialogues), which I read as a freshman in Columbia's humanities course, presented me not only with a flurry of ideas and a way of investigating them and thinking them through but also with a figure, Socrates, vividly portrayed, who embodied these ideas and lived this inquiry. The issues and the figure have stayed with me.

R. Duncan Luce and Howard Raiffa. *Games and Decisions: Introduction and Critical Survey.* New York: John Wiley, 1957.

Sometime late in college I stumbled across R. Duncan Luce and Howard Raiffa's *Games and Decisions,* a lucid and conceptually sophisticated presentation of utility theory and game theory. Its fitting of complicated aspects of human behavior into abstract mathematical structure intrigued me—and by a roundabout route I returned to this subject in doing a doctoral dissertation on decision theory.

Friedrich August von Hayek. *Individualism and Economic Order.* Chicago: University of Chicago Press, 1948.

Ludwig Von Mises. *Socialism* (orig. *Die Gemeinwirtschaft,* 1922). J. Kahane, trans. Indianapolis: Liberty-Classics, 1981. (Pb)

Friedrich August von Hayek. *The Constitution of Liberty* (1960). Chicago: Regnery, 1972.

While in graduate school I encountered the writings of Friedrich Hayek and Ludwig Von Mises, which shook me out of my then socialist beliefs. There was Hayek's book of essays, *Individualism and Economic Order,* and Mises's wide-ranging and unsettling *Socialism,* which showed me I had not thought through any details—economic, social or cultural—of how socialism would work. One of their arguments in particular, about the impossibility of rational economic calculation under socialism, dumbfounded me. Whether or not the argument was ultimately judged to be correct, it was *amazing,* something I never would have thought of in a million years. Soon afterward I read Hayek's then recently published and magisterial *Constitution of Liberty,* which impressed me with the depth of its thinking about society.

William Shakespeare. *Shakespeare: Complete Works* (1592–1611). Alfred Harbage, ed. New York: Penguin, 1969.

The works I have listed affected, in different ways, my first book, a book of political philosophy. Since then my own thinking has not centered on the political or social realm. However, it is harder for me to pick out *individual* works since then that have had large impact. Perhaps the greater the weight of intellectual baggage we acquire as we grow older, the harder it is for one new thing to move us. But I cannot close without saying that back then and since then, there has been, always, presenting the world complete and not merely from one partial intense perspective, Shakespeare.

Joseph S. Nye, Jr.

Joe Nye is a professor of government at Harvard's John F. Kennedy School of Government and director of the Harvard Center for Science and International Affairs. Professor Nye graduated from Princeton, was a Rhodes Scholar at Oxford, and wrote his Harvard Ph.D. thesis in East Africa. His latest book is Nuclear Ethics *(1986).*

In a world of sovereign states and nuclear weapons, it is too dangerous to think one can know all the answers, but it is essential to be clear about the key questions and one's values. These books have helped me with both. They are listed chronologically.

Leo Tolstoy. *War and Peace* (1865–69). Louise Maude and Aylmer Maude, trans. George Gibian, ed. New York: W. W. Norton, 1966.

Tolstoy introduced me to the complexity of history; to the enormous gap between what humans intend and what transpires; and to the importance of being clear about one's own core values. And what a good read!

Joseph A. Schumpeter. *Capitalism, Socialism, and Democracy* (1942). New York: Harper & Row, 1983. (Pb)

Schumpeter's celebration of the achievements of capitalism, and particularly the role of the entrepreneur and "creative destruction," is combined with a paradoxical prognosis of capitalism "killing itself by its successes." I wrote my undergraduate thesis about the question of whether that conclusion followed from his premise. I am still not sure that it does. This great book sets a great puzzle.

Alfred J. Ayer. *Language, Truth and Logic* (1936). New York: Dover, 1952. (Pb)

While I would no longer subscribe to such a simple positivist epistemology, the experience of studying "Oxford philosophy" left me with a lifelong skeptical approach to tangled questions. Before trying to cut tall trees, start by clearing away the obstructing underbrush. Ayer set a high standard.

Hans J. Morgenthau. *Politics Among Nations: The Struggle for Power and Peace* (1948). 5th ed. New York: Knopf, 1978.

A flawed book can have a great influence on one's life. This "Realist" text dominated the field when I began graduate study of international politics. It was too good to dismiss, but something was missing. My book (with Robert Keohane), *Power and Interdependence,* was in part a product of this wrestling match with Morgenthau. I am grateful for the great provocation.

Elenore Smith Bowen [Laura Bohannan]. *Return to Laughter* (1954). New York: Doubleday, 1964.

This sensitive fictionalized account of an anthropologist's coming to terms with cultural relativism helped me to understand why I could admire so much of life in Uganda when I lived there in the early 1960s, yet still refuse to accept certain things I felt to be wrong.

David J. Duncan. *The River Why* (1983). New York: Bantam, 1984. (Pb)

Long after I knew that I am often happiest when waist deep in a rushing river casting flies to rising trout, I read this book on an Alaskan float trip. Its droll portrayal of the fine line between fishing and philosophy allowed me both to laugh at myself and to feel justified in continuing as I would in any case. One can love books for many reasons.

Laurie D. Olin

Laurie Olin is a professor of landscape architecture at Harvard's Graduate School of Design. He teaches a landscape-design studio and lectures on the history and evolution of landscapes. He has received Guggenheim and Rome Prize Fellowships for study in landscape architecture, which he has taught at the University of Washington, the University of Pennsylvania and Harvard. He is a founding partner of Hanna/Olin Ltd., a landscape-architectural firm located in Philadelphia.

These books should dispel either of two notions: the first that the world and our society are fixed or complete, and the second that any particular current trend is destiny. Things can and must change, but to a surprising degree such change can be shaped by dreams and design just as it can by chance or the forces currently at work in society.

Holling C. Holling. *Tree in the Trail.* Boston: Houghton Mifflin, 1942.

Of all the books from childhood, I place this one ahead of *Winnie the Pooh, Alice, The Leather-stocking Tales,* and so on (which are better literature), because it gave an exciting history of a place. The protagonist was a cottonwood tree that witnessed three hundred years of American evolution from buffalo herds and Indian migrations through the exploration and settling of the West by European immigrants. It opened my eyes at age eight to social and ecological history. The elegant drawings, paintings and maps on every page conveyed as much or more content as the text, another lesson that shaped my future self-expression.

Frank Lloyd Wright. *An American Architecture.* Edgar Kaufmann, ed. New York: Bramhall House, 1955.

One of the several books about Frank Lloyd Wright's work. As a young architecture student I found this book was truly an inspiration. The clear exposition of Wright's ideas concerning the relationship between buildings and society, between structure and form, between ornament and materials, and his attitudes toward society, work and art opened up the possibilities of architecture and imagination.

Loren C. Eiseley. *The Immense Journey* (1957). Alexandria, Va.: Time–Life Books, 1981.

The first and possibly the best of his many books. More than Rachel Carson's *Silent Spring,* which came later, this collection of essays explicated an ecological point of view to which I still aspire. Eiseley follows Thoreau as one who presents the longer view of man as a part of nature, who struggles with this truth and the beauty of evolution and its unfinished workings and experiments.

Theodore Roethke. *Words for the Wind* (1957). Seattle: University of Washington Press, 1981. (Pb)

The third volume of poetry published by one of the most influential teachers I ever had. Roethke introduced me to all the modern poets as well as to the seventeenth-century metaphysical ones, but it was in the close reading of his work that I began to see how one of my own contemporaries could make art from a living language, using material from his own experience and mine, and give it form based upon classical and historical precedents. It was intelligent, passionate and beautiful. More importantly, like William Carlos Williams and Wallace Stevens, the two American poets I came to value the most, his poetry seemed always fresh and to admonish you to "change your life."

W. G. Hoskins. *The Making of the English Landscape.* New York: Penguin, 1970.

This deceptively concise and readable book by the current preeminent cultural geographer of Britain led me to spend several years of my life involved in the study of the evolution of landscapes in Europe and Britain. It also led me to classical archaeology, to the history of settlement patterns and agriculture, to the persistence of archetypes and themes in the design of gardens and parks, and finally to make comparisons and connections between social, ecological and artistic history and theory. More importantly, it led me to want both to share such views with others through teaching and to add my contribution to the palimpsest of design on the land.

Certain historic comic strips and movies were equally important to my drawing and graphic development.

Richard D. Parker

Richard Parker is a professor of constitutional law and criminal law at the Harvard Law School. He is well known to his colleagues for his eclectic interests and voracious reading. Before joining the Harvard Law faculty he practiced law in Paris and clerked for Justice Potter Stewart.

Friedrich Nietzsche. *The Birth of Tragedy* (1872). Walter Kaufmann, trans. New York: Random House, 1967.

A "scholarly" discourse on Greek tragedy that boldly celebrates the passionate, the lyrical, the personal—as contrasted to the dryly rational, the "soundly" balanced, the impersonal "virtue" of mainstream scholarship.

Alan J. P. Taylor. *English History, 1914–1945* (1965). New York: Oxford University Press, 1985.

Exemplifies a kinetic vision of politics and history expressed idiosyncratically and provocatively and joining detailed sensitivity to contingencies with insistence on simple, deep structural tendencies.

Roberto M. Unger. *Knowledge and Politics.* New York: Free Press, 1975. (Pb)

An amazingly comprehensive, ambitious and mind-opening critique of liberalism combining (once again) systematics and bold, passionate commitment.

Alexander M. Bickel. *The Least Dangerous Branch: The Supreme Court at the Bar of Politics* (1962). New Haven: Yale University Press, 1986.

The best book so far on American constitutional law, exploring—in a highly personal style—the politics at the heart of the law.

James Agee and **Walker Evans.** *Let Us Now Praise Famous Men*
   (1941). New York: Ballantine, 1974. (Pb)

   A cumulatively stunning expression and evocation of passionate, lyrical, personal idealism, embedded in a concrete description of the texture of sharecroppers' lives.

Vladimir Nabokov. *Lolita* (1955). Berkeley, Calif.: Berkeley
   Press, 1984. (Pb)

   A beautiful novel-of-authenticity, fusing romantic and empirical sensibilities in a way rather like the first two, otherwise
dissimilar, books I have listed.

Orlando Patterson

Orlando Patterson was born in Jamaica. He was educated and has taught at the University of the West Indies and the London School of Economics before he came to Harvard in 1969. He is the author of three books on historical and comparative sociology and of three novels. He is presently completing a work on the historical sociology of freedom.

These works are as important for the way they approach their subjects as for the subjects they treat. By illuminating past and present in wholly new ways, they teach us how to understand the future when it becomes the present.

Immanuel Kant. *Groundwork on the Metaphysics of Morals* (orig. *Moral Law,* 1797). H. J. Paton, trans. New York: Harper & Row, n.d. (Pb)

This is the greatest work of philosophy. Through it Kant became my intellectual father-figure. When I first read it as an undergraduate I was awed, but not scared by its great themes and insights. Under the forbidding Teutonic surface I soon discovered a very human, deeply compassionate presence. The *Groundwork* was my path to the serious study of philosophy. It taught me intellectual discipline and provided me with an inexhaustible philosophical foundation for any later thinking.

It has two windows: one looks out on the Enlightenment and all that's best in modern culture, the other looks back at ancient cultures and their greatest achievement, stoicism. The connections are not immediately obvious. Discovering them has been one of the abiding pleasures of my intellectual growth.

Albert Camus. *The Myth of Sisyphus* (1942). Justin O'Brien, trans. New York: Random House, 1959. (Pb)

There are books such as the *Groundwork* which one grows with, and there are books one grows out of. Camus's *The Myth of*

Sisyphus was one such work for me. I first came across it in high school, did not understand it, but was deeply drawn to it. I read it repeatedly through college. It is the perfect work for a young, searching mind concerned with the problems of identity and the meaning of existence. Absurdity and exile were just the themes I needed to explore as I came to terms with a decolonizing society (Jamaica) similar to the one in which Camus grew up (Algeria). Camus taught me intellectual nimbleness, the serious art of playing with ideas. And I learned confidence from him. When, finally, I came to understand him fully, I came to see not only that he was wrong but that I could think more creatively about the ideas to which he had introduced me. These ideas inspired my first novel, *The Children of Sisyphus* (1964).

Karl R. Popper. *The Open Society and Its Enemies* (1945). Volume 1. Princeton: Princeton University Press, 1966.

This great work was an eye-opener for me. It completely overturned my conventional views on ancient society and thought, especially that of Plato. It made me realize how it is possible for a whole tradition of scholarship to distort systematically the interpretation of a period. This work taught me the importance of interpreting the past and the classics for oneself.

Eric E. Williams. *Capitalism and Slavery: The Caribbean* (1944). New York: André Deutsch, 1964. (Pb)

This masterful historical work showed me how a powerful mind can turn long-cherished views of history upside down. It was also important for all West Indian intellectuals growing up in the 1950s and 1960s—history as a political force. The work taught me two things: the importance of slavery in the rise of the modern West and the courage to take on big ideas and great themes.

Karl Marx. *Economic and Philosophical Manuscripts of 1844* (1844). Dirk J. Struik, ed., Martin Milligan, trans: New York: International, 1964. (Pb)

This work, along with the *Preface to the Critique of Political Economy,* restored my respect for Marx after a long love affair with, and ultimate rejection of, *Das Kapital* during my early years of graduate school at the London School of Economics. This is the early, humanistic side of Marx. A profound critique of the central human problem of capitalism—alienation. From this work I could move back to Hegel and forward to Weber, Laski and other modern thinkers in the development of my own sociological thought.

David Riesman, with Reuel Denny and Nathan Glazer. *The Lonely Crowd* (1950). New Haven: Yale University Press, 1973. (Pb)

One of the greatest works of modern interpretive sociology. This is the work that finally turned me on to sociology. It does for the interpretation of modern American society what Alexis de Tocqueville did for the first part of the nineteenth century. Like the latter's work, it transcends the deeper period to which it is addressed. The work brought me a deeper understanding of American society and a lasting fascination with it. More important, it became my model of informed macrosociological analysis; the interpretive sociological imagination at its best.

Reginald Phelps

Dr. Phelps attended public schools in western Massachusetts, received his A.B. in 1930 from Harvard and spent the following year in Europe, primarily in Germany. He has led a life of educational administration, teaching and scholarship chiefly at Harvard University. During the stresses of the 1930s, his early interest in German literature developed into the study of European and American history. His writings include many articles, largely on twentieth-century Germany. He has also written, with Jack Stein, a useful reading text entitled The German Heritage.

I don't know that these books prepared me for the challenges of the twentieth century, and I doubt that they would prepare our successors for those of the twenty-first century. What they did was to help me to understand the European and American past and present.

As introduction: any such list is subjective and temporary. The books are chosen from my present view of my experience, and are not necessarily the books I would have selected ten or thirty years ago. Mostly they have affected me by their literary qualities, not their "messages," since most philosophies and (quasi-)theologies sound equally persuasive if skillfully presented. These are books that have stayed with me for years, hence the absence of contemporary writing.

William Shakespeare. *King Lear* (1605). New York: Penguin, 1984. (Pb)

————. *Macbeth* (1606). Maynard Mack and Robert E. Boynton, eds. New York: Random House, 1981. (Pb)

William Shakespeare's plays; specifically *King Lear* and *Macbeth,* both read in G. L. Kittredge's famous course. Close to them, *Othello, Julius Caesar* and *The Tempest.* Among these *Lear* seems greatest, perhaps because of seeing an overwhelming performance of it in London during the war.

The Bible. King James version (1611).

The Bible, specifically the Psalms, in the King James version, as we heard and sometimes recited them in Massachusetts public schools from the first grade on; and in Luther's German translation. Why? The beauty of the words, and, I suppose, the religious *Urerlebnis* they express. And, like so many writings, musical associations enhance their effect—American, English, German hymns; Brahms's *Requiem,* with Toscanini conducting, heard in the Salzburg church fifty years ago.

Johann Wolfgang von Goethe. *Faust, part I* (1770). John Prudhoe, trans. Manchester: Manchester University Press, 1974. (Pb).

Goethe, *Faust* I (not *Faust* II) and many of his youthful lyric poems. A word artist who matches Shakespeare, and a drama that somehow symbolizes occidental man, with its theme of eternal striving; and a personal tragedy of such force that it might well, like Goethe's second major emotional creation, *The Sorrows of Young Werther,* have wrung tears from stones. Beside these, even young Schiller's splendid dramas, the artistic beauties of Stefan George and Rainer Maria Rilke, the rhetoric of German expressionist drama, and the arts and crafts of Thomas Mann, all of which once appealed very strongly, do not quite stand equal.

John Dos Passos. *Nineteen Nineteen* (1932). New York: New American Library, n.d. (Pb)

Sidney B. Fay. *The Origins of the World War* (1928). 2 vols. New York: Macmillan, 1954.

Erich Maria Remarque. *All Quiet on the Western Front* (1928). New York: Fawcett, 1979. (Pb)

John Dos Passos's powerful novel *Nineteen Nineteen* came quite early in the wave of revisionism and disillusion with World War I that reached these shores well before the Depression. For the scholarly world, Sidney B. Fay's *The Origins of the World War* led to revisionism. For the general reader, such works as Erich Maria Remarque's *All Quiet on the Western Front,* and the magnificent film made from it, led to disillusion. If you want to know why my generation was so reluctant to go to war in the 1930s, these books will help you find out.

Thomas Wolfe. *Look Homeward, Angel* (1929). New York: Scribner's, 1982. (Pb)

For my generation, perhaps the great American novel— its rooted/rootless hero, its ironic naturalism, its waves of stunning rhetoric; coming of age in this century in the small towns of eastern America. Less "literary" than Faulkner. A wider range than that almost perfect novel about Harvard, George Weller's *Not to Eat, Not For Love.* Not as universal, doubtless, as Herman Melville's *Moby Dick* but a clearer, more human, less strained presentation of such American themes as wandering, roots, grand visions.

Immanuel Kant. *Critique of Pure Reason* (1781). New York: St. Martin's, 1969. (Pb)

————. *Critique of Practical Reason and Other Writings in Moral Philosophy* (1788). Lewis Beck, trans. New York: Garland, 1977.

The philosopher who, like his medieval precursor Cardinal Nicholas Cusanus, defines and sets limits for human capacities and presents, one may hope, guidelines for ethics and behavior more satisfying than those provided by hubris and wills to power.

Richard Pipes

Richard Pipes is the Frank B. Baird, Jr. Professor of History at Harvard and has been a member of the Harvard faculty since 1950. From 1981 to 1982, Professor Pipes was director of Eastern European and Soviet affairs on the National Security Council. His many works include: Survival Is Not Enough *(1984);* U.S.–Soviet Relations in the Era of Détente *(1981); and* Formation of the Soviet Union *(1954).*

I did not provide a list of the most important books but only of those which have had a strong personal influence on me. They may do nothing for others.

Friedrich Nietzsche. *The Basic Writings of Nietzsche* (1872–95). Walter Kaufman, ed. and trans. New York: Modern Library, 1968.

The first author to make a great impression on me was Friedrich Nietzsche, whom I "discovered" at the age of fifteen. I devoured all he wrote (in the original German). He suited well my adolescent sense of rebellion. Once I reached seventeen I found him less and less palatable, and I have not been able to read him since.

Rainer Maria Rilke. *Selected Poetry of Rainer Maria Rilke* (1897–1923). Stephen Mitchell, ed. New York: Random House, 1982.

The poetry of Rainer Maria Rilke I first read at the age of nineteen or twenty. Its profound lyricism, its serenity have affected me more than any other poetry and do so to this day.

François P. Guizot. *The History of Civilization in Europe* (1828). William Hazlitt, trans. Darby, Penn.: Arden Library, 1983.

I discovered this book while I was a soldier and it showed me that history can be a form of philosophy and literature. It persuaded me to become a professional historian.

The Bible (so-called "Old Testament").

I first read it late, at the age of twenty-eight or so, in connection with tutoring in history and literature, where it was obligatory. I was overwhelmed by nearly all of it, but especially the Book of Job and the Psalms.

Michel de Montaigne. *Selections from the Essays* (1595). Donald M. Frame, ed. and trans. Arlington Heights, Ill.: Harlan Davidson, 1973. (Pb)

I tried to read the *Essays* (in the Florio translation) at the age of twenty-five but it bored me. Then I read it again at the age of forty-seven and found it the wisest book ever written. I never fail to be impressed and influenced by Montaigne's outlook.

Sir Max Beerbohm. *Works and More* (1930). St. Clair Shores, Mich.: Scholarly Press, 1969.

Max Beerbohm has had a much smaller influence on me and yet I love reading him: his quiet elegance, detachment, serenity appeal to me greatly, as does his exquisite humor. I first read him when I was fifty or so.

Willard V. Quine

Willard Quine has retired from his teaching career at Harvard University, where he is the Edgar Pierce Professor of Philosophy Emeritus. His distinguished work as a mathematical logician and philosopher of language continues. Retirement allows him to produce such forthcoming works as Bits and Pieces *(Harvard University Press). He is the subject of a volume in the "Library of Living Philosophers" series. Best known for writing* Mathematical Logic *and* Word and Object, *his autobiography,* Time of My Life, *was published in 1985.*

Bertrand Russell. *Introduction to Mathematical Philosophy* (1919). New York: Simon & Schuster, 1971. (Pb)

Introduction to Mathematical Philosophy was my introduction to the rigors of modern logic and the mysteries of infinite numbers. It brought new clarity to familiar old mathematical concepts as well, by reducing them to pure logic and set theory. The charms of the subject matter and of Russell's writing combined to launch me on a career of mathematical philosophy.

Alfred North Whitehead and **Bertrand Russell.** *Principia mathematica* (1910–12). 3 vols. New York: Cambridge University Press, 1962. (Pb)

Written mostly in mathematical symbols, these volumes provided the solid fare for which Russell's book above had whetted my appetite. Here the derivation of classical mathematics from logic and set theory is carried through in strict formal detail.

Sir Arthur S. Eddington. *The Nature of the Physical World* (1928). Folcroft, Penn.: Folcroft Library Editions, 1935.

This was perhaps the most memorable of several books of popular science that both fired and helped to gratify my curiosity about the basis, bounds and inner workings of physical reality.

Bertrand Russell. *Our Knowledge of the External World* (1914). 2d ed. Atlantic Highlands, N.J.: Humanities Press, 1972.

The two philosophical interests noted above—the logico-mathematical and the physical—are here brought into contact. A program is sketched for deriving our knowledge of nature from our sensory evidence with the help of modern logical techniques.

Rudolf Carnap. *Der logische Aufbau der Welt* (1928). Hamburg: Meiner, 1974.

The program that Russell had thus sketched is here undertaken in earnest and explicit technical detail, bristling with logical symbols. It is a work of admirable vision and ingenuity.

Rudolf Carnap. *Logische Syntax der Sprache.* Vienna: J. Springer, 1934.

This work, the writing of which I was privileged to witness for a while, brought logical positivism to full flower. It develops the philosophy of science as the logic and syntax of the language of science. Carnap and I diverged from it in opposite directions after a few years, but the book has influenced me deeply.

Walter W. Skeat, ed. *An Etymological Dictionary of the English Language* (1879). Oxford: Oxford University Press, 1924.

The foregoing six books sparked and nourished interrelated interests that took on professional proportions. But this book has been the faithful support for fifty-seven years of another and independent interest that I somehow acquired in my late teens: a consuming interest in the origins of words.

Howard Raiffa

Howard Raiffa has a joint appointment to Harvard's John F. Kennedy School of Government and the Harvard Business School, where he is the Frank P. Ramsey Professor of Managerial Economics. He is the first director of the International Institute for Applied Systems Analysis in Vienna. He has a worldwide reputation as an applied mathematician, statistician, game theorist, decision analyst and negotiation analyst.

My thesis is that some rather straightforward, simple, systematic, nonesoteric analysis of complex decisions can make a net positive difference in society. These books collectively contribute to this noble quest.

Kenneth J. Arrow. *Social Choice and Individual Values* (1951). New Haven: Yale University Press, 1970. (Pb)

This book profoundly influenced my research agenda. In controversial arenas where one has to choose an alternative and there are conflicting principles of fairness or of rationality, it is helpful to articulate desiderata of a "good" solution and to investigate the compatibility and implications of these desiderata (or axioms). Arrow was a pathfinder and deserved his Nobel Prize for this work.

John G. Kemeny et al. *Introduction to Finite Mathematics* (1957). Englewood Cliffs, N.J.: Prentice-Hall, 1974.

One of the earliest books written by mathematicians to expose social scientists to the power and beauty of mathematical thinking in a truly accessible way.

John Von Neumann and **Oskar Morgenstern.** *Theory of Games and Economic Behavior* (1944). Princeton: Princeton University Press, 1980. (Pb)

A mathematical tour de force. The first really profound mathematical treatise written about a subject at the crossroads of economics, sociology and psychology.

Thomas C. Schelling. *The Strategy of Conflict.* Cambridge: Harvard University Press, 1960. (Pb)

One of the first books to exploit game-theoretic thinking, but it breaks away from the overly rigid structures of formal game theory. Profound and insightful . . . and a delight to read.

Robert Schlaifer. *Analysis of Decision Under Uncertainty* (1965). Huntington, N.Y.: Krieger, 1978.

A first-rate pedagogical contribution that uses exclusively case analysis for instructional purposes. The book is written in a heavy style that does not appeal to students, but subsequent authors have written follow-on versions that make the subject matter more enjoyable. The Schlaifer book was the pioneering effort in the teaching of quantitative techniques by the case method.

David Lax and **James Schenius.** *The Manager as Negotiator.* New York: Free Press, 1986.

Though written by mathematically oriented authors, this book should be readily accessible to managers. It should be required reading for students in public policy and business.

Robert B. Reich

Robert B. Reich teaches political economy and management at Harvard's John F. Kennedy School of Government. Mr. Reich is the author of numerous books and articles concerning the relationships among law, politics and economics. Among his most recent books are New Deals: The Chrysler Revival and the American System *and* The Next American Frontier. *A former Rhodes Scholar, Professor Reich has served in Washington as assistant to the solicitor general and as director of policy planning for the Federal Trade Commission.*

Whether the immediate problem is described as arms control, Soviet expansionism, economic growth and competitiveness or social justice to the poor and disadvantaged—the deeper issue is the same. That is, how should we define the border between "us" and "them"? Our overarching goal must be to expand the first realm ("us"), and contract the second ("them"). These books suggest how we might begin this formidable task.

Fernand Braudel. *Civilization and Capitalism, 15th–18th Century* (1967, 1982–84). Siân Reynolds, trans. 3 vols. New York: Harper & Row, 1985, 1986. (Pb)

Braudel weaves detailed threads into stirring tapestries. These volumes reveal the fragility of our societies—their vulnerabilities to war, plague and human misery—but also, wondrously, their capacity to endure. Braudel is a master.

Ellis W. Hawley. *The New Deal and the Problem of Monopoly, 1934–1938* (1959). Princeton: Princeton University Press, 1966. (Pb)

Hawley unwraps politics and finds economics. He then unwraps economics and finds ideology. He peers through ideology and discovers our most basic hopes and fears for ourselves, our families and our nation. His insights explain much of our current condition.

Joseph A. Schumpeter. *Capitalism, Socialism, and Democracy* (1942). New York: Harper & Row, 1983. (Pb)

This rich inkblot of a book is many different things to many different people. But above all else it suggests that the political and economic universe we inhabit is in flux; it grows on itself, reaching outward in many directions at once, like organic matter. Instead of equilibrium, there is omnipresent disequilibrium. Instead of secured values, there is the constant danger that values we hold dear will be subsumed.

Samuel P. Huntington. *American Politics: The Promise of Disharmony* (1981). Cambridge: Harvard University Press, 1983. (Pb)

Huntington skillfully identifies the yearnings at the heart of American politics. As a nation, we are always "to be," we never are. We feel, alternatively, guilt, anxiety, anger and resolution about our ideals. But we are animated by myths that can never be fulfilled. A powerful and critically important book.

John Kenneth Galbraith. *The Affluent Society* (1958). New York: New American Library, 1978. (Pb)

As fresh and insightful today as it was thirty years ago. Galbraith reconfigures our way of thinking about a nation's economy and the society of which the economy is but a part. How do we define economic success? What do we want for ourselves, anyway? The influence of this book, and of the towering figure behind it, cannot be overstated.

Mark Twain. *The Adventures of Huckleberry Finn* (1884). New York: Harper & Row, 1984. (Pb)

I have learned more about American society, and, not incidentally, human nature, from reading and rereading Huck's accounts of life on the Mississippi River than I have from any other single source. His knowledge always runs deep; his insights are on target; he can smell duplicity from a mile away.

David Riesman

David Riesman is a professor emeritus of sociology at Harvard University. One of the world's leading sociologists, his opinion is often sought on a wide range of topics, frequently the sociology of American higher education. His most notable works include The Lonely Crowd: A Study of the Changing American Character *and* Faces in the Crowd: Individual Studies in Character and Politics. *He may well be the most prolific letter writer on Harvard's campus. The following comments are excerpted from Riesman letters to the editors of this guide.*

It seems to me that in many cases it is not a particular book, though often of course it is just that, but a particular author who opens new visions and impels new curiosities.

Louis Auchincloss. *The Rector of Justin* (1964). Boston: Houghton Mifflin, 1980. (Pb)

Niccolò Machiavelli. *The Prince* (1513). Peter E. Bondanella and Mark Musa, trans. New York: Oxford University Press, 1984.

Alexis de Tocqueville. *Democracy in America* (1835–40). G. Laurence, trans. New York: Random House, 1981. (Pb)

I was thinking about Louis Auchincloss the other day. He is an unduly deprecated author because, while a full-time practicing lawyer and responsible New York citizen, he has written a large number of novels dealing, as did much of Henry James and Edith Wharton, with the upper class, or at least the upper professional class, such as old Wall Street law firms. His novel *The Rector of Justin* is about a private-school headmaster of an earlier day and, I think, a wonderful book. But it is perhaps less relevant to some than one of his books dealing with Wall Street life and its ethical problems, similar to those faced in other professional callings.

It is the author, not the particular book, to whom one would want to call the reader's attention. You will recall, of course, that the Bible is itself a collection of books, poetry, history and much else. There are of course salient books, whether Machiavelli's *The Prince* or de Tocqueville's *Democracy in America,* but in these cases it is the author whom one would want also to bring to the reader's attention.

Marc Roberts

Marc Roberts holds a joint appointment with Harvard's School of Public Health and the Kennedy School of Government as a professor of political economy and health policy. He has taught primarily in the fields of industrial organization, cost-benefit analyses, environmental economics and health economics. He is a consultant to public agencies, including the Environmental Protection Agency and the Massachusetts Department of Public Health, and author of books that examine environmental and health challenges in modern society.

Ernest Hemingway. *For Whom the Bell Tolls* (1940). New York: Scribner's, 1982. (Pb)

I think almost everyone reads a novel when they are still young that first brings them face to face with the reality of life and death. I read this my freshman year and argued about it endlessly late at night sitting in cafeterias while the traffic lights glistened in the rain on the streets outside. Best of all, I liked the Spanish woman, Pilar, and years later felt vindicated in my preference when I discovered Hemingway had named his favorite boat after her.

Thomas S. Kuhn. *The Structure of Scientific Revolutions* (1962). Chicago: University of Chicago Press, 1970. (Pb)

I read this my first year in graduate school. For years I told people about the book, how much it had to say about all academic work and the ways in which we all think. For years it was an underground classic and I was an ardent devotee. Now it has received its well-deserved fame.

Max Weber. *On the Methodology of the Social Science* (1904–17). Edward A. Shils and Henry A. Finch, trans. Glencoe, Ill.: Free Press, 1949.

I read this my last year in graduate school. Since reading Kuhn, I had been struggling with the question of how, if at all, social science was "different." What role should numerical measurements play in such work? How could I make sense of the tendency of economic models to oscillate from descriptive to prescriptive and back again? The translation was obscure, the ideas flashed across my mind like skyrockets. I now urge every graduate student to read the essay "Science as a Vocation."

John Rawls. *A Theory of Justice* (1971). Oxford: Oxford University Press, 1972. (Pb)

I have struggled with this book for the past ten years. It took two readings for me to figure out what it meant and one more to find out where and how I disagreed with it. The effort to define my reactions has been extraordinarily educational but it is not one for the faint-hearted nor a task to be undertaken lightly.

John A. McPhee. *Encounters with the Archdruid.* New York: Farrar, Straus & Giroux, 1971. (Pb)

Since I was introduced to McPhee five years ago, I have read almost everything. This is certainly one of the best. It is about both people as individuals and people as representatives of ideas and causes. It reminds us that those we like most may not be those we think are right and that there should be room in our lives for both kinds of regard. It reminded me why I used to belong to the Sierra Club and made me unembarrassed by that youthful enthusiasm.

Jeffrey Sachs

Jeffrey Sachs is a professor of economics at Harvard College and a former junior fellow in Harvard's Society of Fellows. An adviser to many Latin American governments, Professor Sachs has also been a consultant to the World Bank and the International Monetary Fund. He is a member of the Brookings Panel of Economists and a contributor to newspapers and magazines in the United States and Japan.

These studies make clear that economic processes can only be understood in conjunction with politics and other social forces. The world's economic problems cannot be solved through any simple fix of technical economics, but only through the broadest understanding of the role of economics in the larger social order.

Max Weber. *The Protestant Ethic and the Spirit of Capitalism* (1904). Talcott Parsons, trans. New York: Scribner's, 1977. (Pb)

In this and related studies (for example, *General Economic History)* Max Weber brilliantly illuminated the social organization and belief system that contributed to the rise of modern capitalism.

Fernand Braudel. *Civilization and Capitalism, 15th–18th Century* (1967, 1982–84). Siân Reynolds, trans. 3 vols. New York: Harper & Row, 1985, 1986. (Pb)

This is a magnificent history of the material development of modern society. Braudel uses paintings, literature and other surprising sources in a remarkable evocation of day-to-day life in the formative period of modern society.

John Maynard Keynes. *Essays in Persuasion* (1931). New York: W. W. Norton, 1963. (Pb)

This is a series of remarkable and pithy essays by the greatest political economist of this century. Keynes comments brilliantly and with great prescience on the major economic issues of his day. In the process we see the unfolding of the modern science of macroeconomics.

Joseph A. Schumpeter. *Capitalism, Socialism, and Democracy* (1942). New York: Harper & Row, 1983. (Pb)

Schumpeter captured the essence of modern economic development with his focus on technological change and the "creative destruction" that it brings about. Added to this focus are Schumpeter's trenchant insights into political competition in the industrial democracies and the role of the intellectual in the capitalist order.

John Kenneth Galbraith. *The Affluent Society* (1958). New York: New American Library, 1978. (Pb)

This is political economy at its polemic best. Galbraith helped to define modern American liberalism with his call for an enlarged role for the public sector. Worth rereading in a period of shrinking government and widespread budget cutting.

Moshe Safdie

Moshe Safdie is an internationally known architect and urban designer with a practice in Montreal, Cambridge, Massachusetts and Jerusalem. He has been director of Harvard's Urban Design Program of the Graduate School of Design and is the Ian Woodner Professor of Architecture and Urban Design. He has written three books: Beyond Habitat, For Everyone a Garden *and* Form and Purpose. *In addition to lecturing frequently at conferences and on campuses, his current projects range from the Momilla business district in Jerusalem to the Montreal waterfront, a Hebrew school in Mexico City, housing in the Republic of Singapore, the National Gallery of Canada in Ottawa and Columbus Circle in New York City.*

By definition, an architect's principal source of inspiration and learning is the study of the visual environment, cities and buildings, observed in reality and in reproductions of drawings and photographs. The architect's eye is a greater scanner sorting out relevancies, perceived and hidden orders, organization and patterns. The written word coexists as stimulation with the image.

I have chosen three books. The impact of the first has been to place my consciousness within an ethical and moral framework. The second is a book of science that connects the body theory of design to a greater universal context. The third is a book specifically about architecture and cities, to give particular emphasis to the significance of one set of images and experiences over others.

The Bible. King James version (1611). Book of Job.

The first book is the Book of Job and, in particular, its entirety but for the last four chapters. Job's starting point is the comfortable world where virtue is rewarded, evil punished. Through a series of devastating experiences this simple con-

struct falls apart. Seeking virtue cannot be pursued for want of
immediate rewards in this life, nor for Job (as for myself) does
the promise of a reward in an afterlife form a part of his consciousness. Invariably there must be other motives to seek virtue. It comes down to the fundamental level of acting in a way
that, when multiplied into the collective behavior of all humanity, makes this planet a livable, comfortable place to be. It builds
upon the ancient Hebrew saying "Thou shall not do unto others
. . ." as a more elementary construct for one's personal morality
than the crime-and-punishment constructs that followed, aim-
ing to control a fundamentally aggressive and selfish humanity.
And though the last four chapters (considered by many scholars
to have been added later) soften the message, as God repents
and rewards Job in this life upon the earth, I've always remained with the lamentation of Job's dilemma and the conviction that what must govern my ethical base and morality as an
architect and as an individual must rest upon a vision of my own
behavior and actions being multiplied to the infinity of collective behavior and its impact upon the species.

Sir D'Arcy W. Thompson. *On Growth and Form* (1917). 2 vols.
New York: Cambridge University Press, 1984. (Pb)

Architects trained through the tradition of art history tend
to think of architecture as a series of culturally based developments, buildings and cities shaped by behavioral and psychic
forces, styles evolving from one generation to the other shaped
primarily by the will of human beings. D'Arcy Thompson's *On
Growth and Form,* published in 1917, which laid the foundation for the science of morphology, has reshaped my understanding of the process and meaning of design. Introduced to
the book by Louis Kahn and Ann Tyng at age twenty-three, I
came to appreciate the inseparable connection between design
by nature and design by man. What Thompson had proposed
and demonstrated was that the forms or organisms in nature,
from the simplest to the most complex, evolved in the Dar-
winian sense to satisfy the criteria essential to survival. From

the overused example of the Nautilus shell to the more subtle demonstrations in the shapes of various plants; sea, land and air, fauna and flora, the bond structure of the vulture's wing; the geometry of leaves of plants in the desert and the tundra, Thompson forever seeks and demonstrates the connection of form to purpose.

It becomes possible to distinguish those developments in architecture and urbanism rooted in purpose, in the constraints of the physical environment, of materials and place, and of life-style from those capricious and arbitrary explorations that surely must have occurred in every age and engaged the builders of every period. It is in the nature of the human psyche to explore with the same certainty that molecules and cells mutate and, in the long run, the history of architecture sorts out the explorations worthy of survival and repetition from those destined to become dead ends.

If before D'Arcy Thompson I might have conceived the act of design as shaping in one's own image, after Thompson I was conscious that form must evolve from the deep understanding and response to the physical and psychological structures and constraints that shape our environment in a similar even though more complex manner as in morphology.

Bernard Rudofsky. *Architecture Without Architects* (1964). Garden City, N.Y.: Doubleday, 1969. (Pb)

With Thompson absorbed it was natural to seek in architecture that mode of building which most closely approximates morphology in the linkage between form and purpose. The third book, Bernard Rudofsky's *Architecture Without Architects,* really an exhibition catalog, is more in the tradition of architectural picture books. At a time that in our culture the architect reigned supreme as form-giver—the one to give shape not only to buildings and cities, but to society itself—Rudofsky cried out that the emperor was naked. Illustrating buildings and villages designed by nonarchitects, untrained human beings building "in the vernacular," he demonstrated a world of immense beauty and complexity and, like D'Arcy Thompson, made the connection showing how a particular form evolved in response to the inventive use of available technologies and materials, of site and climate, where decoration emerged from myth and ritual, where efficiency, in the morphological sense, begets a sense of order, fitness and, perhaps most relevantly, spiritual uplift.

Rudofsky establishes criteria that transcend the standard fare of art-history evaluations, suggesting the greater and more fundamental measure from which no architect should attempt to escape. In an art world that proclaims that all is possible, D'Arcy Thompson and Rudofsky suggest that the search is not for that which is possible, an infinity of choices, but for that which is appropriate, a diminishing set of choices in search of truth.

Michael J. Sandel

Michael J. Sandel is an associate professor of government at Harvard, where he teaches political philosophy. He is the author of Liberalism and the Limits of Justice. *His course "Justice" consistently fills Sanders Theater, and he is regarded by undergraduates as one of Harvard's best lecturers.*

These seem to be among the books that can help us reflect on the moral and political conditions of liberal democracy in contemporary America.

Hannah Arendt. *The Human Condition* (1958). Chicago: University of Chicago Press, 1970. (Pb)

Arendt offers the most compelling modern case for the ancient claim that politics is essential to the good life, not merely instrumental to the pursuit of private interests and ends.

Sir Isaiah Berlin. *Four Essays on Liberty* (1969). New York: Oxford University Press, 1979. (Pb)

Berlin grounds liberalism in the idea that the human good is ultimately plural, that there is no single, overarching value that orders all the rest. To acknowledge the tragic possibility that inheres in moral and political life is to respect above all people's freedom to pursue their own ends, to negotiate their own moral circumstance.

G. W. F. Hegel. *Philosophy of Right (Grundlinien der Philosophie des Rechts,* 1821). T. M. Knox, trans. Oxford: Oxford University Press, 1965.

Hegel contrasts the idea of a civil society, where people cooperate to further their interests, with the idea of a political community as an ethical life that enlarges the self-knowledge of the participants.

Fred Hirsch. *Social Limits to Growth.* Cambridge: Harvard
   University Press, 1976. (Pb)

Hirsch recasts economics as political economy, and political economy as moral economy. Cost-benefit analysis to the
contrary, he shows that the market is not a neutral way of
evaluating goods. Not all values can be translated without loss
into commodity values, nor does all economic growth produce
greater welfare.

Michael J. Oakeshott. *Rationalism in Politics and Other Essays*
   (1962). New York and London: Methuen, 1981. (Pb)

Oakeshott's romantic conservatism contrasts powerfully
(and eloquently) with more familiar libertarian versions.
Against a philosophy of abstract principles and natural rights,
he conceives politics "as the pursuit of intimations."

John Rawls. *A Theory of Justice* (1971). Oxford: Oxford University Press, 1972.

Rawls provides the most important philosophical defense
of liberalism in our time. Individual rights cannot be overridden
by utilitarian considerations, he argues, and the principles of
justice that specify our rights do not presuppose any particular
conception of the good life.

Thomas C. Schelling

Thomas Schelling is the Lucius N. Littauer Professor of Political Economy at Harvard's John F. Kennedy School of Government and a professor in the Department of Economics. He is the author of numerous works including The Strategy of Conflict *(1961),* Arms and Influence *(1966),* Micromotives and Macrobehavior *(1978), and* Choice and Consequence *(1984). In addition to teaching at Harvard since 1958, he is director of Harvard's Institute for the Study of Smoking Behavior and Policy, which fulfills his research interest in addictive and habitual behaviors and other issues in self-management. His other research interests include national security and climate changes.*

These books give readers a taste of the best in natural science, social science, classical and modern history and literary style.

Charles Darwin. *The Origin of Species* (1859). New York: Penguin, 1982. (Pb)

I have had a fascination with evolutionary biology, provoked by such beautiful books as George Gaylord Simpson's *This View of Life,* but had never picked up a copy of Darwin's original work until ten years ago. I have rarely had such pleasure and excitement in reading a sustained piece of scientific reasoning and presentation of evidence. It is technically accessible to any intelligent reader. It is a genuinely participatory experience.

Thucydides. *History of the Peloponnesian War* (ca. 431–404 B.C.). Richard Livingstone, ed. New York: Oxford University Press, 1960.

I knew that classical Greece produced people at least as smart as people anywhere today, but until I read this I had no idea how modern they were in their thinking. Nothing written in this century can touch Thucydides (or the people he quotes) for subtlety of political and diplomatic discourse and strategy. I like Rex Warner's translation in the Penguin edition, but some readers may need large print. If you like it go on to Herodotus and Xenophon.

Erving Goffman. *Interaction Ritual: Essays in Face-to-Face Behavior* (1967). New York: Pantheon, 1982. (Pb)

I was hooked on Goffman from the time I read "On Face Work," the first essay in this collection. If you like this try "Stigma," "Forms of Talk," and "Asylums." He looks at the same people we look at doing the same things we see them doing, and he sees things we can't see without his help. He once pointed out to me that a woman can be naked with her husband without embarrassment, naked with her sister without embarrassment, but not naked without embarrassment in the presence of both.

Laurence Sterne. *Tristram Shandy* (1759–67). New York: Oxford University Press, 1983. (Pb)

I bought a copy in 1943 because it fit in my pocket and I was vaguely aware that it was a classic. I read it for an hour on a streetcar and was captivated by the story, the style and the purported author. It is an endlessly digressive autobiography that begins with his conception and barely gets up to his birth. Sterne writes a lovely, leisurely sentence that can wind on for three hundred words and you never lose your way or have to look back.

John Keegan. *The Face of Battle* (1976). New York: Penguin, 1983. (Pb)

I have a book on baseball that says fear is the fundamental factor in hitting, and hitting with the bat is the fundamental act of baseball. For John Keegan, a distinguished military historian, fear is the fundamental factor in exposing oneself to enemy weapons, and exposing oneself is the fundamental act of combat, as he vividly describes, at the level of the individual soldier, the battles of Agincourt, Waterloo and the Somme. A superbly thoughtful history of military combat.

Bruce Scott

Bruce Scott first joined the Harvard Business School as an M.B.A. student in 1954. Since then he has become widely respected for his international research and course development in national economic strategies. In 1973 he was appointed the first Paul Whiton Cherington Professor of Business Administration.

These readings should raise a question of the adequacy of the role and direction of current economic theory as it affects business policy and public policy in the United States and Europe.

Alfred D. Chandler, Jr. *Strategy and Structure.* Cambridge, Mass.: M.I.T. Press, 1962. (Pb)

———. *The Visible Hand.* Cambridge: Harvard University Press, 1977. (Pb)

Two prize-winning books showing how senior managers of large corporations broke away from the static notions of microeconomics to fashion strategies based in part on internalizing market forces rather than remaining dependent upon them.

Chalmers A. Johnson. *MITI and the Japanese Miracle: The Growth of Industrial Policy, 1925–1975.* Stanford, Calif.: Stanford University Press, 1982. (Pb)

Miyohei Shinohara. *Industrial Growth, Trade and Dynamic Patterns in the Japanese Economy.* Tokyo: University of Tokyo Press, 1982.

Ezra F. Vogel. *Japan as Number One: Lessons for America* (1979). New York: Harper & Row, 1985. (Pb)

Three views on how and why Japan has become more competitive than any of the older industrial countries. Shinohara explains Japan's departure from Western economic theory to create a growth-oriented economic strategy. Johnson explains how it was conceived, by whom, and how it has been implemented. Vogel explains why Japan is not and does not wish to become a consumer-oriented welfare state.

Thomas S. Kuhn. *The Structure of Scientific Revolutions* (1962). Chicago: University of Chicago Press, 1970. (Pb)

Pierre Wack. "Scenarios: Uncharted Waters Ahead." *Harvard Business Review* (19 September 1985).

Wack explains the value of scenarios as alternative theories of the case. Kuhn explains revolutionary changes in the sciences as occurring only when one theory replaces another.

Ihor Ševčenko

Ihor Ševčenko is a byzantinist in Harvard's Department of the Classics. His principal interest is Byzantine cultural history. The first entry in his own extensive bibliography —a translation into Polish of an excerpt from Voltaire— was written when Ševčenko was a sixteen-year-old student in Warsaw. His Harvard career as a professor of Byzantine history and literature has been spent in Cambridge, Massachusetts; Dumbarton Oaks, Washington, D.C.; and as a visiting professor at colleges around the world. As an avid dryfly trout fisherman those same travels permit his pursuit of the Arctic grayling.

The books by Souvarine and de Man will be forgotten. The others will continue yielding insights into the minds and feelings of men and into the behavior of groups with a depth and immediacy that cannot be gotten from treatises on psychology or sociology. St. Mark's Gospel will remain a concise message that helps explain the appeal of the most successful mass movement of our civilization to date.

Thucydides. *History of the Peloponnesian War* (ca. 431–404 B.C.). Richard Livingstone, ed. New York: Oxford University Press, 1960. (Pb)

The most difficult Greek prose author I had previously encountered. Absorbing the whole of Thucydides was painful, but the task, once accomplished, determined my choice of Greek texts as subject of study for the rest of my life. Reading Thucydides was a make-or-break enterprise. I never encountered a more difficult, more concise and more deeply thinking Greek author in my subsequent career as a classicist or a byzantinist. The Melian Dialogue and the passages devoted to Alcibiades' career stuck with me for the duration.

The collected works of Fyodor Dostoevsky (1844–1880) (no standard collection in English).

Reading Dostoevsky is like going through an imaginary illness of late adolescence and early adulthood that, when overcome, increases the chances of survival for the rest of one's life. The novel that produced the greatest impact was *The Demons.* I looked at it (and most of my friends did the same) as a distorted but magic and prophetic mirror that revealed the doings of those who were to stage the Revolution of November 1917 and of those whom the Revolution was to topple. The quest after the meaning of human existence—a query to which I later chose a negative answer—first became an "accursed question" during the reading of Dostoevsky. Critics say that Dostoevsky's prose is drab. I did not feel it at all in this second of my massive immersions in Russian literary prose (the first was Gogol) and I was overawed by it.

Rainer Maria Rilke. *Selected Poetry of Rainer Maria Rilke* (1897–1923). Stephen Mitchell, ed. New York: Random House, 1982.

Rilke has been my companion throughout my life. My preferred collection of poems include: *Neue Gedichte* (1907) and *Neue Gedichte Anderer Teil* (1908). They represnt my life's most intimate contact with poetry. As with all intimate contacts, it is difficult to put in words. Rilke led to my discovery of German as a language in which modern poetry can be written, admiration for subdued elegance of form and economy of linguistic means, and for the languid subtlety of the message. I translated some of Rilke's poems into Polish and Ukranian. All of it was lost in 1945.

Boris Souvarine. *Stalin: A Critical Survey of Bolshevism* (1935). New York: Arno, 1972.

How could the Revolution have been betrayed and perverted? How could its "pure" message be discerned and preserved? These, along with the problem of right and might, were the preoccupying questions of my late adolescence. Souvarine's book gave a scholarly and, on the surface, dispassionate answer to those emotional questions, that both made sense of the past and satisfied the expectations for the future (expectations not borne out by events, of course). At the time, I did not know the extent of Souvarine's engagement in the Trotskyite movement. Still a book to read.

James Joyce. *Ulysses* (1918–20). New York: Random House, 1976. (Pb)

This was the second major English prose classic I worked through in the original, *Vanity Fair* having been the first. *Ulysses*'s role in my biography as a reader was analogous to the one Thucydides had played some ten years earlier: it was a make-or-break affair. I had no conception of Dublin or its pubs, but was by my own makeup attuned to the stream of consciousness and went along with Joyce on his heroes' rounds. Result: a lasting admiration for the flexibility of English and for the author's own virtuoso play on that instrument (and on other languages as well: remember the list of ambassadors!). Mrs. Bloom's inner monologue, a model of empathy, will remain the kind of text I wish I were able to write.

Gospel According to St. Mark. The Bible.

I chose the shortest among the Gospels, for I wanted to read one of them in Greek. Two insights resulted from the reading: realizing the power and universal appeal of the Christian message at a time when its ethical elements were questioned by word and deed all around me; understanding that there was more to antiquity, in terms of "lasting" values, than high classics. This was the starting point for my ultimately opting for the science of antiquity and its aftermath rather than pure classical philology.

Hendrik de Man. *The Psychology of Socialism (Die sozialistische Idee*, 1933). Eden Paul and Cedar Paul, trans. New York: Arno, 1974.

At a time that seemingly "eternal" values were contradicted by reality, relativized, or made into constructs that expressed the social interest of those who propounded them, de

Man offered reasoned and scholarly solutions to a young man's doubts: stress on the writings of young Marx; the concept of intellectuals as a "free-floating" stratum, not shackled in their perceptions by their social backgrounds; the relative autonomy of ideas; the relativization of Marxism; the derelativization of the notions of Truth, Beauty and Justice; viewing conscience as an instinct rather than as interiorized ideology.

Sigmund Freud. *Civilization and Its Discontents* (1929). Joan Riviere, trans. London: Hogarth, 1930.

————. *The Future of an Illusion* (1926). James Strachey, ed. and trans. New York: W.W. Norton, 1961.

————. *Psychopathology of Everyday Life* (1901). A.A. Brill, ed. and trans. New York: Macmillan, n.d.

————. *Totem and Taboo* (1913). James Strachey, ed. and trans. New York: W.W. Norton, 1962.

Otto Immisch. *Wie studiert man klassische Philologie?* (1909). 2d ed. Stuttgart: W. Violet, 1920.

Plato. *The Republic* (370–360 B.C.). James Adam, ed. 2 vols. New York: Cambridge University Press, 1963.

If it were possible to enlarge to ten, I would add the following three names: (1) Sigmund Freud, whose writings influenced me more than several of the books I discussed in some detail above. I just did not think of him when I was taking down the names of "influential" books as they were spontaneously coming to mind; I wonder why. I record this *Fehlleistung* here as a tribute to his delightful *Psychopathology of Everyday Life* (1901). Other books by him that determined my intellectual climate for years were *Totem and Taboo* (1913) (even if based on assumptions no longer shared by anthropologists); *The Future of an Illusion* (1927); and *Civilization and Its Discontents* (1929). (2) Plato, *Republic,* Book 1 for its insights into the mechanisms of naked power. (3) Otto Immisch, *Wie studiert man klassische Philologie?,* merely for autobiographical reasons: this sensible small book confirmed me in the resolve to study the classics and helped map out the beginnings of my study program.

Judith Shklar

Judith Shklar was born in Riga, Latvia. She describes herself as having attended, off and on, various useless schools, but was educated at McGill and Harvard Universities. She became interested in political theory as an undergraduate and has taught it at Harvard since 1954. She is the John Cowles Professor of Government. In 1984, she was a recipient of the MacArthur Award. Among her books are Men and Citizens: A Study of Rousseau's Social Theory *and her most recent work,* Ordinary Vices.

These books do not prepare anyone for anything in particular. They can only enhance our intellectual imagination and understanding.

Plato. *The Republic* (370–360 B.C.). James Adam, ed. 2 vols. New York: Cambridge University Press, 1963.

The first book I read in my late adolescence which I had to recognize as both perfect and wholly alien. It set me off to asking the question that has preoccupied me as a political theorist since then: How are we to think about our personal lives and experiences in a world order that is entirely remote from us, but nevertheless impinges upon us constantly and often incomprehensibly? All the other books I list play upon this theme.

St. Augustine. *The City of God* (A.D. 413–426). David Knowles, ed. New York: Penguin, 1984. (Pb)

Both as an account of what Christian religiosity implies and also as the most extreme vision of a moral and material order in which we must fail especially when we think that we are behaving well.

Michel de Montaigne. *Selections from the Essays* (1595). Donald M. Frame, ed. and trans. Arlington Heights, Ill.: Harlan Davidson, 1973. (Pb)

The question of how a skeptic can live his life as a social and political agent is often asked, and here it is examined in "attempts," or thought experiments. Nothing is asserted and everything can be doubted without despair or destructiveness. For me it is the model of how to think.

Leo Tolstoy. *War and Peace* (1865–69). Louise Maude and Aylmer Maude, trans. George Gibian, ed. New York: W.W. Norton, 1966.

I read it when I was very young and have reread it many times. It is both a complete world in which one lives while one reads on and the most successful of all attempts to integrate public history and private lives.

Thomas Mann. *The Magic Mountain* (1924). H.T. Lowe-Porter, trans. New York: Random House, 1969. (Pb)

The political novel achieves the same effect as *War and Peace,* but in a different way. It allows us to rush helplessly into the First World War, not knowing why but how the European world committed collective suicide.

In some indefinable way the mass of historical novels I read as a child turned me into a historian. Everything from Alexandre Dumas, Sir Walter Scott and Dickens's *Tale of Two Cities* to an endless number of far less distinguished romances, not least those of Rafael Sabatini, inspired an enduring passion for history. The mixture of this inbred taste for the past and the need to explain the events of my childhood, as a refugee in and out of the Europe of the Second World War, have structured my work as a political theorist from the first.

B. F. Skinner

B. F. Skinner is the Edgar Pierce Professor of Psychology Emeritus at Harvard University. A pioneer in the field of operant behavior, Dr. Skinner began his work primarily with rats and pigeons, extending his techniques to the human organisms in the study of psychotic behavior, the analysis of verbal behavior, the design of instructional devices, the care of infants and the analysis of cultures. The author of more than eighteen books, he published volume three of his autobiography, Upon Further Reflection, *in the summer of 1986.*

Sir Edwin Durning-Lawrence. *Bacon is Shake-speare.* London and New York: Gay & Hancock, 1910.

Asa Gray. *How Plants Grow: A Simple Introduction to Structural Botany.* 3d ed. New York: Ivison and Phinney; Chicago: Gregg, 1859.

Ivan P. Pavlov. *Conditioned Reflexes: An Investigation of the Physiological Activity of the Cerebral Cortex.* G. V. Anrep, ed. and trans. London: Oxford University Press, 1927.

Bertrand Russell. *The Problems of Philosophy* (1911). New York: Oxford University Press, 1959. (Pb)

John B. Watson. *Behaviorism* (1925). New York: W. W. Norton, 1970. (Pb)

——. *Psychology, from the Standpoint of a Behaviorist* (1919). 3d ed. Philadelphia and London: J. B. Lippincott, 1929.

The books that have been most important in leading me to my present position as a behaviorist are not books that I would recommend to anyone seeking to understand that position. They were important, not so much because of their content, but because of their bearing on my life at the time I read them. A mere accident sent me to Sir Edwin Durning-Lawrence's *Bacon is Shake-speare,* and that book sent me in turn to all I could find of, and about, Francis Bacon. I have acknowledged the role of three great Baconian principles in my life, but I would not send anyone to Durning-Lawrence to discover them.

Gray's *How Plants Grow,* my high-school botany text, taught me, with the example of the radish, how living things pass on to the future the contributions they have received from the past. Later I found the same theme in Hervieu's "La Course du Flambeau," but I would not send anyone there for further instruction. I was greatly influenced by the first third of Bertrand Russell's *Problems of Philosophy.* According to his biographer it was "written at speed for the American market," and it certainly is not regarded as one of Russell's great books. Pavlov's *Conditioned Reflexes* taught me the importance of controlling laboratory conditions, but I soon departed from the Pavlovian paradigm. John B. Watson was important, of course, but I read only his *Behaviorism,* a book written for the general public. I am not sure I ever read his *Psychology, from the Standpoint of a Behaviorist.*

This is all perfectly reasonable, since, after all, if anything I have done is "creative," should we expect to find it in anything I have read?

Anne Whiston Spirn

Anne Whiston Spirn is associate professor of landscape architecture at Harvard's Graduate School of Design. Her research and publications grow out of her work on theories of nature and city design, best illustrated in her recent award-winning book The Granite Garden: Urban Nature and Human Design. *She was a fellow of the Bunting Institute at Radcliffe in 1978 and a Noyes fellow in 1985. She holds a B.A. from Radcliffe College and a M.L.A. from the University of Pennsylvania.*

It was only after writing these notes that I realized that all five of the books are in one way or another a product of Harvard. Eliot was an undergraduate at Harvard College, McHarg and Alexander studied at the Harvard Graduate School of Design, and John Dewey delivered *Art as Experience* as a Harvard lecture series founded in memory of William James.

Thomas Stearns Eliot. *Four Quartets* (1935–42). New York: Harcourt, Brace, 1968. (Pb)

I bought my first copy of the *Four Quartets* in a bookstore in Copenhagen. I was sixteen, living for a year on a farm and going to school in Denmark. The *Four Quartets* was one of a handful of books in English that I read and reread. At first these books were a linguistic refuge, the still center in a storm of unfamiliar words. Later, when Danish became a comfortable everyday language, the words of the poems acquired a newness, as if heard for the first time. Eliot's use of the garden as metaphor, his juxtaposition of nature's time and human time, struck a deep resonance. I was a city girl (suburban, really) exposed for the first time to the violent vicissitudes of nature and a life founded on nature's rhythms as well as man's. Over the past twenty years, I have returned to the *Four Quartets* again and again. They drive me to find a way to design landscapes that embody time past, time present, and time future, that highlight the poignant contrast between nature's time and human time.

John Dewey. *Art as Experience.* New York: Minton, Balch, 1934.

I first read *Art as Experience* as a Radcliffe undergraduate struggling to strike a balance between art and scholarship. I had meant to major in painting, only to find upon arrival that in Harvard's fine-arts department, one studied the history of art, not its making. The idea that aesthetic experience was not the special property of an educated elite, but was knowable, an important and universal human phenomenon engaging the senses and capable of being experienced on many different levels, was attractive. By sketching an aesthetic theory that related to everyday experience as well as to extraordinary moments, Dewey constructed a bridge for me between the making of art and its history, between high art and craft. This has since defined my own approach to the aesthetics of design, one that is grounded in both sensual experience and intellectual meaning.

Ian L. McHarg. *Design with Nature* (1969). New York: Natural History Press, 1971. (Pb)

Design with Nature introduced me to my profession. Through this book, I learned that landscape architecture consisted of more than the design of gardens, that it extended to the park, the parkway, the region. Through this profession I hoped to create "useful" art and thereby to fuse the poetic imagery of Eliot and the pragmatic aesthetic of Dewey. I subsequently studied landscape architecture with McHarg at the University of Pennsylvania and later worked for five years in his professional office on a wide variety of planning and design projects. These projects ranged in scope from a study of an entire metropolitan region to portions of cities, from plans for new communities to park designs. In the office, I gained a different appreciation for the book: for its power to shape values and to create the demand for a particular type of professional practice. *Design With Nature* demonstrated for me the potential of a book to change the way the environment is perceived and built. But McHarg neglected the city, and that was the seed for my own book.

Christopher Alexander. *Notes on the Synthesis of Form.* Cambridge: Harvard University Press, 1964. (Pb)

———— et al. *A Pattern Language which Generates Multi-Service Centers.* Berkeley, Calif.: Center for Environmental Structure, 1968.

These two books stand for me as one. As a graduate student in landscape architecture, the first provided a theoretical frame and the second the application that made the theory comprehensible and meaningful. Alexander's work opened up new worlds for me. As a visually oriented person trained in a highly verbal educational tradition, I found that the diagrams in *Multi-Service Centers* packed a jolt in the way they fused abstract ideas, empirical data, and physical form. A door opened; this was a language that seemed more native to me than words. Alexander also dispelled the mystique of design; he highlighted a framework within which the real mystery—the flash of insight that illuminates a meaningful pattern—was facilitated.

Zeph Stewart

Zeph Stewart's career at Harvard began in the 1940s as a graduate student and later as a junior fellow in the Society of Fellows. He recently assumed a new position as director of Harvard's Center for Hellenic Studies in Washington, D.C. He continues as the Andrew W. Mellon Professor of the Humanities in the Classics Department. Throughout his professional life, he has written on the literature, philosophy and religion of the Greek and Roman world. His current pursuit focuses on religion of the Hellenistic period.

These works give one some understanding of the human condition, of man's place in the world and of the marvel of human creativity.

Homer. *The Iliad* (ca. 800 B.C.). Robert Fitzgerald, trans. New York: Doubleday, 1975. (Pb).

My choice of career was partly influenced by a comparatively early reading of Homer's *Iliad* (probably in an abridged form). The cast of distinct and memorable characters, the essentially simple but deftly contrived plot, the sombre atmosphere of the opening and closing scenes, the wonderful balance of crowds in action and intimate detail, all picture a whole civilization and yet endure both as types and symbols and as a very human story. I felt in touch with the beginnings and grandeur of both the literature and the history of my own world.

The Bible. Books of Genesis and Exodus.

Perhaps I felt some of the same appeal in these simply and beautifully crafted ideas and anecdotes from the earliest parts of the Bible as I found in Homer, but here the mystery of things unseen and of man's dependence on his faith (whatever it is) come through much more clearly. I was thrilled by the sense of motion and purpose in history, whereas change and motion in the *Iliad* are more personal and psychological.

Thomas Mann. *The Magic Mountain* (1924). H. T. Lowe-Porter, trans. New York: Random House, 1969. (Pb)

Having been brought up on traditional English and American nineteenth-century novels, I was gripped by the inner world and its outward reflections that seemed so modern and powerful in Mann's writing, even when it was most wordy. Such a tour de force as the entrapping snowstorm was frightening and full of meaning, giving character to the physical world and to exterior experience like that found in the post-Impressionists. It led me not only into more reading of Mann but also into an appreciation of much other contemporary literature and art.

Cleanth Brooks. *Modern Poetry and the Tradition.* Chapel Hill, N.C.: University of North Carolina Press, 1970. (Pb)

This critical survey, now a little passé, opened a door for me just at the moment that I was looking for ways to appreciate the new poets (Yeats and Eliot in particular). I found in the New Criticism some of the same methods applied to modern poetry that were familiar in classical scholarship, and Brooks's analyses and connection-making brought me deeper appreciation, but also showed me the limitations of his method in his treatment of Frost.

William Shakespeare. *King Lear* (1605). New York: Penguin, 1984. (Pb)

Many plays and films, from Aeschylus to the present, have moved me deeply, but perhaps none more than *King Lear* in the three superb performances that I have seen. The power of speech to evoke man's most subtle and contradictory insights, the interplay of good and evil in the world, the terror of the irrational and the unknown and the healing power of hope and love are all woven into a single dream.

In the course of my professional work I have of course occasionally read books that have had an enormous impact at the time on my thinking and understanding, but which could often not be recommended to a general audience, particularly an English-reading one. I think of Erwin Rohde's *Der griechische Roman,* or E. R. Dodds's *The Greeks and the Irrational* (fine for a general audience), or of A. J. Festugière's *La révélation d'Hermès Trismégiste.* To someone who is seeking to understand the thinking and literature of another people in another time such books can light up a whole cultural landscape.

John R. Stilgoe

Author of Common Landscape of America, 1580 to 1845, Metropolitan Corridor: Railroads and the American Scene *and a forthcoming book on American suburbs, John R. Stilgoe teaches the analysis of landscapes at Harvard's Graduate School of Design. He farms as an avocation.*

These five books introduce five scales of space—from the Mediterranean basin to an obscure New England farm—and offer a feast of perceptual biases and techniques; whatever the challenges of the next century, the delight that so often accompanies disciplined scrutiny of the physical environment will continue to hearten alert travelers and readers, and perhaps make the challenges less daunting.

Fernand Braudel. *The Mediterranean and the Mediterranean World in the Age of Philip II* (1949). Siân Reynolds, trans. New York: Harper & Row, 1976. (Pb)

One of the few genuinely masterful works of modern geographical–historical writing, Braudel's fourteen-hundred-page *Mediterranean* defines a region ecologically (from the southern limits of the date palm to the northern limits of the olive tree) and culturally (from the Arab east and south to the Catholic north and west), demonstrating in intricate detail the complex and fragile interaction of physical environment and human effort in one moment of time past. No recent work better displays the sumptuous richness of meanings implicit in the word *region.*

Henry James. *The American Scene* (1907). Leon Edel, ed. Indianapolis: Indiana University Press, 1968. (Pb)

Written after a self-imposed absence of some two decades, *The American Scene* is James's nonfiction account of stupendous change in the landscape and life of the eastern United States, change best designated as "modernization" perhaps, but

certainly change that no participant—and no foreign visitor—
perceived so crisply. James left an essentially agricultural nation
and returned to one urban, industrialized, and ensnared in
mechanized haste; high-speed trains, rural trolley cars and mo-
torcars had changed forever the traveler's perception of landscape, foreshortening distances, twisting angles of vision and
blurring detail, making the whole visual environment a sort of
scene.

Timothy Dwight. *Travels in New England and New-York*
(1821–22). 4 vols. Cambridge: Harvard University Press,
1969.

At the close of the eighteenth century, the president of
Yale College began riding horseback (and later by chaise)
through the northeastern part of the new Republic. His *Travels*
details not only thousands of landscape constituents—everything from the texture of soil to the shape of bridges to the color
of meetinghouses—along his winding routes, but interprets the
landscape emerging from wilderness as the emblem of dis-
tinctly American virtues—order, simplicity, individualism, self-
reliance. His volumes offer a glimpse of slow, self-paced, me-
thodical wandering and a wealth of insight into the cultural
baggage any observer of landscape and customs brings to a
region, and particularly to his own.

Henry David Thoreau. *Cape Cod* (1865). New York: Thomas Y.
Crowell, 1972. (Pb)

As Thoreau walked the edge of the land, he found real
wilderness, a spray-soaked zone of eroding sand, shipwreck,
packs of wild dogs, sharks and people inured to assaults by wind,
tide and surf, a zone that disconcerted the lover of Concord
woodlots and fields. *Cape Cod* grapples with the concept of the
margin, the amorphous zone neither wholly landscape nor
wholly sea. There Thoreau encountered the edge of fear, the
awesome recognition that tiny Cape Cod thrusts into an alien
element, an element so powerful that it shapes not only Cape

Cod landscape, but Cape Cod life. *Cape Cod* unmasks the Thoreau disguised in *Walden,* reveals the incredible fragility of a small land continuously besieged, and rams home the terrible intimacy of the walker exploring alien space.

Donald Hall. *String Too Short to Be Saved* (1961). Boston: David R. Godine, 1979. (Pb)

A New Hampshire hill farm in the Depression and the early years of World War II forms the setting for autobiographical memory. But more than memory suffuses this brilliant book. Hall inquires deeply into the love of a farmer for his farm and its neighborhood, the love for individual rocks and blueberry plantings, for old cellar holes and hay fields, for neighbors as individuals; and he scrutinizes the survival of nineteenth-century (and earlier) agricultural techniques and attitudes into the twentieth century. On the slopes of Ragged Mountain endure an earlier landscape and an earlier way of living almost wholly isolated from the world-shaking events far off in cities, in Europe, in the Pacific. Stewardship, simplicity, forbearance, compassion—such are the virtues manifested in the fields and buildings city folk scorn as scrubby, rundown, or old-fashioned as their automobiles race past.

Samuel Thorne

Fifty-five years ago, Sam Thorne graduated from the Harvard Law School, where he now serves as the Charles Stebbins Fairchild Professor of Legal History Emeritus. He has lectured "to generations" on medieval legal history. He wonders if today's parents read to their children as his parents read Sir Walter Scott to him.

The books listed had a significant influence on *me*, sixty years ago, opening up a new field. They are superseded and out of date today, their place being taken by more recent studies.

H. A. L. Fisher. *Frederic William Maitland, Downing Professor of the Laws of England: A Biographical Sketch.* Cambridge: Cambridge University Press, 1910.

A biography of the great legal historian, which awakened and then nurtured my interest in the field on which my life has been spent.

Edward Pollock and **Frederic W. Maitland.** *The History of English Law Before the Time of Edward I* (1895). 2 vols. New York: Cambridge University Press, 1968. (Pb)

A magnificent survey of the field, which may be understood by any literate layman, written in a style that is sure to enthuse the reader.

Oliver Wendell Holmes, Jr. *The Common Law* (1881). Boston: Little, Brown, 1964. (Pb)

A valuable account of some of the great formative ideas of English law. It was one of the eye-opening books on law; one that I read a number of times with the greatest interest.

C. H. McIlwain. *The High Court of Parliament and Its Supremacy* (1910). J. P. Mayer, ed. Salem, N.H.: Ayer, 1979.

A work which threw new light on the history of Parliament and set its history in a new frame. It provided a fresh point of departure and set the stage for much new and exciting work.

Heinrich Brunner. *Die Entstehung der Schwurgerichte* (1871). Aalan (Germany): Scientia Verlag, 1967.

An epoch-making treatise. For many years the best authority on the history of the jury which set the much-disputed question in a new light.

C. Peter Timmer

C. Peter Timmer is the John D. Black Professor of Agriculture and Business at the Harvard Business School and has an appointment in the Department of Economics. In addition, he is a faculty fellow at the Harvard Institute for International Development. He grew up on a farm near Tipp City, Ohio, which his family still operates. An interest in food systems, he writes, combines his agricultural background with his training as an economist; the major applications are in food policy for developing countries. Food Policy Analysis *is his best-known book.*

All of these books deal directly or indirectly with the dynamics of complex systems and the message that intuitive understanding will provide a richer guide to the future than formal economic models.

Alexander Gerschenkron. *Economic Backwardness in Historical Perspective.* Cambridge: Harvard University Press, 1962.

Important for its understanding of the way governments respond to the challenge of underdevelopment as presented by more developed neighbors and political rivals. Shows clearly that "market forces" were not the driving mechanism in the development of the latecomers to industrial modernization and provides a powerful sense of the *dynamics* of economic change which cannot be captured in simple economic-growth models.

Albert O. Hirschman. *Development Projects Observed.* Washington, D.C.: Brookings Institution, 1967. (Pb)

Develops the principle of the "hiding hand," which argues that the difficulties of actually implementing a complex project are "hidden" from the designers, who then overlook them. But in compensation, the creativity of project managers is often greater than designers anticipated, so many projects are successful because the two effects offset each other. The book provides, above all, a sobering picture of the limits of planning and the power of learning by doing.

George L. Clarke. *Elements of Ecology* (1954). New York: Wiley, 1965.

A comprehensive introduction to the principles of ecology, which provide an essential framework of linkages among biological systems. Ecology has many parallels with economics, especially the need to explain the functioning of entire systems of relationships as well as of individual behavior. Much of my own effort to understand the links between the micro- and macro-levels of economic systems stems from my early training in ecology.

Clifford Geertz. *Agricultural Involution: The Processes of Ecological Change in Indonesia.* Berkeley: University of California Press, 1963. (Pb)

This is perhaps the most influential attempt to incorporate ecological factors into an explanation of social change (in rice cultivation on Java) by one of the world's foremost anthropologists. Although much of Geertz's historical interpretation has been challenged by recent scholars, the paradigm of interacting social and ecological forces remains.

John K. Fairbank. *Chinabound: A Fifty-Year Memoir.* New York: Harper & Row, 1983. (Pb)

This is a favorite book for highly personal reasons, as it traces the career of a Midwesterner at Harvard. Fairbank's efforts to create a new academic field in the form of East Asian Studies has parallels to my own efforts to create a field in food-policy analysis. The difficulties in crossing academic disciplines and departments, and his eventual success, provide both a model and a mystery quality to the book.

Yujiro Hayami and **Vernon W. Ruttan.** *Agricultural Development: An International Perspective* (1971). Baltimore: Johns Hopkins University Press, 1985. (Pb)

Without a doubt the most influential and comprehensive analysis of agricultural development. The model of "induced innovation" removes technological change from the "manna from heaven" category and places it firmly in the hands of societies and market forces. Because technological change is the primary force driving economic development, an understanding of its origins and impact is crucial indeed to our efforts to speed the process in the poorer countries.

Helen Vendler

Helen Vendler is a professor of English at Harvard as well as poetry critic of The New Yorker. *She is the author of books on Yeats, Stevens, Herbert and Keats as well as essays on modern American poetry, collected in* Part of Nature, Part of Us. *She is the editor of* The Harvard Book of Contemporary American Poets.

The stuff of poetry, the life of the affections, the speculations of the mind and the contradictions of existence, are as alive in Homer as in us, for readers and writers alike. The patterning of language—present in every culture—seems likely to be with us 'til the end of time.

The poets who have "had a significant influence on thinking and life" for me might not be the right ones for anyone else. In poetry, affinities are strong and personal links of temperament and disposition. I think others should find for themselves, by skimming through anthologies, poets who will mean to them what Yeats, Stevens, Herbert, and Keats have meant to me. For one reader, it will be Whitman, for another, Marvell, for another, Dickinson. As Dickinson said, "The soul selects her own Society—Then—shuts the Door."

Sidney Verba

Sid Verba is the Carl H. Pforzheimer University Professor and director of the Harvard University Library. He is also on the board of the Harvard University Press but, as a serious political scientist, reserves time to teach government at Harvard.

Mark Twain. *The Adventures of Huckleberry Finn* (1884). New York: Harper & Row, 1984. (Pb)

It taught me about being an American—about growing up, about whites and blacks, about escape, about big rivers.

Chaim Grade. *Rabbis and Wives* (1982). Harold Rabinowitz and I. H. Grade, trans. New York: Random House, 1983. (Pb)

It describes the world of the Eastern European *sktetl*—the world of my grandparents. Grade, like Dickens, gives the texture of life.

Alexis de Tocqueville. *Democracy in America* (1835–40). G. Laurence, trans. New York: Random House, 1981. (Pb)

Probably still the greatest book about American society and politics.

William Shakespeare. *Henry IV, Parts 1 and 2* (1596–97). Arthur Quiller-Couch et al., eds. New York: Cambridge University Press, 1965. (Pb)

———. *Richard II* (1595). New York: Penguin, 1981. (Pb)

All the Histories—especially these two—are great treatises on politics, maturity and responsibility.

V. O. Key, Jr. and **Alexander Heard.** *Southern Politics in State* *and Nation* (1949). Knoxville: University of Tennessee Press, 1984. (Pb)

The first book that taught me to think like a social scientist. Still a classic account of a past political world.

Avis C. Vidal

Avis Vidal is an associate professor of city and regional planning at Harvard's John F. Kennedy School of Government and specializes in urban economic development, housing and urban policy. Her current research focuses on the effectiveness of public–private partnerships formed to promote urban development by supporting the activities of community-based organizations.

J. D. Salinger. *Franny and Zooey: Two Novellas* (1961). New York: Bantam, 1969. (Pb)

Buddy's letter to Zooey is the best and most enduring reminder I have had of the importance of discovering the things that really matter to you, and then doing them with *zest* because that's the way they *deserve* to be done.

Chaim Potok. *My Name Is Asher Lev* (1972). New York: Fawcett, 1978. (Pb)

A powerful exploration of the clarity of purpose that a natural gift or calling makes possible, and of the anguish that comes with being forced to choose between two highly valued claims on one's identity.

Anthony Lewis. *Gideon's Trumpet.* New York: Random House, 1964. (Pb)

Bob Woodward and **Scott Armstrong.** *The Brethren* (1979). New York: Avon, 1980. (Pb)

Two very different accounts of the wonder and power of the law and the people who make it work—when it works.

Charlotte Brontë. *Jane Eyre* (1847). New York: Putnam, 1982.

My former husband and I read this book aloud. When we finished I asked him whether he liked it. "It's good . . . okay

. . . but it gets a little tiresome because it's all from *her* point of view."

Chaim Potok. *The Book of Lights.* New York: Fawcett, 1981. (Pb)

A book that illustrates the potential power of religious and cultural tradition in helping one come to terms with the inescapable presence of death and evil.

Willa Cather. *My Ántonia* (1918). Boston: Houghton Mifflin, 1926. (Pb)

The only thing I ever read that helped me understand why people like the Midwest.

Ezra F. Vogel

Ezra Vogel is a professor of sociology at Harvard and director of the U.S.-Japan Program at Harvard's Center for International Affairs. He is well known in the United States and East Asia for his research and teaching on contemporary Chinese society, Japanese society and economy, and industrial East Asia. He is the author of Japan as Number One *and, most recently,* Comeback.

Talcott Parsons. *The Social System* (1951). Glencoe, Ill.: Free Press, 1964. (Pb)

Talcott Parsons did not always find the simplest, most concise way to express his views, but he was constantly thinking about the general characteristics of society, and his book *The Social System* was a powerful effort to think systematically about the linkages between different parts of society. I have found his framework an extraordinarily stimulating general perspective from which to think about all societies, present and future. It provides a broader framework for considering all the implications of policies than the narrower, more mechanical perspectives provided by economics, decision-making theory, law and the like.

Daniel Bell. *The Coming of Post-Industrial Society* (1973). New York: Basic Books, 1976. (Pb)

Daniel Bell is one of the best-read social scientists anywhere, and his work on the year 2000, and his thoughts about the transition from an industrial society to a post-industrial society, though ten years old, still provide a powerful intellectual framework for thinking about changes in the future.

Richard W. Bolling and **John Bowles.** *America's Competitive Edge.* New York: McGraw-Hill, 1982.

Dick Bolling for decades was one of the most knowledgeable and systematic thinkers in Congress, and his work with

John Bowles represents a deep understanding of how our national politics work and presents a vision of what might be possible within our American system.

George C. Lodge and **Bruce R. Scott**, eds. *U.S. Competitiveness in the World Economy.* Boston: Harvard Business School Press, 1985.

The work that George Lodge and associates have done at the Harvard Business School, more than that of any other group that I know, has charted the nature of the new competitive international economic climate in which we find ourselves. They have been thinking systematically about the changing nature of business and of the world's political and economic climate from a broad-gauged yet well-grounded perspective. These factors will have a far greater impact on the future than myopic Americans realize, and they provide a framework for thinking about these issues.

Organization for Economic Cooperation and Development. *Industrial Policy of Japan.* Paris: O.E.C.D., 1972.

No country has done more to chart a meaningful program for guiding national economies than Japan. When Japan was admitted to O.E.C.D. membership, they were asked to present a report to the O.E.C.D. explaining their industrial policy. This is the result, MITI's classic statement about how it approached questions of economic strategy.

I know of no good book in any language that charts the future developments in Japanese commerce and industry, but I am convinced that just as America in the 1960s and 1970s was the country to observe because it was at the cutting edge, so Japan is the country to observe in thinking about the future because it is replacing us at the cutting edge. I am amazed how provincial most American intellectuals are, how little they understand about the most dynamic part of the world and how blind they are to the impact East Asia will have on the United States. I find that the best way to think about the world's future is to visit Japan and know intimately the grassroots of Japanese research, industry, agriculture, business and government. Speaking the local language and visiting these places frequently, I now find this field work far more useful in thinking about the future than any book in Japanese or English.

Luise Vosgerchian

Luise Vosgerchian is the Walter W. Naumburg Professor of Music at Harvard University. She has been a teacher and active contributor to the musical life at Harvard University for twenty-six years. In 1971 she became a professor of music, and was appointed to her present chair in 1974. She subsequently served for four years as chairman of the Music Department.

As a concert pianist, Luise Vosgerchian has appeared with major orchestras, including the New York Philharmonic and the Boston Symphony Orchestra, as well as with numerous chamber and ensemble groups in both the United States and Europe. Her recordings include nineteenth- and twentieth-century works by such composers as Brahms, Schumann, Debussy, Ives and Bartok.

I hope the spiritual and intellectual comprehension of the creative process so beautifully expressed in these books will fire young students to act against all that is now and will be potentially destructive.

The following books from my reading list have strongly influenced my teaching from several points of view:
1. The importance of discovering.
2. Awakening the responsibility to the artistic conscience.
3. The importance of total commitment to learning.
4. Stimulating the creative use of knowledge.

Alfred North Whitehead. *The Aims of Education and Other Essays* (1929). New York: Free Press, 1967. (Pb)

Wendell Berry. *Recollected Essays, 1965–1980.* San Francisco: North Point Press, 1981. (Pb)

Ben Shahn. *The Shape of Content.* Cambridge: Harvard University Press, 1957. (Pb)

D. W. Prall. *Aesthetic Analysis.* New York: Thomas Y. Crowell, 1936.

Rainer Maria Rilke. *Letters to a Young Poet* (1929). M. D. Herter Norton, trans. New York: W. W. Norton, 1963. (Pb)

D. H. Lawrence. *Studies in Classic American Literature* (1923). New York: Penguin, 1977. (Pb)

Lloyd Weinreb

Lloyd Weinreb has been a professor of law at the Harvard Law School since 1965. His specialties are criminal law and legal philosophy. In addition to his textbook, Leading Constitutional Cases on Criminal Justice, *he has published* Denial of Justice *and* Law of Criminal Investigation.

Homer. *The Iliad* (ca. 800 B.C.). Robert Fitzgerald, trans. New York: Doubleday, 1975. (Pb)

The great epic, full of the grandeur and pain of the human condition.

Sophocles. *The Three Theban Plays: Antigone, Oedipus the King, and Oedipus at Colonus* (ca. 441–401 B.C.). New York: Penguin, 1984. (Pb)

The unlimited tragic vision. The meaning of human freedom is laid bare.

William Shakespeare. *King Lear* (1605). New York: Penguin, 1984. (Pb)

Everyone must choose which of Shakespeare's plays is closest to him. In this end, I return most often to *Lear. The Tempest* is a close second.

Michel de Montaigne. *Selections from the Essays* (1595). Donald M. Frame, ed. and trans. Arlington Heights, Ill.: Harlan Davidson, 1973. (Pb)

Montaigne is a wise, compassionate friend to accompany one throughout life, ready to converse about every important subject, whatever one's mood.

James Joyce. *Dubliners* (1914). New York: Penguin, 1976. (Pb)

Small lives seen closely enough to disclose eternal truths. *Ulysses* is as good for the same reason.

William H. McNeill. *The Rise of the West: A History of the Human Community* (1963). Chicago: University of Chicago Press, 1970. (Pb)

Truly great history.

Fred R. Whipple

Fred R. Whipple arrived at Harvard in 1931 "with his bright and shining Ph.D. and a position of observer at the observatory." In the ensuing fifty-five years, he has brought more than distinction to Harvard's astronomy reputation. He was responsible for the Smithsonian astrophysical observatory's coming to Harvard. The Collected Contribution of Fred R. Whipple *(2 vols.) describes much of his work. The Phillips Professor of Astronomy Emeritus, he retired from teaching in the late 1970s and continues research and prolific writing. He will spend much of 1986 observing Halley's Comet from Paris, Moscow and West Germany.*

When I think of books that have influenced me, I can only think of those books I selected so eagerly from the library in Red Oak, Iowa as a very young man. I was a very independent only child. I read much more than other children—I read much more than my parents, who spent most of their lives working very hard, too tired to read.

Alexandre Dumas. *The Count of Monte Cristo* (1844–45). New York: Bantam, 1981. (Pb)

———. *The Three Musketeers* (1844). New York: Penguin, 1982. (Pb)

Sir H. Rider Haggard. *She* (1887). New York: Airmont, n.d. (Pb)

The first books I picked out of the library were fairy tales in all the different colors. I remember the *Thousand and One Nights*—the expurgated version for a nice Presbyterian boy. After reading everything that amused me, I moved on to Greek legends. I considered them mediocre, second-rate fairy tales. It wasn't until college that I realized that Greek legends had a value far beyond fairy tales.

My next pursuit was science fiction—which continued for

years. I read by author, not title. All of H. G. Wells, Edgar Allan Poe, Sir H. Rider Haggard. Everyone should remember *She*. Science-fiction magazines allowed me to live in another world with visual circumstances so different from mine. Hugh Gernsbach's *Electrical Experimenter* and, later, *Amazing Stories* were particular favorite magazines. So was my friend Isaac Asimov's science fiction.

I perfected my French with amusing French novels. *The Count of Monte Cristo* and *The Three Musketeers* stick in my mind. My parents' only suggestion to this reading were Zane Grey and Edgar A. Guest. I think I must have read them all. I found Mark Twain on my own and know I read all of his wonderful work.

Gordon R. Willey

Gordon Willey is the Bowditch Professor of Mexican and Central American Archaeology and Ethnology Emeritus and, currently, a senior professor in anthropology at Harvard University. He has long-time research interests in Mesoamerican archaeology, especially in Mayan studies, and has conducted fieldwork in Belize, Guatemala and Honduras. He has also had field experience in Nicaragua, Panama and Peru.

In selecting the following books I have tried to strike a balance between the impact they made upon me at first reading and the impressions they have left with me ever since. It is a very personalized list, most of it closer to me than to my profession. Indeed, only one of the six books is strictly archaeological, and four of the six are works of fiction. I shall take them up in the chronological order of my first reading them.

Robert Louis Stevenson. *The Strange Case of Dr. Jekyll and Mr. Hyde* (1886). New York: Dodd, Mead, 1979.

My first reading of this was in 1922, when I was nine years old; since then I have reread it on several occasions. The magic of this fascinating fable of good and evil never fails. While as a youngster I was undoubtedly first captured by its "mystery and horror" aspects, I think even then I was aware of the moral tragedy Stevenson depicted so wonderfully.

F. Scott Fitzgerald. *The Great Gatsby* (1925). New York: Scribner's, 1981.

I read this first at the right time—as an undergraduate in college—but it continues to be an old and dear favorite. Fitzgerald's lyric masterpiece tells us about the dreams, desires and heartbreaks that "float in the wake" (to use a good Fitzgeraldian phrase) of the search for money and power. The whole narrative is also pervaded by the ever-present concern for social class and status that lay—and still lies—just below the surface of American life.

Oswald Spengler. *The Decline of the West* (1919–22). Charles
Francis Atkinson, trans. 2 vols. New York: Knopf, 1975.

I was bowled over by this vast, absurd, learned, pretentious book when I read it in 1936. I suppose it was the first "Big
Book" I had ever read. I don't go back to it much now. As an
archaeologist I am interested in many of the things Spengler has
to say, though I think many of Spengler's ideas are wrong-
headed and even bad. At the same time, the book has value.

Vere Gordon Childe. *The Danube in Prehistory* (1929). New
York: AMS Press, 1976.

This was read as part of my graduate professional education
in 1939–40. I select it as one of the finest professional and technical works of this greatest of modern archaeologists. In it Childe
shows the way archaeological syntheses should be written. It
made an initial and a lasting impression upon me and my career.

Anthony Powell. *A Dance to the Music of Time* (1962–75). 12
vols. Boston: Little, Brown, 1976.

I read the twelve volumes of this splendid novel serially as
they appeared, and since then I have reread the whole series
twice, each time with new pleasure. I seem never to tire of it.
Perhaps it is not up to Proust's *Remembrance of Things Past,*
but I like it better. It is witty, sensitive, involved yet remote; my
sense of empathy with Nicholas Jenkins, the narrator, seems
always complete.

Vladimir Nabokov. *Pale Fire* (1962). New York: Putnam, 1980. (Pb)

This is a very strange book, and I do not really understand
why I am so entranced by it. Many of Nabokov's other things I
don't care for, but I have read this at least three times. One thing
about it is that Nabokov is an extraordinarily visual writer. The
imagery is superb; it is like dreaming in Color-Vision. The story is
ridiculous, poignant, and enchanting, but it opens up a world of
the imagination that becomes more real than the real world.

Edward O. Wilson

Edward Wilson is the Frank B. Baird, Jr. Professor of Science at Harvard and curator of entomology at the university's Museum of Comparative Zoology. One of the nation's leading biologists, Professor Wilson received the Pulitzer Prize for nonfiction in 1979 for his work entitled On Human Nature. *One of the most entrenched biological predispositions Wilson finds among human beings is biophilia—the love for other forms of life such as plants and animals—which is also the title of his most recent book (*Biophilia, *1984).*

I was an adolescent, from fifteen to eighteen years of age, when I encountered the books that were to have the most profound and lasting influence on my life. Thereafter I read thousands of books, many of equal or superior quality, and put most to good use; but I have to confess that individually they have had a steadily declining effect on my world view, style and ambition. Hence I can only offer you works that might, either literally or as examples of a genre, influence a certain kind of young person to take up a career as a biologist and naturalist. More I cannot promise.

Sir Arthur Conan Doyle. *Lost World* (1912). New York: Random House, 1959.

Even as a small child I dreamed of going on faraway expeditions to collect insects and other animals. This book set my imagination on fire, and I was thereafter a *nesiophile,* a lover of islands, the concrete symbols of new worlds awaiting exploration. The compulsion was one of the mental factors that led me in later years to develop (with Robert H. MacArthur) the theory of island biogeography, which has become an influential part of ecology.

Trofim D. Lysenko. *Heredity and Its Variability* (1943). Moscow: Foreign Languages, 1954.

Although I was later to see Lysenkoism for what it was,
false in conception, political in aim, and very nearly the death
of Soviet genetics, I was enchanted by this little book when I
encountered it at the age of sixteen. It appealed to my mood of
rebelliousness. It seemed to me that Lysenko was offering a
radical and effective challenge to conventional science, and
that even the callow and inexperienced might have a chance to
proceed directly to new realms of discovery.

Philip Wylie. *An Essay on Morals* (1947). Westport, Conn.:
Greenwood, 1978.

———. *Generation of Vipers* (1942). Marietta, Ga.: Larlin, 1979.

When I was a seventeen-year-old college student, these
Menckenesque essays broke me out of the fundamentalist Protestant faith in which I had been raised and moved me toward
the secular humanism with which I increasingly identify today.
I still find Wylie a delightful read.

Sinclair Lewis. *Arrowsmith* (1925). New York: New American
Library, 1982. (Pb)

The perfect young man's book: a vision of a pure life devoted to the search for scientific truth, above money grubbing
and hypocrisy. How I longed to be like Arrowsmith, to find my
mentor in a real Gottlieb. The feeling was intensified when I
discovered Jack London's *Martin Eden* shortly afterward.

Erwin Schrödinger. *What Is Life?* (1946). New York: Cambridge University Press, 1967.

This taut little book, which I encountered as a college
freshman, invited biologists to think of life in more purely physical terms. Schrödinger was right of course, as witness the rise
of molecular biology soon afterward. For me his arguments
suggested delicious mysteries and great challenges. (Later, I
was especially pleased when a reviewer likened my own book

Genes, Mind, and Culture, published with C. J. Lumsden in 1981, to *What Is Life?* saying that it offered a comparable challenge from biology to the social sciences.)

Ernst Mayr. *Systematics and the Origin of Species from the Viewpoint of a Zoologist* (1942). New York: Columbia University Press, 1982. (Pb)

By defining the biological species in strong, vital language and connecting the process of species formation to genetics, Mayr opened a large part of natural history to a more scientific form of analysis. This is an example of a very heuristic work, which invited young scientists to join an exciting quest in field research. More than forty years after its publication, I am still wholly involved in this effort.

Marcus Aurelius. *Meditations* (ca. A.D. 160). G. M. A. Grube, ed. and trans. Indianapolis: Hackett, 1984. (Pb)

I hope that I have not missed the editors' purpose entirely by listing books that affected one rather rebellious adolescent in the 1940s, but I was quite surprised myself when I came up with this list after careful reflection. Let me make partial amends by citing the work that I pull off the shelf most often, and gives me the greatest pleasure, now that I am in my fifties: *Meditations,* by Marcus Aurelius. For this work reflects the point to which I have come, in company with such a magnificent spirit who "bears in mind that all that is rational is akin, and that it is in man's nature to care for all men, and that we should not embrace the opinion of all, but of those alone who live in conscious agreement with Nature."

James Q. Wilson

James Wilson is the Henry Lee Shattuck Professor of Government at Harvard University and professor of management at the University of California, Los Angeles. Prior to these appointments, Professor Wilson was chairman of Harvard's Task Force on the Core Curriculum from 1976 to 1977; chairman of the Department of Government from 1969 to 1973; and director of the Joint Center for Urban Studies of M.I.T. and Harvard from 1963 to 1966. An expert on crime and the penal system, Professor Wilson has served on numerous commissions and task forces including the attorney general's 1981 Task Force on Violent Crime and the 1967 White House Task Force on Crime.

Aristotle. *The Politics* (ca. 335 B.C.). Carnes Lord, trans. Chicago: University of Chicago Press, 1984.

The greatest statement of human nature and political life ever written.

Alexander Hamilton, John Jay, and **James Madison.** *The Federalist [Papers]* (1788). Benjamin F. Wright, ed. Cambridge: Harvard University Press, 1961. (Pb)

A brilliant subtle argument for a non-Aristotelian regime.

Chester I. Barnard. *The Functions of the Executive* (1938). Thirtieth anniversary ed. Cambridge: Harvard University Press, 1968. (Pb)

After nearly fifty years, it is still the best account of what it means to maintain cooperative human activity.

Philip Selznick. *Leadership in Administration: A Sociological Interpretation* (1957). Berkeley: University of California Press, 1983. (Pb)

The runner-up to Barnard.

James Boswell. *The Life of Samuel Johnson* (1791). New York: Random House, 1964. (Pb)

A brilliant account of how a man may sustain a powerful moral vision in an imperfect world.

Fyodor Dostoevsky. *The Brothers Karamazov* (1915). Andrew MacAndrew, trans. New York: Bantam, 1981. (Pb)

An eerie foretelling of the notion of ideological fanaticism and totalitarianism.

Abraham Zaleznik

Abraham Zaleznik is the Konosuke Matsushita Professor of Leadership at the Harvard Business School. He has taught at Harvard since 1947 and is known internationally for his research and teaching in the field of social psychology in the business setting, and for his investigations into the distinguishing characteristics of managers and leaders. A psychoanalyst, Professor Zaleznik maintains that he studied psychoanalysis because the way to advance in our understanding of people at work is first to understand people. His courses not only examine leadership within the business organization but also address issues such as the family, the individual's emotional life and the tension between career goals and personal aspirations. His works include: Human Dilemmas of Leadership *(1966),* Power and the Corporate Mind *(1975) and* The Managerial Mystique: The Changing Realities of Business Leadership *(1985).*

If you believe as I do that human beings change only microscopically in their biological and psychological structure, then you will believe that the books I have listed will probably have enduring value into the next century.

Sigmund Freud. *The Complete Psychological Works: Standard Edition.* James Strachey, ed. and trans. 25 vols. New York: W.W. Norton, 1976.

Sigmund Freud has had the most influence on my intellectual life. I cannot restrict myself to only one of his books. Among the most important, I would list his *The Interpretation of Dreams, Three Essays on Sexuality,* and his case studies, including *Dora, Little Hans, The Rat Man,* and *The Wolf Man.* For those who want to study Freud seriously, I would recommend that they read Ernest Jones's three-volume biography, *The Life and Work of Sigmund Freud.*

F. J. Roethlisberger and **William J. Dickson.** *Management and the Worker* (1934). Cambridge: Harvard University Press, 1946.

This book was my introduction to the study of human relations in business, and it opened my eyes to a field of study as it changed the way executives thought about their work and about themselves.

Bronislaw Malinowski. *Argonauts of the Western Pacific* (1960). New York: Waveland Press, 1984. (Pb)

Alfred R. Radcliffe-Brown. *The Andaman Islanders.* New York: Free Press, 1964. (Pb)

Conrad M. Arensberg. *The Irish Countryman.* Garden City, N.Y.: Natural History Press, 1968. (Pb)

William F. Whyte. *Street Corner Society* (1943). Chicago: University of Chicago Press, 1981. (Pb)

My third selection is a group of books. They were written by anthropologists and opened my eyes to the aesthetics of field work in the scientific examination of social organization.

George C. Homans. *The Human Group* (1950). London: Routledge and Kegan Paul, 1975.

———. *Social Behavior: Its Elementary Forms.* New York: Harcourt Brace Jovanovich, 1974.

George C. Homans wrote two books that taught me something about evidence and inference in social research.

Saul Bellow. *Humboldt's Gift* (1975). New York: Avon, 1976. (Pb)

Saul Bellow's novels lifted the veil that hides the dilemmas of modern man; the intellectual, the artist and the humanist. *Humboldt's Gift* is a powerful book.

Arthur Miller. *Death of a Salesman* (1966). New York: Penguin, 1977. (Pb)

———. *The Price* (1967). New York: Penguin, 1985. (Pb)

———. *A View from the Bridge* (1957). New York: Penguin, 1977. (Pb)

The plays of Arthur Miller taught me about survival in a world that is for some tragic heroes a very unfriendly place. Three of his plays are especially important to me: *Death of a Salesman, The Price* and *A View from the Bridge.*

INDEX OF WORKS CITED

UNATTRIBUTED WORKS

The Bhagavad Gītā (ca. A.D. 1). Franklin Edgerton, trans. Cambridge: Harvard University Press, 1944. [Eck]

The Bible. King James version (1611). [Bate, Coles, Gavin, Keppel, Lord, Mills, Phelps]
  Book of Exodus. [Stewart]
  Book of Genesis. [Stewart]
  Book of Job. [Gould, Safdie]
  Gospel According to St. Mark. [Ševčenko]
  Old Testament. [Pipes]

The Book of Common Prayer (1549). New York: Oxford University Press, 1928. [Chatfield]

The Epic of Gilgamesh (seventh century B.C.). R. Campbell Thompson, ed. New York: AMS Press, 1981. [Lord]

New York Times (1948 to date). [Keppel]

Organization for Economic Cooperation and Development. *Industrial Policy of Japan.* Paris: O.E.C.D., 1972. [Vogel]

The Scientific American. [Bossert]

ATTRIBUTED WORKS

Adams, Henry. *The Education of Henry Adams* (1907). Ernest Samuels, ed. Boston: Houghton Mifflin, 1973. (Pb) [Neustadt]

Adler, Mortimer J., ed. *The Great Ideas: A Syntopicon of Great Books of the Western World* (1952). Chicago: Encyclopaedia Britannica, 1955. (Vols. 2 and 3 of *Great Books of the Western World.*) [Bell]

Agee, James and Walker Evans. *Let Us Now Praise Famous Men* (1941). New York: Ballantine, 1974. (Pb) [Niebuhr, Parker]

Alberts, Bruce, et al. *Molecular Biology of the Cell.* New York: Garland, 1983. [Doty]

Alexander, Christopher. *Notes on the Synthesis of Form.* Cambridge: Harvard University Press, 1964. (Pb) [Spirn]

―――― et al. *A Pattern Language which Generates Multi-Service Centers.* Berkeley, Calif.: Center for Environmental Structure, 1968. [Spirn]

Allison, Graham T. *Essence of Decision: Explaining the Cuban Missile Crisis.* Boston: Little, Brown, 1971. (Pb) [Collins]

Arendt, Hannah. *The Human Condition* (1958). Chicago: University of Chicago Press, 1970. (Pb) [Sandel]

Arensberg, Conrad M. *The Irish Countryman.* Garden City, N.Y.: Natural History Press, 1968. (Pb) [Zaleznik]

Ariosto, Ludovico. *Orlando Furioso* (1532). New York: Oxford
University Press, 1983. (Pb) [Della-Terza]
Aristotle. *Nicomachean Ethics* (ca. 350 B.C.). New York: Oxford
University Press, 1980. (Pb) [Mansfield]
———. *The Politics* (ca. 335 B.C.). Carnes Lord, trans. Chicago:
University of Chicago Press, 1984. [Moore, J. Wilson]
Aron, Raymond. *Peace and War: A Theory of International Relations*
(1962). Richard Howard and Annette Baker Fox, trans. Garden
City, N.Y.: Doubleday, 1966. [Allison, Hoffman]
Arrow, Kenneth J. *Social Choice and Individual Values* (1951). New
Haven: Yale University Press, 1970. (Pb) [Raiffa]
Auchincloss, Louis. *The Rector of Justin* (1964). Boston: Houghton
Mifflin, 1980. (Pb) [Riesman]
Augustine, St. *The City of God* (A.D. 413–426). David Knowles, ed. New
York: Penguin, 1984. (Pb) [Shklar]
———. *The Confessions* (ca. A.D. 400). Rex Warner, trans. New York:
Penguin, 1961. (Pb) [Miles]
Aurelius, Marcus. *Meditations* (ca. A.D. 160). G. M. A. Grube, ed. and
trans. Indianapolis: Hackett, 1984. (Pb) [E. Wilson]
Austen, Jane. *Pride and Prejudice* (1813). Tony Tanner, ed. New York:
Penguin, 1972. (Pb) [McArdle]
Ayer, Alfred J. *Language, Truth and Logic* (1936). New York: Dover,
1952. (Pb) [Nye]
Bach, J. S. *The Goldberg Variations* (1747). R. K. Kirkpatrick, ed. New
York: Schirmer, 1938. [Montgomery]
Bailey, Stephen K. *Congress Makes a Law: The Story Behind the
Employment Act of 1946* (1950). Westport, Conn.: Greenwood
Press, 1980. [Chandler]
Bailyn, Bernard. *The Ideological Origins of the American Revolution*
(1965). Cambridge: Harvard University Press, 1967. (Pb) [May]
Barber, James D. *The Lawmakers: Recruitment and Adaptation to
Legislative Life* (1965). Westport, Conn.: Greenwood Press, 1980.
[Linsky]
Barnard, Chester I. *The Functions of the Executive* (1938). Thirtieth
anniversary ed. Cambridge: Harvard University Press, 1968. (Pb)
[Andrews, J. Wilson]
Barth, Karl. *The Epistle to the Romans* (1918). Edwyn C. Hoskyns,
trans. 6th ed. New York: Oxford University Press, 1968. (Pb)
[Kaufman]
Barthes, Roland. *The Pleasure of the Text.* Richard Miller, trans. New
York: Hill & Wang, 1975. (Pb) [Ackerman, Miles]
Bateson, Gregory. *Steps to an Ecology of Mind* (1972). New York:
Ballantine, 1975. (Pb) [Hodgson]
Baum, L. Frank. *The Wizard of Oz* (1900). New York: Penguin, 1983.
(Pb) [Mack]

Bedford, Sybille. *A Legacy* (1956). New York: Ecco Press, 1976. (Pb)
   [Ford]

Beerbohm, Sir Max. *Works and More* (1930). St. Clair Shores, Mich.:
   Scholarly Press, 1969. [Pipes]

Bell, Daniel. *The Coming of Post-Industrial Society* (1973). New York:
   Basic Books, 1976. (Pb) [Vogel]

Bellah, Robert N. *The Broken Covenant: American Civil Religion in a Time
   of Trial* (1975). Minneapolis, Minn.: Winston, 1976. (Pb) [Epps]

Bellow, Saul. *Humboldt's Gift* (1975). New York: Avon, 1976. (Pb)
   [Zaleznik]

Benedict, Ruth F. *Patterns of Culture* (1934). Boston: Houghton Mifflin,
   1961. [Chall, Frazier]

Berle, Adolph A., Jr. *Power Without Property: A New Development in
   American Political Economy.* New York: Harcourt, Brace, 1959.
   [Christensen]

Berlin, Sir Isaiah. *Four Essays on Liberty* (1969). New York: Oxford
   University Press, 1979. (Pb) [Sandel]

Bernanos, Georges. *The Diary of a Country Priest* (1936). Pamela
   Morris, trans. New York: Carroll & Graf, 1984. (Pb) [Coles]

Bernard, Claude. *An Introduction to the Study of Experimental
   Medicine* (1865). H. C. Greene, trans. New York: Dover, 1957.
   (Pb) [Adelstein]

Berry, Wendell. *Recollected Essays, 1965–1980.* San Francisco: North
   Point Press, 1981. (Pb) [Vosgerchian]

Beveridge, William I. B. *The Art of Scientific Investigation* (1951). New
   York: Random House, 1960. (Pb) [Christensen]

Bickel, Alexander M. *The Least Dangerous Branch: The Supreme Court
   at the Bar of Politics* (1962). New Haven: Yale University Press,
   1986. [Parker]

Boccaccio, Giovanni. *The Decameron* (ca. 1348). New York: New
   American Library, 1982. (Pb) [Della-Terza]

Bolling, Richard W. and John Bowles. *America's Competitive Edge.*
   New York: McGraw-Hill, 1982. [Vogel]

Bonhoeffer, Dietrich. *The Cost of Discipleship* (1948). R. H. Fuller,
   trans. Magnolia, Mass.: Peter Smith, 1983. [Mills]

Bork, Robert H. *The Antitrust Paradox: A Policy at War with Itself*
   (1978). New York: Basic Books, 1980. (Pb) [McCraw]

Borrow, George Henry. *Lavengro.* 3 vols. London: J. Murray, 1851.
   [Aaron]

Boswell, James. *The Life of Samuel Johnson* (1791). New York: Random
   House, 1964. (Pb) [Bate, J. Wilson]

Bowen, Elenore S. [Laura Bohannan]. *Return to Laughter* (1954). New
   York: Doubleday, 1964. [Nye]

Bowen, Elizabeth. *The House in Paris* (1935). New York: Avon, 1979.
   (Pb) [Alfred]

Braudel, Fernand. *Civilization and Capitalism, 15th–18th Century*
    (1967, 1982–84). Siân Reynolds, trans. 3 vols. New York: Harper
    & Row, 1985, 1986. (Pb) [Reich, Sachs]
———. *The Mediterranean and the Mediterranean World in the Age of
    Philip II* (1949). Siân Reynolds, trans. New York: Harper & Row,
    1976. (Pb) [Stilgoe]
Bridgman, Percy W. *The Logic of Modern Physics* (1927). New York:
    AMS Press, 1980. [Frazier]
———. *Reflections of a Physicist* (1950). Bernard I. Cohen, ed. Salem,
    N.H.: Ayer, 1980. [Fiering]
———. *The Way Things Are* (1959). New York: Viking, 1961.
    [Ackerman]
Briggs, Jean L. *Never in Anger.* Cambridge: Harvard University Press,
    1970. (Pb) [Kagan]
Brontë, Charlotte. *Jane Eyre* (1847). New York: Putnam, 1982. [Vidal]
Brooks, Cleanth. *Modern Poetry and the Tradition.* Chapel Hill, N.C.:
    University of North Carolina Press, 1970. (Pb) [Stewart]
Browning, Elizabeth Barrett. *Sonnets from the Portuguese* (1850). New
    York: Crown, 1977. [Fiering]
Brunner, Heinrich. *Die Entstehung der Schwurgerichte* (1871). Aalan
    (Germany): Scientia Verlag, 1967. [Thorne]
Buck, Pearl S. *The Good Earth* (1931). New York: Washington Square
    Press, 1983. (Pb) [Horner]
Bullock, Alan L., ed. *The Harper Dictionary of Modern Thought.* New
    York: Harper & Row, 1977. [Bell]
Burke, Kenneth. *Permanence and Change* (1935). Indianapolis:
    Bobbs-Merrill, 1965. [Aaron]
Burns, James MacGregor. *Roosevelt: The Lion and the Fox* (1956). New
    York: Harcourt, Brace, 1963. (Pb) [Champion]
Bury, John B. *The Idea of Progress: An Inquiry into Its Origin and
    Growth* (1920). Westport, Conn.: Greenwood Press, 1982.
    [Herrenstein]
Caesar, Julius. *The Gallic Wars* (ca. 40 B.C.). Boston: David R. Godine,
    1980. [Hodgson]
Caldwell, Erskine. *God's Little Acre* (1933). New York: New American
    Library, n.d. (Pb) [Fiering]
Camus, Albert. *The Myth of Sisyphus* (1942). Justin O'Brien, trans. New
    York: Random House, 1959. (Pb) [Patterson]
Carnap, Rudolf. *Der logische Aufbau der Welt* (1928). Hamburg:
    Meiner, 1974. [Quine]
———. *Logische Syntax der Sprache.* Vienna: J. Springer, 1934. [Quine]
Carr, Edward H. *What Is History?* (1961). New York: Random House,
    1967. (Pb) [Atkinson, Christensen]
Carroll, J. B. "Developmental Parameters of Reading Comprehension"

(1974). In J. T. Guthrie, ed., *Cognition, Curriculum, and Comprehension*. Newark, Del.: International Reading Association, 1977. (Pb) [Chall]

Cary, Joyce. *Art and Reality: Ways of the Creative Process* (1958). Freeport, N.Y.: Books for Libraries Press, 1970. [Dunlop]

Cather, Willa. *My Ántonia* (1918). Boston: Houghton Mifflin, 1926. (Pb) [Vidal]

Chandler, Alfred D., Jr. *Strategy and Structure*. Cambridge: M.I.T. Press, 1962. (Pb) [McCraw, Scott]

———. *The Visible Hand*. Cambridge: Harvard University Press, 1977. (Pb) [Scott]

Chaucer, Geoffrey. *The Canterbury Tales* (ca. 1390). New York: Penguin, 1951. (Pb) [Buchanan]

Chekhov, Anton. *Plays and Letters* (1884–1904). New York: W. W. Norton, 1977. (Pb) [Brustein]

Chesterton, G. K. *The Napoleon of Notting Hill* (1904). New York: Paulist Press, 1978. (Pb) [Gavin]

Childe, Vere Gordon. *The Danube in Prehistory* (1929). New York: AMS Press, 1976. [Willey]

Chodorow, Nancy. *The Reproduction of Mothering: Psychoanalysis and the Sociology of Gender*. Berkeley: University of California Press, 1978. [Miles]

Churchill, Winston S. *History of the English-Speaking Peoples* (1956–58). 4 vols. New York: Dodd-Mead, 1983. (Pb) [Allison]

———. *The Second World War* (1948–53). 6 vols. Boston: Houghton Mifflin, 1983. [Allison, Doty, Herrenstein, Mills]

Clarke, George L. *Elements of Ecology* (1954). New York: Wiley, 1965. [Timmer]

Cochran, Thomas C. *Railroad Leaders, 1845–1890: The Business Mind in Action*. Cambridge: Harvard University Press, 1953. [Chandler]

Coleridge, Samuel Taylor. *Aids to Reflection* (1825). James Marsh and H. N. Coleridge, eds. Burlington: Chauncey Goodrich, 1840. [Niebuhr]

———. *Biographia literaria* (1817). J. Shawcross, ed. London: Oxford University Press, 1962. [Niebuhr]

———. *The Poetical Works* (1796–1819). New York: Oxford University Press, 1969. [Niebuhr]

Collingwood, R. G. *An Essay on Metaphysics* (1940). Lanham, Md.: University Press of America, 1984. (Pb) [Kaufman]

———. *The Idea of History* (1946). T. M. Knox, ed. New York: Oxford University Press, 1956. (Pb) [Kaufman]

Collins, Michael. *Carrying the Fire: An Astronaut's Journeys*. New York: Farrar, Straus & Giroux, 1974. [Doty]

Conant, James B. *Education in a Divided World* (1948). New York:
     Greenwood Press, 1969. [Keppel]
Coomaraswamy, Ananda K. *Yakshas* (1928–31). 2 vols. New Delhi:
     Munshiram Manoharlal, 1971. [Eck]
Cooper, James Fenimore. *The Leather-stocking Tales* (1823–41). New
     York: Avon, 1980. (Pb) [Heclo]
Cover, Robert M. *Justice Accused: Antislavery and the Judicial Process*
     (1975). New Haven: Yale University Press, 1984. (Pb) [Edley,
     Minow]
Cremin, Lawrence A. *American Education.* 2 vols. to date. New York:
     Harper & Row, 1982–. (Pb) [Glazer, Keppel]
Curie, Ève. *Madame Curie* (1937). Vincent Sheean, trans. New York:
     Doubleday, Doran, 1938. [Adelstein]
Dale, Edgar. *The Higher Literacy: Selections from the Writings of Dr.
     Edgar Dale.* Champaign: University of Illinois Film Center, 1982.
     [Chall]
Daly, Mary. *Beyond God the Father: Toward a Philosophy of Women's
     Liberation.* Boston: Beacon, 1973. [Eck]
————. *Gyn/Ecology: The Metaethics of Radical Feminism* (1978).
     Boston: Beacon, 1979. (Pb) [Miles]
Dante Alighieri. *The Divine Comedy* (ca. 1307–21). New York: Penguin,
     1984. (Pb) [Della-Terza]
Darwin, Charles. *The Origin of Species* (1859). New York: Penguin,
     1982. (Pb) [Friedman, Gould, Herrenstein, Schelling]
Davies, Robertson. *The Deptford Trilogy.*
     Fifth Business (1970). New York: Penguin, 1977. (Pb) [Galbraith]
     The Manticore (1972). New York: Penguin, 1977. (Pb) [Galbraith]
     World of Wonders (1975). New York: Viking, 1977. (Pb)
     [Galbraith]
DeKruif, Paul H. *Microbe Hunters* (1926). New York: Harcourt, Brace,
     1966. (Pb) [Hiatt, Livingston]
Dermoût, Maria. *The Ten Thousand Things* (1958). E. M. Beekman, ed.,
     Hans Koning, trans. Amherst: University of Massachusetts Press,
     1983. [Knowlton]
Derrida, Jacques. *Of Grammatology.* Gayatri C. Spivak, trans.
     Baltimore: Johns Hopkins University Press, 1976. (Pb) [Frug]
DeWaal, Frans. *Chimpanzee Politics: Power and Sex Among Apes.*
     Janet Milnes, trans. New York: Harper & Row, 1983. (Pb)
     [Allison]
Dewey, John. *Art as Experience.* New York: Minton, Balch, 1934.
     [Spirn]
Dickens, Charles. *Bleak House* (1853). New York: Bantam, 1983. (Pb)
     [McArdle]
————. *David Copperfield* (1850). New York: Advent, 1983. (Pb)
     [Friedman]

————. *Little Dorrit* (1857). Harvey P. Sucksmith, ed. New York: Oxford University Press, 1982. (Pb) [Coles]

————. *A Tale of Two Cities* (1859). New York: Bantam, 1981. (Pb) [Livingston]

Dickinson, Emily. *The Complete Poems of Emily Dickinson* (mid-nineteenth century). Thomas H. Johnson, ed. Boston: Little, Brown, 1960. [Horner]

Di Maggio, Joe. *Lucky to be a Yankee* (1946). New York: Grosset & Dunlap, 1951. [Gould]

Dinnerstein, Dorothy. *The Mermaid and the Minotaur: Sexual Arrangements and Human Malaise.* New York: Harper & Row, 1976. (Pb) [Dalton]

Djilas, Milovan. *The New Class: An Analysis of the Communist System* (1957). San Diego: Harcourt Brace Jovanovich, 1982. [Mills]

Dos Passos, John. *Nineteen Nineteen* (1932). New York: New American Library, n.d. (Pb) [Phelps]

————. *Three Soldiers* (1921). Boston: Houghton Mifflin, 1964. (Pb) [Alfred]

Dostoevsky, Fyodor. *The Brothers Karamazov* (1915). Andrew MacAndrew, trans. New York: Bantam, 1981. (Pb) [Frazier, J. Wilson]

————. *Notes from Underground* (1864). Jessie Coulson, ed. and trans. New York: Penguin, 1972. (Pb) [Mack]

Doyle, Sir Arthur Conan. *Lost World* (1912). New York: Random House, 1959. [E. Wilson]

DuBois, W. E. B. *Black Reconstruction in America* (1935). New York: Atheneum, 1969. (Pb) [Haskins]

————. *The Souls of Black Folk* (1903). New York: New American Library, 1969. (Pb) [Epps]

Dumas, Alexandre. *The Count of Monte Cristo* (1844–45). New York: Bantam, 1981. (Pb) [Grabar, Whipple]

————. *The Three Musketeers* (1844). New York: Penguin, 1982. (Pb) [Grabar, Whipple]

Duncan, David J. *The River Why* (1983). New York: Bantam, 1984. (Pb) [Nye]

Durning-Lawrence, Sir Edwin. *Bacon is Shake-speare.* London and New York: Gay & Hancock, 1910. [Skinner]

Dwight, Timothy. *Travels; in New England and New-York* (1821–22). 4 vols. Cambridge: Harvard University Press, 1969. [Stilgoe]

Dyson, Freeman J. *Disturbing the Universe: A Life in Science* (1979). New York: Harper & Row, 1981. (Pb) [Knowlton]

Eddington, Sir Arthur S. *The Nature of the Physical World* (1928). Folcroft, Penn.: Folcroft Library Editions, 1935. [Quine]

Edgeworth, Maria. *Castle Rackrent* (1800). New York: Oxford University Press, 1982. (Pb) [Kelleher]

Edwards, Jonathan. *A Treatise Concerning Religious Affections* (1746). New York: Baker, 1982. (Pb) [Niebuhr]

Einstein, Albert and Leopold Infeld. *Physik als Abenteuer der Erkenntnis (The Evolution of Physics,* 1938). New York: Simon & Schuster, 1967. (Pb) [Bloembergen]

Eiseley, Loren C. *The Immense Journey* (1957). Alexandria, Va.: Time–Life Books, 1981. [Olin]

Eisenstein, Hester and Alice Jardine, eds. *The Future of Difference* (1980). New Brunswick, N.J.: Rutgers University Press, 1985. (Pb) [Dalton, Minow]

Elgin, Suzette Haden. *Native Tongue.* New York: Donald A. Wollheim, 1984. (Pb) [Dalton]

Elias, Norbert. *The History of Manners* (1978). Edmund Jephcott, trans. New York: Pantheon, 1982. (Pb) [Frug]

Eliot, George [Mary Ann Evans Cross]. *Daniel Deronda* (1876). New York: New American Library, 1979. (Pb) [Gould]

——. *Middlemarch* (1871–72). New York: Bantam, 1985. (Pb) [Coles, McArdle]

——. *The Mill on the Floss* (1860). New York: Penguin, 1980. (Pb) [McArdle]

Eliot, Thomas Stearns. *Four Quartets* (1935–42). New York: Harcourt, Brace, 1968. (Pb) [Spirn]

Ellison, Ralph. *Shadow and Act.* New York: Random House, 1964. (Pb) [Epps]

Fairbank, John K. *Chinabound: A Fifty-Year Memoir.* New York: Harper & Row, 1983. (Pb) [Timmer]

——. *The United States and China* (1958). 4th ed. Cambridge: Harvard University Press, 1983. (Pb) [MacFarquhar]

Faulkner, William. *Absalom! Absalom!* (1936). New York: Random House, 1972. (Pb) [Bailyn, Brinkley, McKinsey]

——. *Intruder in the Dust* (1948). New York: Random House, 1967. (Pb) [Mills]

——. *The Sound and the Fury* (1929). New York: Random House, 1967. (Pb) [Mills]

Fay, Sidney B. *The Origins of the World War* (1928). 2 vols. New York: Macmillan, 1954. [Phelps]

Feuerbach, Ludwig. *The Essence of Christianity* (1841). E. Graham Waring and F. W. Strothmann, eds. New York: Frederick Ungar, 1975. (Pb) [Kaufman]

Fisher, H. A. L. *Frederic William Maitland, Downing Professor of the Laws of England: A Biographical Sketch.* Cambridge: Cambridge University Press, 1910. [Thorne]

Fitzgerald, F. Scott. *The Great Gatsby* (1925). New York: Scribner's, 1981. (Pb) [Willey]

Flack, Isaac H. *Eternal Eve* (1950). London: Hutchinson, 1960.
[Friedman]

Follett, Mary Parker. *Dynamic Administration* (1940). Henry C.
Metcalf and L. Urwick, eds. London: Pitman, 1973. [Andrews]

Ford, Ford Madox. *The Good Soldier* (1915). New York: Random
House, 1951. (Pb) [Livingston]

Foucault, Michel. *Discipline and Punish: The Birth of a Prison.* New
York: Random House, 1979. (Pb) [Miles]

France, Anatole. *The Gods Will Have Blood (Les dieux ont soif,* 1912).
Frederick Davies, trans. New York: Penguin, 1979. (Pb) [Ford]

Frank, Anne. *Anne Frank: The Diary of a Young Girl* (1947). New
York: Doubleday, 1967. (Pb) [Fiering]

Freud, Sigmund. *Civilization and Its Discontents* (1929). Joan Riviere,
trans. London: Hogarth, 1930. [Ševčenko]

———. *The Complete Psychological Works: Standard Edition.* James
Strachey, ed. and trans. 25 vols. New York: W. W. Norton, 1976.
[Zaleznik]

———. *The Future of an Illusion* (1926). James Strachey, ed. and trans.
New York: W. W. Norton, 1961. [Ševčenko]

———. *A General Introduction to Psychoanalysis* (1909, 2d ed., 1920).
New York: Boni & Liveright, 1977. (Pb) [Kennedy]

———. *The Interpretation of Dreams* (1900). New York: Avon, 1980.
(Pb) [Horner, Mack]

———. *Psychopathology of Everyday Life* (1901). A. A. Brill, ed. and
trans. New York: Macmillan, n.d. [Ševčenko]

———. *Totem and Taboo* (1913). James Strachey, ed. and trans. New
York: W. W. Norton, 1962. [Ševčenko]

Fry, Christopher. *The Lady's Not for Burning* (1949). New York:
Oxford University Press, 1977. (Pb) [Howe]

Fry, Roger. *Vision and Design* (1920). New York: Oxford University
Press, 1981. (Pb) [Ackerman]

Fulton, John F. *Harvey Cushing: A Biography* (1946). Salem, N.H.:
Ayer, 1980. [Friedman]

Fu Shên. *Chapters from a Floating Life* (ca. 1800). Shirley M. Black,
trans. New York: Oxford University Press, 1960. [Green]

Gabriel, Ralph Henry. *The Course of American Democratic Thought*
(1940). New York: Ronald Press, 1956. [Chandler]

Galbraith, John Kenneth. *The Affluent Society* (1958). New York: New
American Library, 1978. (Pb) [Reich, Sachs]

Gandhi, M. K. *Gandhi, an Autobiography: The Story of My
Experiments with Truth* (1927–29). Mahadev Desai, trans., 2 vols.
New York: Dover, 1983. (Pb) [Eck]

Gaskell, Philip. *A New Introduction to Bibliography.* New York: Oxford
University Press, 1972. [Collins]

Gaulle, Charles de. *The Complete War Memoirs of Charles de Gaulle* (1954–59). J. Griffin and R. Howard, trans. New York: Simon & Schuster, 1964. [Hoffman]

Geertz, Clifford. *Agricultural Involution: The Processes of Ecological Change in Indonesia.* Berkeley: University of California Press, 1963. (Pb) [Timmer]

Gernsback, Hugo, ed. *The Experimenter: Electricity, Radio, Chemistry* (1921–26). [Whipple]

Gerschenkron, Alexander. *Economic Backwardness in Historical Perspective.* Cambridge: Harvard University Press, 1962. [Timmer]

Giedion, Sigfried. *Space, Time, and Architecture.* Cambridge: Harvard University Press, 1941. [Ackerman]

Gilbert, Felix. *Machiavelli and Guicciardini* (1965). New York: W. W. Norton, 1984. (Pb) [Ford]

Goethe, Johann Wolfgang von. *Faust, part I* (1770). John Prudhoe, trans. Manchester: Manchester University Press, 1974. (Pb) [Phelps]

Goffman, Erving. *Interaction Ritual: Essays in Face-to-Face Behavior* (1967). New York: Pantheon, 1982. (Pb) [Schelling]

Golding, William G. *Lord of the Flies* (1954). New York: Putnam, 1978. [MacFarquhar]

Gombrich, E. H. *Art and Illusion: A Study in the Psychology of Pictorial Representation* (1960). Princeton: Princeton University Press, 1961. (Pb) [Ackerman]

Grade, Chaim. *Rabbis and Wives* (1982). Harold Rabinowitz and I. H. Grade, trans. New York: Random House, 1983. (Pb) [Verba]

Gray, Asa. *How Plants Grow: A Simple Introduction to Structural Botany.* 3d ed. New York: Ivison and Phinney; Chicago: Gregg, 1859. [Skinner]

Guizot, François P. *The History of Civilization in Europe* (1828). William Hazlitt, trans. Darby, Penn.: Arden Library, 1983. [Pipes]

Gwaltney, John Langston, ed. *Drylongso: A Self-Portrait of Black America* (1980). New York: Random House, 1981. (Pb) [Haskins]

Haggard, Sir H. Rider. *She* (1887). New York: Airmont, n.d. (Pb) [Whipple]

Halberstam, David. *The Best and the Brightest* (1972). New York: Penguin, 1983. (Pb) [Livingston]

Hall, Donald. *String Too Short to Be Saved* (1961). Boston: David R. Godine, 1979. (Pb) [Stilgoe]

Hamilton, Alexander, John Jay, and James Madison. *The Federalist [Papers]* (1788). Benjamin F. Wright, ed. Cambridge: Harvard University Press, 1961. [Champion, Chatfield, Keppel, Neustadt, J. Wilson]

Harris, Richard. *Freedom Spent.* Boston: Little, Brown, 1976 (out of print). Appeared in *The New Yorker,* June 17 and 24, 1974; August 18, 1975; November 3, 10, and 17, 1975; and April 5, 12, and 19, 1976. [Linsky]

Harrod, Roy F. *The Life of John Maynard Keynes* (1951). New York: W. W. Norton, 1983. (Pb) [Cooper]

Hartz, Louis. *The Liberal Tradition in America.* New York: Harcourt, Brace, 1962. (Pb) [Lodge]

Hasek, Jeroslav. *The Good Soldier Svejk and His Fortunes in War* (1922). Cecil Parrott, trans. Cambridge, Mass.: Robert Bentley, 1980. [Della-Terza]

Hawley, Ellis W. *The New Deal and the Problem of Monopoly, 1934–1938* (1959). Princeton: Princeton University Press, 1966. (Pb) [Reich]

Hayami, Yujiro and Vernon W. Ruttan. *Agricultural Development: An International Perspective* (1971). Baltimore: Johns Hopkins University Press, 1985. (Pb) [Timmer]

Hayek, Friedrich August von. *The Constitution of Liberty* (1960). Chicago: Regnery, 1972. [Knowlton, Nozick]
———. *Individualism and Economic Order.* Chicago: University of Chicago Press, 1948. [Nozick]

Hegel, G. W. F. "The Independence and Dependence of Self-Consciousness: Master and Slave." Chapter IV.A. of *The Phenomenology of Spirit* (*Die Phänomenologie des Geistes,* (1807). New York: Oxford University Press, 1977. (Pb) [Dalton]
———. *The Phenomenology of Mind* (1807). J. B. Baillie, ed. and trans. New York: Harper & Row, 1967. (Pb) [Kennedy]
———. *Philosophy of Right* (*Grundlinien der Philosophie des Rechts,* 1821). T. M. Knox, trans. Oxford: Oxford University Press, 1965. [Heclo, Sandel]

Heilbroner, Robert L. *The Great Ascent: The Struggle for Economic Development in Our Time.* New York: Harper & Row, 1963. [Cooper]

Hemingway, Ernest. *A Farewell to Arms* (1929). New York: Scribner's, 1982. (Pb) [Galbraith]
———. *For Whom the Bell Tolls* (1940). New York: Scribner's, 1982. (Pb) [Roberts]

Hersey, John. *Hiroshima* (1946). New York: Bantam, n.d. (Pb) [Hiatt]

Hinton, William. *Fanshen: A Documentary of Revolution in a Chinese Village.* New York: Random House, 1968. (Pb) [Haskins]

Hirsch, Fred. *Social Limits to Growth.* Cambridge: Harvard University Press, 1976. (Pb) [Sandel]

Hirschman, Albert O. *Development Projects Observed.* Washington, D.C.: Brookings Institution, 1967. (Pb) [Timmer]

Hoffer, Eric. *The True Believer: Thoughts on the Nature of Mass Movements* (1951). New York: Harper & Row, 1966. (Pb) [Cooper]

Hofstadter, Richard. *Academic Freedom in the Age of the College.* New York: Columbia University Press, 1955. (Pb) [Glazer]

———. *The Age of Reform: From Bryan to F.D.R.* New York: Knopf, 1955. [Brinkley]

———. *Anti-Intellectualism in American Life* (1963). New York: Random House, 1966. (Pb) [McCraw]

Holling, Holling C. *Tree in the Trail.* Boston: Houghton Mifflin, 1942. [Olin]

Holmes, Oliver Wendell, Jr. *The Common Law* (1881). Boston: Little, Brown, 1964. (Pb) [Thorne]

Homans, George C. *The Human Group* (1950). London: Routledge and Kegan Paul, 1975. [Andrews, Zaleznik]

———. *Social Behavior: Its Elementary Forms.* New York: Harcourt Brace Jovanovich, 1974. [Zaleznik]

Homer. *The Iliad* (ca. 800 B.C.). Robert Fitzgerald, trans. New York: Doubleday, 1975. (Pb) [Holton, Lord, Stewart, Weinreb]

———. *The Odyssey* (ca. 800 B.C.). Robert Fitzgerald, trans. Franklin Center, Penn.: Franklin Library, 1976. [Lord]

Horowitz, Donald L. *Ethnic Groups in Conflict.* Berkeley: University of California Press, 1985. [Glazer]

Hoskins, W. G. *The Making of the English Landscape.* New York: Penguin, 1970. [Olin]

Hough, Henry Beetle. *Country Editor* (1940). Greenwich, Conn.: Chatham, 1974. (Pb) [Linsky]

Housman, A. E. *The Collected Poems of A. E. Housman* (1867–1936). New York: Holt, Rinehart and Winston, 1971. (Pb) [Howe]

Hugo, Victor. *Les Misérables* (1862). New York: Penguin, 1982. (Pb) [Friedman]

Huneker, James G. *Egoists, a Book of Supermen* (1909). New York: AMS Press, 1975. [Aaron]

———. *Iconoclasts, a Book of Dramatists* (1905). Westport, Conn.: Greenwood, 1969. [Aaron]

———. *Ivory, Apes and Peacocks* (1915). Philadelphia: Richard West, 1973. [Aaron]

———. *Unicorns* (1917). New York: AMS Press, 1976. [Aaron]

Huntington, Samuel P. *American Politics: The Promise of Disharmony* (1981). Cambridge: Harvard University Press, 1983. (Pb) [Reich]

———. *Political Order in Changing Societies* (1968). New Haven: Yale University Press, 1969. (Pb) [Lodge, Montgomery]

Hurston, Zora Neale. *Their Eyes Were Watching God* (1937). Urbana: University of Illinois Press, 1978. [McKinsey]

Ibsen, Henrik. *Complete Major Prose and Plays* (ca. 1880s). Rolf
    Fjelde, trans. New York: New American Library, n.d. (Pb)
    [Brustein]
————. *Speeches and New Letters* (ca. 1880s). Arne Kildal, trans.
    Brooklyn: Haskell, 1972. [Brustein]
Immisch, Otto. *Wie studiert man klassische Philologie?* (1909). 2d ed.
    Stuttgart, W. Violet, 1920. [Ševčenko]
Ingalls, Albert G., ed. *Amateur Telescope Making* (1926). 3 vols. New
    York: Munn, 1945. [Bossert]
Jaeger, Werner W. *Paideia: The Ideals of Greek Culture* (1934). Gilbert
    Highet, trans. New York: Oxford University Press, 1965. (Pb)
    [Bate, Keppel]
Jakobson, Roman. "Linguistics and Poetics." In *Style in Language*,
    Thomas A. Sebeok, ed. Cambridge: Technology Press of M.I.T.,
    1960. [Grabar]
James, Henry. *The American Scene* (1907). Leon Edel, ed. Indianapolis:
    Indiana University Press, 1968. (Pb) [Stilgoe]
————. *The Bostonians* (1886). New York: New American Library,
    1984. (Pb) [Green]
————. *The Wings of the Dove* (1902). New York: Penguin, 1974. (Pb)
    [Chall]
James, William. *Pragmatism* (1907). Cambridge: Harvard University
    Press, 1978. (Pb) [Andrews, Niebuhr]
————. *The Varieties of Religious Experience* (1902). New York:
    Penguin, 1982. (Pb) [Mills]
Jauch, Josef Maria. *Foundations of Quantum Mechanics.* Reading,
    Mass.: Addison-Wesley, 1968. [Edley]
Joad, C. E. M. *Introduction to Modern Political Theory* (1924). Oxford:
    Oxford University Press, 1953. [MacFarquhar]
Johnson, Chalmers A. *MITI and the Japanese Miracle: The Growth of
    Industrial Policy, 1925–1975.* Stanford, Calif.: Stanford University
    Press, 1982. (Pb) [Scott]
Jones, Ernest. *The Life and Work of Sigmund Freud* (1953–57). 3 vols.
    New York: Basic Books, 1961. (Pb) [Bailyn, Zaleznik]
Joyce, James. *Dubliners* (1914). New York: Penguin, 1976. (Pb)
    [Weinreb]
————. *Ulysses* (1918–20). New York: Random House, 1976. (Pb)
    [Brustein, Kelleher, Ševčenko]
Jung, Carl G. *Memories, Dreams, Reflections* (1963). Aniela Jaffé, trans.
    New York: Random House, 1965. (Pb) [Kao]
Jungk, Robert. *Brighter Than a Thousand Suns* (1954). James Cleugh,
    trans. New York: Harcourt, Brace, 1970. (Pb) [MacFarquhar]
Juster, Norton. *The Phantom Tollbooth.* New York: Epstein & Carroll,
    1961. (Pb) [Minow]

Kafka, Franz. *Amerika* (1938). Edwin Muir, trans. New York: New Directions, 1946. (Pb) [Herrenstein]

———. *The Castle* (1926). Willa Muir and Edwin Muir, trans. New York: Random House, 1974. (Pb) [Herrenstein]

———. *The Trial* (1937). Willa Muir and Edwin Muir, trans. New York: Penguin, 1953. (Pb) [Herrenstein]

Kant, Immanuel. *Critique of Practical Reason and Other Writings in Moral Philosophy* (1788). Lewis Beck, trans. New York: Garland, 1977. [Kaufman, Phelps]

———. *Critique of Pure Reason* (1781). New York: St. Martin's, 1969. (Pb) [Kaufman, Phelps]

———. *Groundwork on the Metaphysics of Morals* (orig. *Moral Law,* 1797). H. J. Paton, trans. New York: Harper & Row, n.d. (Pb) [Patterson]

Kantorowicz, Ernst H. *Frederick the Second* (1927). E. O. Lorimer, trans. New York: Frederick Ungar, 1957. [Grabar]

Keegan, John. *The Face of Battle* (1976). New York: Penguin, 1983. (Pb) [Schelling]

Kehr, Eckart. *Schlachtflottenbau und Partei-Politik 1894–1901.* Berlin: E. Ebering, 1930. [May]

Kelly, Joan. *Women, History, and Theory.* Chicago: University of Chicago Press, 1984. [Atkinson]

Kemeny, John G. et al. *Introduction to Finite Mathematics* (1957). Englewood Cliffs, N.J.: Prentice-Hall, 1974. [Raiffa]

Kempe, Margery. *The Book of Margery Kempe.* Hope Emily Allen and Sanford Brown Meech, eds. London: Oxford University Press, 1940. [Atkinson]

Kennan, George F. *Memoirs* (1967). 2 vols. New York: Pantheon, 1983. [Brinkley]

Kerouac, Jack. *On the Road* (1957). New York: Penguin, 1979. (Pb) [Collins]

Key, V. O., Jr. and Alexander Heard. *Southern Politics in State and Nation* (1949). Knoxville: University of Tennessee Press, 1984. (Pb) [Verba]

Keynes, John Maynard. *Essays in Persuasion* (1931). New York: W. W. Norton, 1963. (Pb) [Sachs]

Keyserling, Hermann Alexander. *The Recovery of Truth* (1927). Paul Fohr, trans. New York: Harper and Brothers, 1929. [Green]

———. *The Travel Diary of a Philosopher* (1912). J. Holroyd Reece, trans. New York: Harcourt, Brace, 1928. [Green]

Kipling, Rudyard. *Collected Works* (1886–1932). 22 vols. Garden City, N.Y.: Doubleday, Page, 1927. [Howe]

Klitgaard, Robert E. *Choosing Elites.* New York: Basic Books, 1985. [Glazer]

Kluger, Richard. *Simple Justice* (1975). New York: Random House, 1977. (Pb) [Edley]

Koestler, Arthur. *Darkness at Noon* (1940). Daphne Hardy, trans. New York: Bantam, 1970. (Pb) [MacFarquhar]

Kristina, Queen of the Swedes, the Goths and the Vandals. *The Works of Christina, Queen of Sweden* (late seventeenth century). Anonymous English trans. London: Wilson and Durham, 1753. [Gavin]

Kuhn, Thomas, S. *The Structure of Scientific Revolutions* (1962). Chicago: University of Chicago Press, 1970. (Pb) [Lodge, Moore, Roberts, Scott]

Lagerqvist, Pär. *The Eternal Smile* (1934). Erik Mesterton et al., trans. New York: Hill and Wang, 1971. [Kagan]

Lao Tsu. *Tao Te Ching.* Witter Bynner, trans. New York: Putnam, 1944. [Kao]

Lardner, Ring. *Gullible's Travels* (1917). Chicago: University of Chicago Press, 1965. [Galbraith]

Lawrence, D. H. *Lady Chatterley's Lover* (1928). Lawrence Durrell, ed. New York: Bantam, 1983. (Pb) [Fiering]

————. *Studies in Classic American Literature* (1923). New York: Penguin, 1977. (Pb) [Vosgerchian]

Lawrence, T. E. *Seven Pillars of Wisdom* (1919). New York: Penguin, 1976. (Pb) [Mack]

Lax, David and James Schenius. *The Manager as Negotiator.* New York: Free Press, 1986. [Raiffa]

Lazarsfeld, Paul F. and Elihu Katz. *Personal Influence: The Part Played by People in the Flow of Mass Communications* (1955). New York: Free Press, 1964. (Pb) [May]

LeDouarain, Nicole. *The Neural Crest.* New York: Cambridge University Press, 1983. [Kagan]

Lewis, Anthony. *Gideon's Trumpet.* New York: Random House, 1964. (Pb) [Vidal]

Lewis, Sinclair. *Arrowsmith* (1925). New York: New American Library, 1982. (Pb) [E. Wilson]

Lightfoot, Sarah Lawrence. *Worlds Apart: Relationships Between Families and Schools.* New York: Basic Books, 1978. (Pb) [Minow]

Lilienthal, David E. *TVA: Democracy on the March* (1954). Westport, Conn.: Greenwood, 1977. [McCraw]

Lippmann, Walter. *Public Opinion* (1922). New York: Free Press, 1965. (Pb) [Linsky]

Lodge, George C. and Bruce R. Scott, eds. *U.S. Competitiveness in the World Economy.* Boston: Harvard Business School Press, 1985. [Vogel]

Lorenzini, Carlo. *Adventures of Pinocchio* (1882–83). New York: Penguin, 1974. (Pb) [Mack]

Lorge, Irving. "Predicting Reading Difficulty of Selections for Children." *Elementary English Review*, 16 (October 1939), 229–33. [Chall]

Luce, R. Duncan and Howard Raiffa. *Games and Decisions: Introduction and Critical Survey*. New York: John Wiley, 1957. [Nozick]

Lysenko, Trofim D. *Heredity and Its Variability* (1943). Moscow: Foreign Languages, 1954. [E. Wilson]

Mach, Ernst. *The Science of Mechanics* (1883). T. J. McCormack, trans. 6th ed. LaSalle, Ill.: Open Court, 1960. (Pb) [Holton]

Machiavelli, Niccolò. *The Prince* (1513). Peter E. Bondanella and Mark Musa, trans. New York: Oxford University Press, 1984. [Mansfield, Neustadt, Riesman]

MacIntyre, Alasdair C. *After Virtue: A Study in Moral Theory* (1981). Notre Dame, Ind.: University of Notre Dame Press, 1982. (Pb) [Kagan]

MacNeill, Eoin. *Celtic Ireland* (1921). Dublin: University Press of Ireland, 1981. [Kelleher]

MacPherson, Crawford B. *The Political Theory of Possessive Individualism: Hobbes to Locke*. Oxford: Oxford University Press, 1962. (Pb) [Lodge]

Mahler, Margaret S., Fred Pine, and Anni Bergman. *The Psychological Birth of the Human Infant: Symbiosis and Individuation*. New York: Basic Books, 1975. [Dalton]

Mailer, Norman. *The Naked and the Dead* (1948). New York: Holt, Rinehart & Winston, 1980. (Pb) [Galbraith]

Malinowski, Bronislaw. *Argonauts of the Western Pacific* (1960). New York: Waveland Press, 1984. (Pb) [Zaleznik]

Man, Hendrik de. *The Psychology of Socialism* (*Die Sozialistische Idee*, 1933). Eden Paul and Cedar Paul, trans. New York: Arno, 1974. [Ševčenko]

Mandelbaum, Maurice H. *History, Man, and Reason: A Study in Nineteenth-Century Thought*. Baltimore: Johns Hopkins University Press, 1971. [Kagan]

Mandel'shtam, Nadezhda. *Hope Against Hope* (1970). Max Hayward, trans. New York: Atheneum, 1976. [Mack]

Mann, Thomas. *Doctor Faustus: The Life of the German Composer, Adrian Leverkühn, as Told by a Friend* (1947). H. T. Lowe-Porter, trans. New York: Random House, 1971. [Bailyn]

——. *Joseph and His Brothers* (1933–43). H. T. Lowe-Porter, trans. 4 vols. New York: Knopf, 1948. [Montgomery]

——. *The Magic Mountain* (1924). H. T. Lowe-Porter, trans. New York: Random House, 1969. (Pb) [Alfred, Shklar, Stewart]

Mannheim, Karl. *Ideology and Utopia* (1929). L. Wirth and G. Shils, trans. San Diego: Harcourt Brace Jovanovich, 1985. (Pb) [Frug, Lodge]

Martin, Judith. *Miss Manners' Guide to Excruciatingly Correct Behavior* (1982). New York: Warner, 1983. (Pb) [Chatfield]

Martin du Gard, Roger. *Les Thibault* (1922–40). New York: Larousse, n.d. (Pb) [Hoffman].

Marx, Karl. *Economic and Philosophical Manuscripts of 1844* (1844). Dirk J. Struik, ed., Martin Milligan, trans. New York: International, 1964. (Pb) [Patterson]

———. *Das Kapital* (1867). Friedrich Engels, ed. Canton, Ohio: International, 1984. (Pb) [Heclo, Kennedy]

Mattingly, Garrett. *The Armada* (1959). Boston: Houghton Mifflin, 1984. (Pb) [Ford]

Maugham, W. Somerset. *Christmas Holiday* (1939). New York: Penguin, 1977. (Pb) [Galbraith]

———. *Of Human Bondage* (1915). New York: Penguin, 1978. (Pb) [Galbraith, Mack]

Mayer, Milton S. *They Thought They Were Free: The Germans, 1933–45* (1955). Chicago: University of Chicago Press, 1966. (Pb) [Haskins]

Mayr, Ernst E. *The Growth of Biological Thought* (1982). Cambridge: Harvard University Press, 1985. (Pb) [Kagan]

———. *Systematics and the Origin of Species from the Viewpoint of a Zoologist* (1942). New York: Columbia University Press, 1982. (Pb) [E. Wilson]

McHarg, Ian L. *Design with Nature* (1969). New York: Natural History Press, 1971. (Pb) [Spirn]

McIlwain, C. H. *The High Court of Parliament and Its Supremacy* (1910). J. P. Mayer, ed. Salem, N.H.: Ayer, 1979. [Thorne]

McNeill, William H. *Plagues and Peoples* (1976). Garden City, N.Y.: Doubleday, 1977. (Pb) [Cooper]

———. *The Rise of the West: A History of the Human Community* (1963). Chicago: University of Chicago Press, 1970. (Pb) [Weinreb]

McPhee, John A. *Encounters with the Archdruid.* New York: Farrar, Straus & Giroux, 1971. (Pb) [Roberts]

Mead, George H. *Mind, Self and Society from the Standpoint of a Social Behaviorist* (1934). Charles W. Morris, ed. Chicago: University of Chicago Press, 1967. (Pb) [Kaufman]

Melville, Herman. *The Confidence-Man; His Masquerade* (1857). Herschel Park, ed. New York: W. W. Norton, 1971. (Pb) [Champion]

———. *Moby Dick* (1851). Berkeley: University of California Press, 1983. (Pb) [McKinsey, Niebuhr]

Memmi, Albert. *The Colonizer and the Colonized* (1957). Howard Greenfield, trans. Chicago: Beacon, 1966. (Pb) [Haskins]

Metzger, Walter P. *Academic Freedom in the Age of the University.*
New York: Columbia University Press, 1955. (Pb) [Glazer]

Miles, Margaret R. *Image as Insight: Visual Understanding in Western
Christianity and Secular Culture.* Boston: Beacon, 1985.
[Buchanan]

Mill, John Stuart. *On Liberty* (1854). Elizabeth Rappaport, ed.
Indianapolis: Hackett, 1978. (Pb) [Nozick]

Miller, Arthur. *Death of a Salesman* (1966). New York: Penguin, 1977.
(Pb) [Zaleznik]

———. *The Price* (1967). New York: Penguin, 1985. (Pb) [Zaleznik]

———. *A View from the Bridge* (1957). New York: Penguin, 1977. (Pb)
[Zaleznik]

Miller, Perry, ed. *Margaret Fuller: American Romantic. A Selection
from Her Writing and Correspondence* (1963). Gloucester, Mass.:
Peter Smith, 1969. [McKinsey]

Miller, Walter M., Jr. *A Canticle for Leibowitz* (1959). New York:
Bantam, 1976. (Pb) [Hodgson]

Montaigne, Michel de. *Selections from the Essays* (1595). Donald M.
Frame, ed. and trans. Arlington Heights, Ill.: Harlan Davidson,
1973. (Pb) [Della-Terza, Pipes, Shklar, Weinreb]

Morgenthau, Hans J. *Politics Among Nations: The Struggle for Power
and Peace* (1948). 5th ed. New York: Knopf, 1978. [Nye]

Morison, Samuel Eliot. *Admiral of the Ocean Sea: A Life of
Christopher Columbus* (1942). Boston: Northeastern University
Press, 1983. (Pb) [Dunlop]

Morrison, Philip, Phylis Morrison, Charles Eames, and Ray Eames.
Powers of Ten. New York: W. H. Freeman, 1982. [Bloembergen]

Munro, H. H. *The Short Stories of Saki* (1894–1916). New York:
Doubleday, 1976. [Chatfield]

Murasaki, Shikubu. *The Tale of Genji* (ca. A.D. 1000). Edward G.
Seidensticker, trans. New York: Random House, 1985. (Pb)
[Bossert]

Murie, Margaret and Olaus Murie. *Wapiti Wilderness: The Life of
Olaus and Margaret Murie in Jackson Hole, Wyoming* (1966).
Jackson Hole, Wyo.: Teton Bookshop, n.d. (Pb) [Mills]

Myrdal, Gunnar, with Richard Sterner and Arnold Rose. *An American
Dilemma: The Negro Problem and Modern Democracy* (1944). 2
vols. New York: Harper & Row, 1969. (Pb) [Graham, Howe]

Nabokov, Vladimir. *Lolita* (1955). Berkeley, Calif.: Berkeley Press,
1984. (Pb) [Parker]

———. *Pale Fire* (1962). New York: Putnam, 1980. (Pb) [Willey]

Needham, Joseph, with Wang Ling. *Science and Civilisation in
China* (1954). Cambridge: Cambridge University Press, 1985.
[Kao]

Neumann, Erich. *The Origins and History of Consciousness* (1949). R. F. C. Hull, trans. New York: Pantheon, 1954. [Kao]

Neustadt, Richard E. *Alliance Politics.* New York: Columbia University Press, 1970. (Pb) [May]

——. *Presidential Power* (1960). New York: Wiley, 1980. (Pb) [Champion, Moore]

Nicolson, Harold G. *Peacemaking 1919* (1933). New York: Grosset & Dunlap, 1965. [May]

Niebuhr, H. Richard. *The Meaning of Revelation* (1941). New York: Macmillan, 1967. (Pb) [Kaufman]

——. *Radical Monotheism and Western Culture.* New York: Harper & Row, 1960. (Pb) [Kaufman]

Nietzsche, Friedrich. *The Basic Writings of Nietzsche* (1872–95). Walter Kaufman, ed. and trans. New York: Modern Library, 1968. [Pipes]

——. *The Birth of Tragedy* (1872). Walter Kaufmann, trans. New York: Random House, 1967. [Parker]

——. *Philosophy and Truth* (1870s). Daniel Breazeale, ed. and trans. Atlantic Highlands, N.J.: Humanities Press, 1979. [Brustein]

Nisbet, Robert. *Prejudices: A Philosophical Dictionary.* Cambridge: Harvard University Press, 1983. [Ford]

Northrop, F. S. C. *The Meeting of East and West.* New York: Oxbow, 1979. (Pb) [Lodge]

Oakeshott, Michael J. *Rationalism in Politics and Other Essays* (1962). New York and London: Methuen, 1981. (Pb) [Sandel]

O'Faoláin, Seán. *The Finest Stories.* Boston: Little, Brown, 1957. [Kelleher]

Omar Khayyam. *Rubaiyat* (early twelfth century). Edward Fitzgerald, trans. Garden City, N.Y.: Doubleday, n.d. (Pb) [Howe]

O'Neill, Eugene. *A Long Day's Journey into Night* (1940) and *A Moon for the Misbegotten* (1943). In *Final Acts,* Judith E. Barlow, ed. Athens: University of Georgia Press, 1985. [Heclo]

Oppenheimer, J. Robert. *Science and the Common Understanding.* New York: Simon & Schuster, 1954. [Adelstein]

Orwell, George. *Coming up for Air* (1940). New York: Harcourt, Brace, 1969. (Pb) [Alfred]

——. *1984* (1949). New York: Signet, 1984. (Pb) [Mills]

Palmer, Tom. *La grande compagnie de colonisation: Documents of a New Plan* (1937). Worcester, Mass.: Clark University Press, 1981. [Gavin]

Parsons, Talcott. *The Social System* (1951). Glencoe, Ill.: Free Press, 1964. (Pb) [Vogel]

——. *The Structure of Social Action* (1937). New York: Free Press, 1968. (Pb) [Dunlop]

Pavlov, Ivan P. *Conditioned Reflexes: An Investigation of the*

Physiological Activity of the Cerebral Cortex. G. V. Anrep, ed.
and trans. London: Oxford University Press, 1927. [Skinner]

Percy, Walker. *The Last Gentleman* (1966). New York: Avon, 1978. (Pb)
[McCraw]

———. *The Moviegoer* (1961). New York: Avon, 1979. (Pb) [Coles,
McCraw]

Piaget, Jean. *Structuralism* (1968). Chaninah Maschler, ed. and trans.
New York: Basic Books, 1970. [Chall]

Pirsig, Robert M. *Zen and the Art of Motorcycle Maintenance* (1974).
New York: Morrow, 1979. (Pb) [Moore]

Plato. *The Republic* (370–360 B.C.). James Adam, ed. 2 vols. New York:
Cambridge University Press, 1963. [Linsky, Mansfield, Nozick,
Ševčenko, Shklar]

Polanyi, Karl. *The Great Transformation* (1944). Boston: Beacon, 1985.
(Pb) [Ford, Heclo]

Pollock, Edward and Frederic W. Maitland. *The History of English
Law Before the Time of Edward I* (1895). 2 vols. New York:
Cambridge University Press, 1968. (Pb). [Thorne]

Popper, Karl R. *The Open Society and Its Enemies* (1945). 2 vols.
Princeton: Princeton University Press, 1966. [Cooper, Patterson]

Potok, Chaim. *The Book of Lights.* New York: Fawcett, 1981. (Pb)
[Vidal]

———. *My Name Is Asher Lev* (1972). New York: Fawcett, 1978. (Pb)
[Vidal]

Potter, David M. *People of Plenty: Economic Abundance and the
American Character.* Chicago: University of Chicago Press, 1954.
(Pb) [McCraw]

Pound, Roscoe. *Social Control Through Law* (1942). Hamden, Conn.:
Archon, 1968. [Dunlop]

Powell, Anthony. *A Dance to the Music of Time* (1962–75). 12 vols.
Boston: Little, Brown, 1976. [Champion, Hodgson, Willey]

Prall, D. W. *Aesthetic Analysis.* New York: Thomas Y. Crowell, 1936.
[Vosgerchian]

Prescott, William H. *History of the Conquest of Mexico* (1839).
Abridgment, Gardiner C. Harvey, ed. Chicago: University of
Chicago Press, 1966. (Pb) [May]

Proust, Marcel. *Remembrance of Things Past* (1913–27). 3 vols. C. Scott
Moncrieff and Terence Kilmartin, trans. New York: Random
House, 1982. (Pb) [Kennedy]

Pym, Barbara. *Excellent Women* (1952). New York: Harper & Row,
1980. (Pb) [Chatfield]

———. *Quartet in Autumn* (1977). New York: Harper & Row, 1980.
(Pb) [Chatfield]

Pynchon, Thomas. *The Crying of Lot 49* (1966). New York: Bantam,
1968. (Pb) [McArdle]

Racine, Jean-Baptiste. *Andromaque* (1667). John Cairncross, trans. New York: Penguin, 1976. (Pb) [Hoffman]

Radcliffe-Brown, Alfred R. *The Andaman Islanders*. New York: Free Press, 1964. (Pb) [Zaleznik]

Rawls, John. *A Theory of Justice* (1971). Oxford: Oxford University Press, 1972. (Pb) [Roberts, Sandel]

Reik, Theodor. *Listening with the Third Ear* (1948). Garden City, N.Y.: Garden City Books, 1951. [Dunlop]

Remarque, Erich Maria. *All Quiet on the Western Front* (1928). New York: Fawcett Book Group, 1979. (Pb) [Bloembergen, Phelps]

Reves, Emery. *The Anatomy of Peace* (1945). Magnolia, Mass.: Peter Smith, 1969. [MacFarquhar]

Rich, Adrienne. *The Dream of a Common Language: Poems.* New York: W. W. Norton, 1978. (Pb) [Minow]

Riesman, David, with Reuel Denny and Nathan Glazer. *The Lonely Crowd* (1950). New Haven: Yale University Press, 1973. (Pb) [Chall, Patterson]

Rilke, Rainer Maria. *Letters to a Young Poet* (1929). M. D. Herter Norton, trans. New York: W. W. Norton, 1963. (Pb) [Vosgerchian]

———. *Selected Poetry of Rainer Maria Rilke* (1897–1923). Stephen Mitchell, ed. New York: Random House, 1982. [Pipes, Ševčenko]

Roethke, Theodore. *Words for the Wind* (1957). Seattle: University of Washington Press, 1981. (Pb) [Olin]

Roethlisberger, F. J. and William J. Dickson. *Management and the Worker* (1934). Cambridge: Harvard University Press, 1946. [Andrews, Zaleznik]

Roosevelt, Theodore. *The Letters of Theodore Roosevelt.* Elting E. Morison, ed. 8 vols. Cambridge: Harvard University Press, 1951–54. [Chandler]

Rostand, Jean. *Can Man Be Modified?* (1956). Jonathan Griffin, trans. New York: Basic Books, 1959. [Christensen]

Rousseau, Jean-Jacques. *Social Contract* (1762). Maurice Cranston, trans. New York: Penguin, 1968. (Pb) [Frug, Hoffman]

Rudofsky, Bernard. *Architecture Without Architects* (1964). Garden City, N.Y.: Doubleday, 1969. (Pb) [Safdie]

Russell, Bertrand. *Introduction to Mathematical Philosophy* (1919). New York: Simon & Schuster, 1971. (Pb) [Quine]

———. *Our Knowledge of the External World* (1914). 2d ed. Atlantic Highlands, N.J.: Humanities Press, 1972. [Quine]

———. *The Problems of Philosophy* (1911). New York: Oxford University Press, 1959. (Pb) [Skinner]

Saint Exupéry, Antoine de. *The Little Prince* (1943). Katherine Woods, trans. New York: Harcourt Brace Jovanovich, 1982. [Hodgson]

Sakharov, Andrei D. *Progress, Coexistence, and Intellectual Freedom* (1968). New York: W. W. Norton, 1970. [Doty]

Salinger, J. D. *Franny and Zooey: Two Novellas* (1961). New York: Bantam, 1969. (Pb). [Vidal]

Samuelson, Paul A. *Economics* (1953). New York: McGraw-Hill, 1980. [Cooper]

Sartre, Jean-Paul. *Critique of Dialectical Reason* (1960). New York: Schocken, 1983. [Kennedy]

Schell, Jonathan. *The Fate of the Earth.* New York: Avon, 1982. (Pb) [Miles]

Schelling, Thomas C. *The Strategy of Conflict.* Cambridge: Harvard University Press, 1960. (Pb) [Allison, Raiffa]

Schlaifer, Robert. *Analysis of Decisions Under Uncertainty* (1965). Huntington, N.Y.: Krieger, 1978. [Raiffa]

Schlesinger, Arthur M., Jr. *The Vital Center: The Politics of Freedom* (1949). London: Deutsch, 1970. [Cooper]

Schrödinger, Erwin. *What Is Life?* (1946). New York: Cambridge University Press, 1967. [Doty, E. Wilson]

Schumpeter, Joseph A. *Capitalism, Socialism, and Democracy* (1942). New York: Harper & Row, 1983. (Pb) [Knowlton, Nye, Reich, Sachs]

Schwarz-Bart, André. *The Last of the Just* (1959). Stephen Becker, trans. Cambridge, Mass.: Richard Bentley, 1981. [Knowlton]

Scott, Paul. *The Raj Quartet.*
  The Jewel in the Crown (1966). New York: Avon, 1979. (Pb) [Galbraith]
  The Day of the Scorpion (1968). New York: Avon, 1979. (Pb) [Galbraith]
  The Towers of Silence (1971). New York: Avon, 1979. (Pb) [Galbraith]
  The Division of the Spoils (1975). New York: Avon, 1979. (Pb) [Galbraith]

Selznick, Philip. *Leadership in Administration: A Sociological Interpretation* (1957). Berkeley: University of California Press, 1983. (Pb) [J. Wilson]

Seuss, Dr. [Theodor Seuss Geisel]. *The Sneetches, and Other Stories.* New York: Random House, 1961. [Horner]

Shaara, Michael. *The Killer Angels* (1974). New York: Ballantine, 1975. (Pb) [Ford]

Shahn, Ben. *The Shape of Content.* Cambridge: Harvard University Press, 1957. (Pb) [Vosgerchian]

Shakespeare, William. *Henry IV, Parts 1 and 2* and *Henry V* (1596–99). Arthur Quiller-Couch et al., eds. New York: Cambridge University Press, 1965. (Pb) [Neustadt, Verba]

———. *King Lear* (1605). New York: Penguin, 1984. (Pb) [Phelps, Stewart, Weinreb]

——. *Macbeth* (1606). Maynard Mack and Robert E. Boynton, eds.
New York: Random House, 1981. (Pb) [Phelps]
——. *Richard II* (1595). New York: Penguin, 1981. (Pb) [Verba]
——. *Romeo and Juliet* (1595). T. J. Spencer, ed. New York: Penguin,
1981. (Pb) [Holton]
——. *Shakespeare: Complete Works* (1592–1611). Alfred Harbage, ed.
Baltimore: Penguin, 1969. [Bate, Lord, Nozick]
Shapiro, David. *Neurotic Styles.* New York: Basic Books, 1965. (Pb)
[Frug]
Sheehy, Eugene Paul. *A Guide to Reference Books.* 9th ed., 2d
suppl. Chicago: American Library Association, 1982. (Pb)
[Collins]
Shelley, Percy Bysshe. *The Complete Poetical Works* (1813–21). New
York: Oxford University Press, 1974. [Collins]
Shinohara, Miyohei. *Industrial Growth, Trade and Dynamic Patterns in
the Japanese Economy.* Tokyo: University of Tokyo Press, 1982.
[Scott]
Silone, Ignazio. *Bread and Wine* (1937). Harvey Ferguson, Jr., trans.
New York: New American Library, 1980. (Pb) [Coles]
Simpson, George G. *The Meaning of Evolution* (1949). New Haven:
Yale University Press, 1967. (Pb) [Gould]
Singer, Isaac Bashevis. *In My Father's Court* (1966). New York:
Fawcett, 1979. (Pb). [Minow]
——. *Stories for Children.* New York: Farrar, Straus, & Giroux, 1985.
[Mills]
Skeat, Walter W., ed. *An Etymological Dictionary of the English
Language* (1879). Oxford: Oxford University Press, 1924. [Quine]
Smith, Earl Baldwin. *Architectural Symbolism of Imperial Rome and
the Middle Ages* (1956). New York: Hacker Art Books, 1978.
[Grabar]
Smith, Hedrick. *The Russians* (1976). New York: New York Times,
1983. [Doty]
Smith, Wilfred Cantwell. *The Meaning and End of Religion* (1962).
New York: Harper & Row, 1978. (Pb) [Eck]
Solzhenitsyn, Alexander I. *The Gulag Archipelago, 1918–1956* (1973).
Thomas P. Whitney, trans. New York: Harper & Row, 1985. (Pb)
[Green, Mansfield]
——. *One Day in the Life of Ivan Denisovich* (1962). Ralph Parker,
trans. Alexandria, Va.: Time–Life Books, 1981. [Knowlton]
Sophocles. *Antigone* (ca. 440 B.C.). Michael Townsend, trans. New York:
Harper & Row, 1962. (Pb) [Frazier]
——. *The Three Theban Plays: Antigone, Oedipus the King, and
Oedipus at Colonus* (ca. 441–401 B.C.). New York: Penguin, 1984.
(Pb) [Weinreb]

Souvarine, Boris. *Stalin: A Critical Survey of Bolshevism* (1935). New York: Arno, 1972. [Ševčenko]

Spade, Mark [Nigel Balchin]. *How to Run a Bassoon Factory, or Business Explained* (1934). Boston: Houghton Mifflin, 1936. [Christensen]

Speare, Morris Edmund, ed. *The Pocket Book of Verse: Great English and American Poems.* New York: Pocket, 1940. [Frazier]

Spengler, Oswald. *The Decline of the West* (1919–22). Charles Francis Atkinson, trans. 2 vols. New York: Knopf, 1975. [Willey]

Spinoza, Benedict. *Ethics* (1675). New York: Scribner's, 1930. [Niebuhr]

Stapledon, W. Olaf. *Last and First Men* (1930). Boston: Gregg, 1976. [MacFarquhar]

Steinbeck, John. *In Dubious Battle* (orig. *Dubious Battle in California*, 1936). New York: Penguin, 1979. (Pb) [Livingston]

———. *The Grapes of Wrath* (1939). New York: Penguin, 1976. (Pb) [Herrenstein]

Stendhal [Marie Henri Beyle]. *The Red and the Black* (1830). Lloyd C. Parks, trans. New York: New American Library, 1970. (Pb) [Aaron]

Sterne, Laurence. *Tristram Shandy* (1759–67). New York: Oxford University Press, 1983. (Pb) [Schelling]

Stevenson, Robert Louis. *The Strange Case of Dr. Jekyll and Mr. Hyde* (1886). New York: Dodd, Mead, 1979. [Willey]

Strauss, Leo. *Natural Right and History* (1950). Chicago: University of Chicago Press, 1965. (Pb) [Mansfield]

Strunk, William, Jr. and E. B. White. *The Elements of Style* (1959). New York: Macmillan, 1979. (Pb) [Atkinson, Friedman]

Swift, Graham. *Waterland: A Novel* (1983). New York: Simon & Schuster, 1984. [Brinkley]

Synge, John Millington. *The Playboy of the Western World* (1907). New York: Barnes & Noble, 1968. [Kelleher]

Talbott, Strobe. *Endgame: The Inside Story of SALT II.* New York: Harper & Row, 1979. [Doty]

Taylor, Alan J. P. *English History, 1914–1945* (1965). New York: Oxford University Press, 1985. [Parker]

Teale, Edwin Way, ed. *The Insect World of J. Henri Fabre* (1949). New York: Harper & Row, 1981. [Christensen]

Thackeray, William. *Vanity Fair* (1847–48). John Sutherland, ed. New York: Oxford University Press, 1983. (Pb) [Livingston]

Thomas, Benjamin P. *Abraham Lincoln* (1952). New York: Knopf, 1974. (Pb) [Bate]

Thompson, Sir D'Arcy W. *On Growth and Form* (1917). 2 vols. New York: Cambridge University Press, 1984. (Pb) [Safdie]

Thomson, David. *Woodbrook* (1974). New York: Irish Book Center, 1981. (Pb) [Bailyn]

Thoreau, Henry David. *Cape Cod* (1865). New York: Thomas Y. Crowell, 1972. (Pb) [Stilgoe]
———. *Walden* (1854). New York: Penguin, 1983. (Pb) [Frazier]
Thucydides. *History of the Peloponnesian War* (ca. 431–404 B.C.). Richard Livingstone, ed. New York: Oxford University Press, 1960. (Pb) [Fiering, Ford, Schelling, Ševčenko]
Tocqueville, Alexis de. *Democracy in America* (1835–40). G. Laurence, trans. New York: Random House, 1981. (Pb) [Frug, Heclo, Riesman, Verba]
Tolman, Edward C. *Purposive Behavior in Animals and Men* (1967). New York: Irvington, 1967. [Horner]
Tolstoy, Leo. *The Death of Ivan Ilych* (1886). Aylmer Maude, trans. New York: New American Library, 1960. (Pb) [Coles]
———. *War and Peace* (1865–69). Louise Maude and Aylmer Maude, trans. George Gibian, ed. New York: W. W. Norton, 1966. [Champion, Doty, Herrenstein, Hoffman, Nye, Shklar]
Trevelyan, George Otto. *The Early History of Charles James Fox* (1880). New York: AMS Press, 1971. [Ford]
Trevor, William. *The Stories of William Trevor.* New York: Penguin, 1983. (Pb) [Bailyn]
Trilling, Lionel. *The Liberal Imagination* (1950). New York: Harcourt Brace Jovanovich, 1979. [Brustein]
Trollope, Anthony. *Barchester Towers* (1857). New York: Penguin, 1983. (Pb) [Galbraith]
———. *The Last Chronicle of Barset* (1867). New York: Penguin, 1981. (Pb) [Galbraith]
———. *The Warden* (1855). New York: Penguin, 1984. (Pb) [Galbraith]
Truman, David B. *The Governmental Process* (1951). New York: Knopf, 1968. [Neustadt]
Truth, Sojourner [Olive Gilbert]. *Narrative of Sojourner Truth* (1878). Salem, N.H.: Ayer, 1968. [Horner]
Twain, Mark [Samuel Clemens]. *The Adventures of Huckleberry Finn* (1884). New York: Harper & Row, 1984. (Pb) [Brinkley, Hodgson, McKinsey, Reich, Verba]
———. *The Adventures of Tom Sawyer* (1876). Berkeley: University of California Press, 1983. (Pb) [Fiering, Holton]
———. *The Comic Mark Twain Reader.* Charles Neider, ed. Garden City, N.Y.: Doubleday, 1977. [Ford]
———. *The Writings of Mark Twain.* Author's National Edition. 25 vols. New York: Harper, 1899–1918. (Also subsequently published letters and other writings by the same author.) [Howe]
Undset, Sigrid. *Kristin Lavransdatter* (1920–22). C. Archer and J. S. Scott, trans. 3 vols. New York: Bantam, 1978. (Pb) [Graham]
Unger, Roberto M. *Knowledge and Politics.* New York: Free Press, 1975. (Pb) [Parker]

Van Vogt, A. E. *The Voyage of the Space Beagle* (1939). New York: Woodhill, 1977. [Kao]

Veblen, Thorstein B. *Theory of the Leisure Class* (1899). New York: Penguin, 1979. (Pb) [Montgomery]

Vico, Giovanni Battista. *Autobiography* (1725–28). M. H. Fisch and T. G. Bergin, trans. Ithaca, N.Y.: Cornell University Press, 1963. (Pb) [Della-Terza]

Vogel, Ezra F. *Japan as Number One: Lessons for America* (1979). New York: Harper & Row, 1985. (Pb) [Scott]

Von Békésy, Georg. *Sensory Inhibition* (1965). Princeton: Princeton University Press, 1967. (Pb) [Kagan]

Von Mises, Ludwig. *Socialism* (orig. *Die Gemeinwirtschaft,* 1922). J. Kahane, trans. Indianapolis: Liberty-Classics, 1981. (Pb) [Nozick]

Von Mises, Richard. *Probability, Statistics, and Truth* (1928). Hilda Geiringer, trans. New York: Dover, 1981. (Pb) [Fiering]

Von Neumann, John and Oskar Morgenstern. *Theory of Games and Economic Behavior* (1944). Princeton: Princeton University Press, 1980. (Pb) [Fiering, Raiffa]

Wack, Pierre. "Scenarios: Uncharted Waters Ahead." *Harvard Business Review* (19 September 1985). [Scott]

Walzer, Michael. *The Revolution of the Saints: A Study in the Orgins of Radical Politics* (1965). Cambridge: Harvard University Press, 1982. (Pb) [Buchanan]

Warren, Robert Penn. *All the King's Men* (1946). New York: Harcourt Brace Jovanovich, 1982. [Brinkley]

Watson, James D. *The Double Helix* (1968). New York: New American Library, 1969. (Pb) [Doty]

Watson, John B. *Behaviorism* (1925). New York: W. W. Norton, 1970. (Pb). [Skinner]

———. *Psychology, from the Standpoint of a Behaviorist* (1919). 3d ed. Philadelphia and London: J. B. Lippincott, 1929. [Skinner]

Waugh, Evelyn. *Decline and Fall* (1928). Boston: Little, Brown, 1977. (Pb) [Galbraith]

———. *Scoop* (1938). Boston: Little, Brown, 1977. (Pb) [Galbraith]

———. *Vile Bodies* (1930). Boston: Little, Brown, 1977. (Pb) [Alfred]

Weber, Max. *From Max Weber: Essays in Sociology* (1946). H. H. Gerth and C. Wright Mills, eds. and trans. New York: Oxford University Press, 1979. (Pb) [Chandler, Ford, Neustadt]

———. *On the Methodology of the Social Science* (1904–17). Edward A. Shils and Henry A. Finch, trans. Glenco, Ill.: Free Press, 1949. [Roberts]

———. *The Protestant Ethic and the Spirit of Capitalism* (1904). Talcott Parsons, trans. New York: Scribner's, 1977. (Pb) [Sachs]

———. *The Theory of Social and Economic Organization* (1922). A. M.

Henderson and Talcott Parsons, trans. New York: Free Press, 1947. (Pb) [Chandler]

Welty, Eudora. *Thirteen Stories.* New York: Harcourt, Brace & World, 1965. (Pb) [McKinsey]

West, E. G. *Education and the State.* 2d ed. London: Institute of Economic Affairs, 1970. [Glazer]

Wheeler-Bennet, Sir John W. *The Nemesis of Power: The German Army in Politics, 1918–1945* (1953). New York: St. Martin's, 1964. [Cooper]

White. T. H. *The Once and Future King.* New York: Putnam, 1958. [Ford]

Whitehead, Alfred North. *The Aims of Education and Other Essays* (1929). New York: Free Press, 1967. (Pb) [Vosgerchian]

———. *Science and the Modern World* (1925). New York: Free Press, 1967. (Pb) [Bate, Dunlop]

——— and Bertrand Russell. *Principia mathematica* (1910–12). 3 vols. New York: Cambridge University Press, 1962. (Pb) [Quine]

Whyte, William F. *Street Corner Society* (1943). Chicago: University of Chicago Press, 1981. (Pb) [Zaleznik]

Wieman, Henry N. *The Source of Human Good* (1946). Carbondale: Southern Illinois University Press, 1964. (Pb) [Kaufman]

Wiener, Norbert. *The Human Use of Human Beings: Cybernetics and Society* (1950). New York: Avon, 1967. [Adelstein]

Wilhelm, Kate. *Where Late the Sweet Birds Sang* (1976). New York: Pocket, 1981. (Pb) [Hodgson]

Williams, Eric E. *Capitalism and Slavery: The Caribbean* (1944). New York: André Deutsch, 1964. (Pb) [Patterson]

Williams, Tennessee. *Three by Tennessee Williams,* including *Night of the Iguana* (1961). New York: New American Library, 1976. [Mills]

Wilson, Edmund. *Axel's Castle: A Study in the Imaginative Literature of 1870–1930* (1931). New York: W. W. Norton, 1984. (Pb) [Aaron]

———. *To the Finland Station* (1940). New York: Farrar, Straus & Giroux, 1972. (Pb) [Herrenstein]

Wittgenstein, Ludwig. *Philosophische Untersuchungen (Philosophical Investigations,* 1953). G. E. Anscome, trans. Frankfurt: Suhrkamp, 1967. [Minow]

Wodehouse, P. G. *Leave It to Psmith* (1923). New York: Random House, 1975. (Pb) [McArdle]

———. *Money for Nothing* (1928). London: Barrie & Jenkins, 1976. [Montgomery]

Wolfe, Thomas. *Look Homeward, Angel* (1929). New York: Scribners, 1982. (Pb) [Phelps]

Wolfson, Harry A. *Religious Philosophy* (1961). New York: Atheneum, 1965. (Pb) [Epps]

Woodward, Bob and Scott Armstrong. *The Brethren* (1979). New York: Avon, 1980. (Pb) [Vidal]

Woolf, Virginia. *The Letters of Virginia Woolf.* Nigel Nicolson, ed. 6 vols. New York: Harcourt Brace Jovanovich, 1975–80. [Bailyn]

———. *A Room of One's Own* (1929). New York: Harcourt Brace Jovanovich, 1981. (Pb) [Atkinson]

———. *Three Guineas* (1928). New York: Harcourt, Brace & World, 1963. (Pb) [Buchanan]

———. *To the Lighthouse* (1927). New York: Harcourt, Brace, 1964. (Pb) [Kennedy]

Wright, Frank Lloyd. *An American Architecture.* Edgar Kaufmann, ed. New York: Bramhall House, 1955. [Olin]

Wylie, Philip. *An Essay on Morals* (1947). Westport, Conn.: Greenwood, 1978. [E. Wilson]

———. *Generation of Vipers* (1942). Marietta, Ga.: Larlin, 1979. [E. Wilson]

X, Malcolm. *The Autobiography of Malcolm X* (1965). New York: Ballantine, 1977. [Edley]

Yeats, William Butler. *The Poems of W. B. Yeats* (1887–1939). Richard Finneran, ed. New York: Macmillan, 1962. (Pb) [Brustein, Kelleher]

York, Herbert F. *Race to Oblivion.* New York: Simon & Schuster, 1970. [Doty]

Zaleznik, Abraham. *Human Dilemmas of Leadership.* New York: Harper & Row, 1966. [Andrews]

Zinsser, Hans. *As I Remember Him: The Biography of R. S.* Boston: Little, Brown, 1940. [Adelstein]

———. *Rats, Lice and History: The Biography of Bacillus* (1935). New York: Little, 1984. (Pb) [Hiatt]

Zipf, George K. *The Psycho-Biology of Language* (1935). Cambridge, Mass.: M.I.T. Press, 1965. [Chall]

READER'S REFLECTION

This section provides an opportunity to complete the thinking that we hope has been stimulated by reading this book. We have found from experience that actually writing down one's choices can be very valuable to an understanding of the effects of reading on thinking.

What books have helped to shape your thinking? Why?

1. Title: _____

   Author: _____

   Comment: _____

   _____

   _____

   _____

2. Title: _____

   Author: _____

   Comment: _____

   _____

   _____

   _____

3. Title: _____

   Author: _____

Comment: _____

_____

_____

_____

4. Title: _____

Author: _____

Comment: _____

_____

_____

_____

5. Title: _____

Author: _____

Comment: _____

_____

_____

_____

READING PLAN

Space is provided below where you may list the books that
you hope to read.

Title: _____
Author: _____
Date Read: _____

Title: _____
Author: _____
Date Read: _____

Title: _____
Author: _____
Date Read: _____

Title: _____
Author: _____
Date Read: _____

Title: _____
Author: _____
Date Read: _____

Title: _____
Author: _____
Date Read: _____

Title: _____
Author: _____
Date Read: _____

THE EDITORS

C. Maury Devine is an avid student of government and politics. A former member of the White House Domestic Policy Staff, she now serves in the Drug Enforcement Administration of the United States Department of Justice.

Claudia M. Dissel is a consultant to management of business and government, Washington, D.C. Now a displaced Westerner, she formerly served as deputy director of the State of Utah Department of Natural Resources. She is supported in her endeavors by her children, Heather Marie and Charles Mitchell.

Kim D. Parrish is a partner in the law firm of Derryberry, Quigley, Parrish & Gooding in Oklahoma City, Oklahoma. He practices law in Oklahoma City to support a serious addiction to New York Yankee baseball and a lesser addiction to golf and tennis.

A percentage of the profits from the sale of this book will be donated to the Center for the Book in Washington, D.C. The center is a partnership of the Library of Congress, corporations and individuals and is designed to focus national attention on books, reading and the written word. Our commitment to such public/private initiatives was reinforced while graduate students at Harvard's Kennedy School of Government, and particularly through its Center for Business and Government. The editors encourage others interested in promoting books and reading to consider contributing to the Center for the Book, The Library of Congress, Washington, D.C. 20540.